INTEGRAL NON-DUALISM

INTEGRAL NON-DUALISM

A Critical Exposition of Vijñānabhikṣu's System of Philosophy

KANSHI RAM

MOTILAL BANARSIDASS PUBLISHERS
PRIVATE LIMITED • DELHI

First Edition: Delhi, 1995

ISBN: 81-208-1212-8

Also available at:

MOTILAL BANARSIDASS

41 U.A. Bungalow Road, Jawahar Nagar, Delhi 110 007
120 Royapettah High Road, Mylapore, Madras 600 004
16 St. Mark's Road, Bangalore 560 001
Ashok Rajpath, Patna 800 004
Chowk, Varanasi 221 001

PRINTED IN INDIA

BY JAINENDRA PRAKASH JAIN AT SHRI JAINENDRA PRESS,
A-45 NARAINA, PHASE I, NEW DELHI 110 028
AND PUBLISHED BY NARENDRA PRAKASH JAIN FOR
MOTILAL BANARSIDASS PUBLISHERS PRIVATE LIMITED,
BUNGALOW ROAD, DELHI 110 007

Dedicated to
Sadguru Bābā Śrī Mastarāmajī
Who was a living embodiment
of Advaita

PREFACE

Vijñānabhikṣu's system of philosophy has been called here 'Integral Non-dualism'. It is mainly his commentary on the *Brahmasūtras*, known as *Vijñānāmṛtabhāṣya*, which has been made the basis to present his system of philosophy. He has himself described his system of thought as *avibhāgādvaita* at several places in the commentary. It means that the Absolute is an integral whole in which *prakṛti* and *puruṣas* inhere as Its real powers. But it should not be confounded with Sri Aurobindo's philosophical system, known as Integral Advaita; the latter differs from the former in many important respects. Aurobindo's philosophy as laid down in the *Life Divine* is widely recognized as a 'double-ladder' (Involution-Evolution)[1] philosophy whereas that of Vijñānabhikṣu may be designated in contrast as a single-ladder (only evolution) system. Vijñānabhikṣu postulates the Eternal Pure-*Sattva*-Adjunct (*Upādhi*) of the Absolute while Sri Aurobindo does not conceive any such principle. Moreover, the conceptions of super-mind, overmind, divine manifestation in matter, etc. which occupy so central a place in Sri Aurobindo are not to be found in Vijñānabhikṣu's works even in a remote sense.

Vijñānabhikṣu advocates the reality of the world and the individual selves along with that of the Absolute. However, in the process of proving the independent status of worldly objects and selves, he lands himself in the dilemma of the less real and the more real. The resolution of this intricate problem defies him. It is indeed baffling when he takes recourse to the concept of Eternal Adjunct of the Absolute in order to lay down that it is only the Absolute Which is ultimately real. Reality according to him consists in the incidence of

---

1. Sri Aurobindo maintains that *Brahman* by 'involution' manifests itself as matter and then progressively brings about an unfolding of its powers through 'evolution'. (*with slight alteration*)
—*The Encyclopedia of Philosophy*, Vol. I, The Macmillan Company and The Free Press, New York, 1967, p. 209.

meaningful activity which is possible only when the *upādhi* is in operation. Excepting the Eternal Pure-*Sattva-Upādhi* of the Absolute, all other *upādhis* of the selves submerge in *prakṛti* along with other manifestations at the time of dissolution (*pralaya*). It means, therefore, that the Pure-*Sattva*-Adjunct of the Absolute continues to remain in operation and performs meaningful activity in the form of perceiving the whole universe. It is this meaningful adjunctival function of the Absolute in virtue of which It is regarded as real at the ultimate level. It implies that other manifestations and the selves are less real. As such a hierarchical status of reality reigns supreme in this system of Integral Non-dualism.

Metaphysics, ethics, epistemology and the *summum bonum* form the basis of a proper system of philosophy. Chapter V on the Theory of Double Reflection fairly represents the epistemological views of Vijñānabhikṣu and his views on ethics are briefly discussed in the chapter on Bondage and Liberation. As such the present attempt may be taken as an exposition of Vijñānabhikṣu's philosophical system.

The chapters second and fifth of the present work were respectively published in *Dharmanīrājanā* (1989), pp. 281-306, a volume dedicated to the memory of Dharmendra Nath Shastri and in *Studies in Indology: Prof. Rasik Vihari Joshi Felicitation Volume* (1988-89), pp. 257-81. The titles under which they were published in the above-mentioned volumes respectively were "Vijñānabhikṣu's Conception of the Absolute" and "Vijñānabhikṣu's Doctrine of Bondage and Liberation". "Vijñānabhikṣu's Theory of Double Reflection" included in the present volume was published in the *Annals of the Bhandarkar Oriental Research Institute,* Vol. LXIX for 1988, pp. 77-92. I thank the respective editors for their permission to include the articles just mentioned.

The present work was submitted to the University Grants Commission in the form of a minor research project entitled "A Critical Exposition of the Philosophy of Vijñānabhikṣu." It was approved for a financial grant in 1985. I take this opportunity to express my gratitude to the University Grants Commission for the same.

It was an act of generosity on the part of Dr. Ramesh Kumar Sharma that he accepted this manuscript for editing. He gave many valuable suggestions for improvement both in content and presentation. I take this opportunity to express my gratitude to him. Thanks are also due to Dr. A.K. Monga and Dr. G.P. Bhatt who read portions of this work and suggested improvements. I also thank Shri N.P. Jain, Managing Director, Motilal Banarsidass Publishers Pvt. Ltd. for its publication.

KANSHI RAM

CONTENTS

ABBREVIATIONS

ALB	*Adyar Library Bulletin*
BhāgPu	*Bhāgavata Purāṇa*
BṛhadUp	*Bṛhadāraṇyaka Upaniṣad*
BS	*Brahmasūtra*
BSS	*Brahmasūtraśāṅkarabhāṣya*
CCA	*Citsukha's Contribution to Advaita*
IPP	*Indian Psychology: Perception*
KUp	*Kaṭha Upaniṣad*
MBH	*Mahābhārata*
MP	*Mārkaṇḍeya Purāṇa*
MuUp	*Muṇḍaka Upaniṣad*
SK	*Sāṅkhyakārikā*
SP	*Studies in Philosophy*
SPB	*Sāṅkhyapravacanabhāṣya*
Srp	*Saura Purāṇa*
SS	*Sāṅkhyasāra*
SSR	*Sāṅkhyasāra* annotated by Ram Shankar Bhattacharya
STK	*Sāṅkhyatattvakaumudī*
SYD	*Sāṅgayogadarśana*
TaittUp	*Taittirīya Upaniṣad*
TP	*Tattvapradīpikā*
TS	*Tarkasaṅgraha*
TV	*Tattvavaiśāradī*
VAB	*Vijñānāmṛtabhāṣya*
VB	*Vyāsabhāṣya*
VK	*Vyākhyākāron kī Dṛṣṭi se Pātañjala Yogasūtra kā Samīkṣātmaka Adhyayana*
VMTP	*Vāsiṣṭhamahārāmāyaṇatātparyaprakāśa*
VP	*Viṣṇu Purāṇa*
VT	*Vidvattoṣiṇī*
YSS	*Yogasārasaṅgraha*
YV	*Yogavārttika*
YVS	*Yogavāsiṣṭha*

1

INTRODUCTION

Philosophy in India has passed through many a change since the time of Upaniṣads which abound in manifold potential conceptualizations about the Absolute and Its relationship with the individual self and the world. The segment of time following the Upaniṣads witnessed development and formulation of some of the seminal ideas contained in them. The result was the emergence of various systems of philosophy. It was mainly the systems of Sāṅkhya and Vedānta which addressed themselves seriously to the philosophically important issues the Upaniṣads actually grappled with. These issues concern the nature of Absolute, individual self, status of the world, their mutual relationship, the phenomenon of plurality, etc. In the case of Vedānta, specially Advaita Vedānta, Śaṅkara ingeniously built up the system of Non-dualism and claimed by implication that the philosophical system propounded by him alone represented the true spirit of the Upaniṣads and hence of the *Bādarāyaṇa-sūtras.* Nevertheless many other attempts were also made by thinkers such as Rāmānuja, Madhva, Vijñānabhikṣu, etc. to interpret the *Brahmasūtras* and to formulate their own systems of thought. Among them it was Vijñānabhikṣu who remained neglected so far as his commentary, that is, *Vijñānāmṛtabhāṣya* on the *Brahmasūtras,* is concerned; he largely remained known for his work on Sāṅkhya, called *Sāṅkhyapravacanabhāṣya.*

Vijñānabhikṣu disagrees with both Śaṅkara and Rāmānuja though he appears to be more akin to the latter. The reason is not very far to seek. Advocating absolute Non-dualism, Śaṅkara rejected the view that lays emphasis on the synthesis of knowledge and action for the attainment of liberation. He steadfastly held the view that it is only knowledge which severs the knot of bondage and frees the individual self. When, with the advent of Rāmānuja, a new cult of devotion gained ascendancy, Vijñānabhikṣu did not remain unaffected. He conceived a system in which both the world and the individual selves also enjoy the status of reality and accorded due importance to both knowledge and action as means to liberation. He believed that it was the philosophy of the unreality of the world which was responsible for man's alienation from his environment and in order to help him overcome the alienation a more meaningful relationship of man with his surroundings and fellow-beings was needed. Devotion relates man to the Lord through the I-and-thou relationship. It is possible only when both the ultimate and the individual self are conceived to be real. This is precisely the reason why Vijñānabhikṣu took up cudgels against the advocates of *māyā* (*prapañca-mithyātva*) and expounded a system in which the world has been accepted as a real transformation (manifestation) of *prakṛti*, the power of the Absolute and hence in which *māyā* has no place in the sense in which it has in the philosophy of Advaita.

To achieve this objective he took clues mainly from the Purāṇic sources and his interpretative observations on them bear out that he was familiar with the prevalent beliefs and traditions. If his comments on and quotations from the Purāṇas are pooled together, the contours of a fairly consistent hermeneutics of the Purāṇas can be comprehended.

His thought is a peculiar blend of knowledge, yoga, and bhakti. Though he is catholic in his views and approach, yet he upholds the principles of *varṇāśrama* tradition. Probably it was the need of the hour when he lived and wrote his works. It is also for this reason that he combined both the idealism of Śaṅkara and the realistic idealism of Sāṅkhya with the prevailing cult of devotion.

He has been considerably influenced by Navya-Nyāya in the method of interpretation. This is clear from his commentaries on the Sāṅkhya, Yoga and Vedānta *sūtras*. It is due to his syncretic zeal that he is even charged with grafting the notions of Nyāya-Vaiśeṣika on Sāṅkhya and those of Sāṅkhya on the philosophy of Vedānta. This is why a proper assessment of Vijñānabhikṣu's philosophy demands that his chronology be decided first after properly examining the attempts made by different scholars in this regard.

Vijñānabhikṣu's Date

Udayavīra Śāstrī and Pulinbihari Chakravarti think that

Vijñānabhikṣu lived about 1400 A.D. The latter bases his observation only on a notation in a catalogue of manuscripts indicating that a manuscript of Vijñāna,[1] entitled *Sāṃkhya-sāra-viveka* was copied in 1516 of the Vikrama era.[2] He also suggests that Vijñānabhikṣu should be placed a century earlier, that is, about 1416 of the Vikrama era which means the later half of the fourteenth century A.D. But on the other hand Udayavīra Śāstrī discusses the date of Vijñānabhikṣu in detail and comes to the conclusion that Vijñānabhikṣu cannot be placed beyond 14th century A.D. In order to examine the grounds given by Udayavīra Śāstrī, it would be of advantage if P.K. Gode's article[3] on the chronology of Vijñānabhikṣu and Bhāvāgaṇeśa is taken up for consideration since Udayavīra Śāstrī's fixing of the date of Vijñānabhikṣu turns on two factors:

(1) Rejection of P.K. Gode's thesis, and
(2) Date of Sadānanda Yati.

P.K. Gode connects the date of Vijñānabhikṣu with that of Bhāvāgaṇeśa, the famous disciple of Vijñānabhikṣu. He thinks that 'Bhāvā is a surname now current among the Citpāvan Brahmins of Mahārāṣṭra as Bhāve.'[4] He further gives the following information based on a stanza[5] found at the beginning of the Oxford Manuscript of *Prabodhacandrodayaṭīkā* called *Ciccandrikā* written by Bhāvāgaṇeśa:[6]

(1) Rāmakṛṣṇa Bhāvā was the illustrious grandfather of Bhāvāgaṇeśa. Gaurī was the name of Rāmakṛṣṇa's wife (1450 -1525 A.D.).
(2) Viśvanātha was the father of Bhāvāgaṇeśa and Bhavānī was his mother (1500-1560 A.D.).
(3) Viśvanātha was also an illustrious person having performed

1. The author apparently takes *Vijñāna* to be Vijñānabhikṣu.
2. Pulinbihari Chakravarti, *Origin and Development of the Sāṁkhya System of Thought,* Munshiram Manoharlal, Delhi, 1975, p. 171.
3. P.K. Gode, "The Chronology of Vijñānabhikṣu and His Disciple Bhāvāgaṇeśa, the Leader of the Citpāvan Brahmins of Benares", *Adyar Library Bulletin*, February, 1944, Vol. VII (Hereinafter referred to as ALB).
4. ALB, *op. cit.*, p. 23.
5. आसीद् भावोपनामा भुवि विदितयशा रामकृष्णोऽतिविज्ञ-
स्तस्माद् गौर्यां विनीतो विविधगुणनिधिर्विश्वनाथोऽवतीर्णः ।
तस्मात्प्रख्यातकीर्तेः विविधमखकृतः प्रादुरासीद् भवान्यां
श्रीमत्यां यो गणेशो भुवि विदितगुणा तस्य चिच्चन्द्रि (का)स्तु ॥1॥
6. ALB, *op. cit.*, p. 20.

many sacrifices, and from him was born Gaṇeśa, the author of *Ciccandrikā* (1550-1600 A.D.).[1]

P.K. Gode identifies Bhāvāgaṇeśa, whose genealogical information has been given above, with 'Bhāvaye Gaṇeśa Dīkṣita' who was a leader of Cipolaṇe or Citpāvan Brahmins of Benares in 1583 A.D. It was the year when a *Nirṇayapatra* was drawn up at Muktimaṇḍapa at Benares.[2] The document known as *Nirṇayapatra* was endorsed by the leaders of different Brahmin communities of Benares in Śaka 1505 (=1583 A.D.). The following notation tops other endorsements in the document:

'*tatra saṃmati. bhāvaye gaṇeśadīkṣita pramukha cipolaṇe*'[3]

P.K. Gode views that if Bhāvāgaṇeśa Dīkṣita and Bhāvaye Gaṇeśa Dīkṣita were accepted to be one and the same person, it would become much easier to decide the date of Bhāvāgaṇeśa Dīkṣita, upon which in turn depends the chronology of Vijñānabhikṣu who, being a teacher of the former, should normally have been his senior contemporary. The author of the article supports this identification with the factual evidence that the Mahārāṣṭra Brahmins now put their surname after the personal name. Assuming that 'Bhāve', a variant of 'Bhāvaye' is equal to 'Bhāvā', he observes that 'Bhāvāgaṇeśa' would be equal to 'Gaṇeśa bhāve' and that the Bhāve community must have lived in Benares in 1583 A.D. In conclusion, P.K. Gode fixes the chronology of Bhāvāgaṇeśa between 1550 A.D. and 1600 A.D. and that of Vijñānabhikṣu between 1525 A.D. and 1580 A.D. [4]

Udayavīra Śāstrī discusses P.K. Gode's paper thoroughly and does not agree with him on the identity of 'Bhāvāgaṇeśa and 'Bhāvaye Gaṇeśa Dīkṣita' who is said to have endorsed the *Nirṇayapatra* in 1583 A.D. He also rejects P.K. Gode's suggestion that *Tattvabodhinī* on *Tarkabhāṣā* is authored by him because of difference in the names of the parents of the two. Burnell's description of the parents of the author of the *Tarkabhāṣāṭīkā* also lends strength to the same view.[5] As such Udayavīra Śāstrī's view is that Bhāvāgaṇeśa and Bhāvaye Gaṇeśa Dīkṣita[6] are different persons. And Suresh Chandra

1. ALB, pp. 24 and 26.
2. *Ibid.*, *op. cit.*, p. 24.
3. *Ibid.*, p. 24.
4. *Ibid.*, p. 28.
5. Udayavīra Śāstrī, *Sāṅkhya Darśana kā Itihāsa*, second ed., 1979, pp. 361-62 (Hereinafter referred to as Śāstrī).
6. ALB, *op. cit.*, p. 20, fn. 2.

Śrīvāstavya's view that since Bhāvā is to be used in Sanskrit, Bhāvāgaṇeśa did not sign as such but as Bhāvaye in the document, seems to be based on conjecture and hence does not wield any significance in the present context.[1]

Udayavīra Śāstrī rightly points out that the fact that the endorser was a leader of the Cipolaṇe or Citpāvan Brahmins does not right away guarantee that he was also a scholar.[2] He also seems to be correct in observing that it is not acceptable that the surname 'Bhāvā' which was used before the personal name has now come to be used after the personal name as Bhāve. G.V. Bhave, the author of *Bhāve-kula-vṛttānta* appears to be supporting Śāstrī's view.[3] In this way after examining P.K. Gode's standpoint critically and rejecting it, Udayavīra Śāstrī expresses the view that the endorsement in the *Nirṇayapatra* of 1583 A.D. by Bhāvaye Gaṇeśa Dīkṣita does not at all deserve to be regarded as the basis for deciding Vijñānabhikṣu's time.[4]

Udayavīra Śāstrī considers Sadānanda Yati's time to be the deciding factor in determining Vijñānabhikṣu's chronology. It now looks proper that his view in this respect be given in a nutshell. He attributes the following works to Sadānanda Yati:

1. *Pañcadaśīṭīkā*
2. *Advaita-dīpikā-vivaraṇa*
3. *Advaitabrahmasiddhi*
4. *Vedāntasāra*
5. *Jīvanmuktiprakriyā*.[5]

Discussing the role of Sadānanda Yati as a staunch defender of Śāṅkara Vedānta he brings home the point that, since Sadānanda Yati has not referred to Vallabha, he cannot have lived after the latter. For, given Sadānanda's disposition, it seems hard to accept that he had ignored Vallabha who lived about the last quarter of 15th century A.D.[6] Udayavīra Śāstrī says that it is, therefore, appropriate to admit that Sadānanda is prior to Vallabha and so flourished before the last quarter of the fifteenth century A.D.

1. Suresh Chandra Śrīvāstavya, *A Study of Vijñānabhikṣu and His Place in Indian Philosophy*, pp. 35-37.
2. Śāstrī, p. 364.
3. ALB, *op. cit.*, p. 26.
4. Śāstrī, p. 365.
5. Works numbering 3 and 4 are significant in the present context.
6. Śāstrī, pp. 366 and 368.

Sadānanda has criticized Vijñānabhikṣu by name.[1] Udayavīra Śāstrī suggests on this basis that by the time Sadānanda Yati wrote *Advaitabrahmasiddhi*, Vijñānabhikṣu must have gained popularity[2] and that if at least half a century is allowed for it,[3] Vijñānabhikṣu can in no circumstances be placed beyond fourteenth century. It is, therefore, proper to accept the view that he lived about the middle of the fourteenth century A.D. (1350 A.D.).[4]

It is obvious from the foregoing account that Udayavīra Śāstrī's attempt to fix Vijñānabhikṣu's date depends upon what he takes to be Sadānanda Yati's time, which, according to him, falls around the later half of the fourteenth century A.D. It seems to us however that such a contention is flawed. It is flawed because Sadānanda Vyāsa, the author of *Vedāntasāra,* is now accepted by every scholar to be a person different from Sadānanda Yati, the author of *Advaitabrahmasiddhi.*[5] It also does not contradict A.B. Keith's view that Sadānanda lived about 1500 A.D. Moreover, Udayavīra Śāstrī's thinking that since Vallabha has not been taken notice of by the author of *Advaitabrahmasiddhi,* the former should not have preceded the latter, seems to be nothing more than a wild conjecture. His view, therefore, about the date of Vijñānabhikṣu can hardly be accepted. More so, because Sadānanda Yati of Kashmir mentions by name Vidyāraṇya Svāmī, Vijñānabhikṣu, Narasiṃhāśrama and Raghunātha Śiromaṇi.[6] He, therefore, should have lived after all the four philosophers he cites in *Advaitabrahmasiddhi,* that is, after 1550 A.D. generally assigned to Narasiṃhāśrama[7] and Raghunātha Śiromaṇi.[8] Sadānanda Yati himself may be assigned the earlier part of the seventeenth century A.D. since it could have taken at least 50 to 60 years for the thoughts of these philosophers to reach Kashmir so that the author of *Advaitabrahmasiddhi* could have referred to them in such a manner. Sadānanda Yati's date having thus been

---

1. एतेन यच्चात्र सांख्यभाष्यकृता विज्ञानभिक्षुणा समाधानत्वेन प्रलपितं तदप्यसङ्गतमेव ।
Advaitabrahmasiddhi, ed. Vāmana Śāstrī, 1981, p. 27.
2. Śāstrī, p. 368.
3. *Ibid.*, p. 370.
4. *Ibid.*, p. 371.
5. S.C. Śrīvāstavya, p. 39.
6. *Advaitabrahmasiddhi*, page numbers are in the respective order of the named—85, 27, 222 and 8.
7. Karl H. Potter, *Encyclopedia of Indian Philosophies,* Delhi, 1983, Vol. I, p. 361.
8. D.H.H. Ingalls, *Materials for the Study of Navya-Nyāya Logic,* Delhi, 1988, p. 9.

shifted to the earlier part of the seventeenth century and Śāstrī's assumption about the date of Vijñānabhikṣu having been proved wrong, it requires more evidential material to determine the probable chronology of Vijñānabhikṣu.

The manner in which Vijñānabhikṣu discusses and interprets philosophical doctrines shows that he was well conversant with the technicalities of the Navya-Nyāya system of philosophy.[1] He joins issue with those who advocate that *viṣayatā* is a separate category and in the course of rejecting it, he puts forth his point of view convincingly.[2] *Viṣayatā* as a separate category might have been conceived and become controversial by the time of Raghunātha Śiromaṇi and Jānakīnātha Bhaṭṭācārya[3] who are said to have lived about the earlier part of the sixteenth century.[4] It may, therefore, be safely assumed that Vijñānabhikṣu could not at least have lived earlier than the earlier half of the sixteenth century.

Besides criticizing Vācaspati and Aniruddha, he discusses the concept of soul's self-luminosity[5] as given by Citsukhācārya in his *Tattvapradīpikā*[6] and rejects it as it does not accord with his philosophical system, particularly his doctrine of double reflection.[7]

Suresh Chandra Śrīvāstavya furnishes substantial and detailed information that Vijñānabhikṣu criticized Sadānanda Vyāsa, the author of *Vedāntasāra*[8] and that it was due to the popularity of *Vedāntasāra* that he felt impelled to write the two compendia: *Sāṅkhyasārasaṃgraha* and *Yogasārasaṃgraha* on the same pattern.[9] In case Śrīvāstavya's argument were accepted, it would be easy to

---

1. T.S. Rukmani, *Yogavārttika of Vijñānabhikṣu*, Vol. I, Introduction, p. 4. Also fns. 4 (a) and (b) on the same page.
2. Ram Shankar Bhattacharya, ed., *Sāṅkhyasūtram Vijñānabhikṣubhāṣyasametam*, Bharatiya Vidya Prakashan, Delhi, p. 56 (Hereinafter referred to as *SPB*).
3. D.C. Guha, *Navya Nyāya System of Logic*, Motilal Banarsidass, Delhi, 1979, p. 103 fns. 1 and 3.
4. Athalye and Bodas, *Tarkasaṃgraha*, Introduction, p. xlvi and Karl H. Potter, *Encyclopedia of Indian Philosophies*, 1983, p. 358.
5. आधुनिकास्तु स्वकल्पितमात्मारोपत्वं सिद्धान्तीकृत्य स्वप्रकाशलक्षणं रचयन्ति अवेद्यत्वे सत्य-परोक्षव्यवहारयोग्यत्वमिति ।

   VAB, p. 43 and also V.A. Sharma, *Citsukha's Contribution to Advaita*, Mysore, 1974, p. 44.
6. अवेद्यत्वे सत्यपरोक्षव्यवहारयोग्यतायास्तल्लक्षणत्वात् ।

   Svāmī Yogīndrānanda, ed. and tr., *Tattvapradīpikā*, Varanasi, 1974, p.16.
7. See chapter 5 of this work.
8. *A Study of Vijñānabhikṣu and His Place in Indian Philosophy*, pp. 41-42.
9. *Ibid.*, p. 42.

assume that Vijñānabhikṣu did not live before fifteenth century A.D.

P.K. Gode cites a passage[1] from Vindhyesvari Prasad's Sanskrit introduction to the Adyar edition of Vijñānabhikṣu's *Yogasāra-saṃgraha* in which he mentions a manuscript of Vijñānabhikṣu's *Brahmamīmāṃsā* dated 1775 of the Vikrama era, that is, 1719 A.D. It is on this basis that Vindhyesvari Prasad concludes that Vijñānabhikṣu should at least be placed earlier than 1719 A.D. Nāgeśa also refers to Vijñānabhikṣu at the end of his *Pātañjalasūtravṛtti.*[2] This famous grammarian-philosopher is believed to have lived about the end of the seventeenth century A.D.[3]

The interval between the fifteenth and the seventeenth centuries can further be reduced on the basis of a manuscript of Vijñānabhikṣu's *Sāṃkhyasāra* in which the time of its copying is given as 1680 of the Vikrama era which in terms of the Christian era comes to 1623 A.D.[4] Taking into consideration Vijñānabhikṣu's reference to the doctrine of *viṣayatā* attributed to Raghunātha Śiromaṇi and Jānakinātha Bhaṭṭācārya who lived about 1550 A.D. it may safely be concluded that he lived between 1550 A.D. and 1623 A.D. This view is supported by N.K. Chattopadhyay when he mentions that Vijñānabhikṣu had been a successor of Lord Caitanya[5] meaning thereby that he had a peculiar blend of *bhakti,*[6] *yoga* and *jñāna,* something which is understandable since he lived during the period when the cult of *bhakti* was in the ascendance and had begun to exert powerful influence upon the minds of people in Bengal and elsewhere.[7] This period also seems to be consonant with his having been influenced both by *bhakti* and the Navya-Nyāya system of philosophy. It is adequately endorsed further by the views held by Winternitz,[8] A.B. Keith,[9]

---

1. अयं विज्ञानभिक्षुराचार्यः कस्मिन्देशे कस्मिन्काल आसीदिति निश्चयः सम्यङ् न भवति, तथापि एतद्विरचितब्रह्ममीमांसाभाष्यपुस्तकस्य विक्रमीय 1775 संवत्सरे लिखितस्य उपलंभात्. . . . पूर्वकालावस्थायी etc. ALB, *op. cit.*, p. 22, fn. 2.
2. पातञ्जलाब्धौ रचितः सेतुर्विज्ञानभिक्षुणा । महापङ्कमूढतमो येन तं तीर्णवानहम् ।।
   quoted in P.K. Gode's article in ALB, *op. cit.*, p. 22, fn. 2.
3. V. Krishnamacharya, ed. *Sphoṭavāda,* Preface, p. v.
4. S.C. Śrīvāstavya, *Study of Vijñānabhikṣu and His Place in Indian Philosophy,* p. 43.
5. *Indian Philosophy—Its Exposition in the Light of Vijñānabhikṣu's Bhāṣya and Yogavārttika: A Modern Approach,* Introduction, p. 11.
6. प्रीयतां मोक्षदो हरिः । *SPB,* p. 2, introductory śloka 6d.
7. N.K. Chattopadhyay, Introduction, p. ii.
8. M. Winternitz, *History of Indian Literature,* Delhi, 1985, vol. III, p. 551.
9. A.B. Keith, *A History of Sāṁkhya Philosophy,* Delhi, 1975, p. 114.

S.N. Dasgupta,[1] Radhakrishnan,[2] G.J. Larson,[3] R.S. Bhattacharya[4] and T.S. Rukmani.[5]

Place

Though it is not possible to say anything definite about the place of birth of Vijñānabhikṣu because of non-availability of information in this regard, yet it can be discussed, at least, where he lived and wrote his works on the basis of such linguistic expressions found in the works written by Vijñānabhikṣu as would, at least, indicate the region where these expressions were likely to be in vogue. Some of them are: *ghoṭaka,*[6] *śīghro mārgaḥ,*[7] *milanam,*[8] *militvā,*[9] *tulyāya-vyayatvam,*[10] *rātridina,*[11] etc. These are clearly Hindi expressions literally translated into Sanskrit and, therefore, provide sufficient help in forming an opinion that the place where Vijñānabhikṣu lived and did his work as a philosopher should have been the region where Hindi was commonly spoken. On the basis of the reports published by the Nāgarī Pracāriṇī Sabhā,[12] Uttar Pradesh, Bihar and North of Madhya Pradesh were some of the regions where Hindi was in use between the fourteenth and the seventeenth centuries both among common people and literary circles. Since Prayāga has been referred to more than once by him, it is appropriate to assume that that was the place where he did most of his philosophical activity.[13] And

1. *History of Indian Philosophy,* Delhi, 1988, vol. I, p. 212.
2. *A Source Book in Indian Philosophy,* p. 426.
3. *Encyclopedia of Indian Philosophies,* vol. IV, ed. G.J. Larson and R.S. Bhattacharya, Delhi, 1987, p. 333. Also see *ibid.*, p. 376.
4. *Ibid.*, p. 376 and also see Introduction to *SPB,* p. 6.
5. T.S. Rukmani, Tr. *Yogavārttika,* vol. I, Introduction, p. 5.
6. *Sāṅgayogadarśanam,* Kashi Sanskrit Series, 110, Benares, 1935, p. 330. (Hereinafter referred to as *SYD*).
7. *Sāṁkhyasāra* of Vijñānabhikṣu, Tr. Shiv Kumar, Eastern Book Linkers, Delhi, 1988, p. 27. (Hereinafter referred to as *SS*).
8. YV in *SYD,* p. 327.
9. *Ibid.*, p. 167.
10. *SPB,* p. 222.
11. YV in *SYD,* p. 343.
12. Suresh Chandra Śrīvāstavya, pp. 26-27.
13. (1) स्वर्गिणां भारतवर्षमागत्य लीलामानुषविग्रहेण प्रयागादौ कर्मानुष्ठानस्य तत्फलस्य च श्रवणादिति । YV in *SYD,* p. 163.
(2) स्यादेव, प्रयागादौ ब्रह्मादीनां यागादिश्रवणात् । तेषां कर्मानधिकारश्च देवादिलोके स्वयागादौ च बोध्यो न तु भारतवर्षे स्वोत्कृष्टदेवतायागे च, अर्थित्वशक्तत्वापर्युदस्तत्वादिभ्य इति । *VAB,* p. 119.

such usages as *Nārāyaṇo 'yaṃ bhāsate,*[1] *mukhalagnām masīmiva*[2], etc. corroborate the same assumption.

Works

Sāṅkhya, Yoga and Vedānta are the three systems of thought Vijñānabhikṣu chose to comment upon and thereby present his system of philosophy: *avibhāgādvaita* (Integral Non-dualism). He wrote *Sāṃkhyapravacanabhāṣya* on the *Sāṅkhyasūtras, Yogavārttika* on *Vyāsabhāṣya,* a gloss on the *Pātañjala-yogasūtras* and *Vijñānāmṛtabhāṣya* or *Brahmasūtrarjubhāṣya* on the *Brahmasūtras.* Two other published compendia are *Sāṃkhyasāra* and *Yogasārasaṃgraha.* The rest have not been published so far.

Aufrecht attributes eighteen works to Vijñānabhikṣu. Among these there are two works listed as *Vedāntāloka* and *Sāṅkhyakārikābhāṣya* which are not accepted as having been written by Vijñānabhikṣu. Suresh Chandra Śrīvāstavya rightly points out that the former is a general name for the commentaries that he wrote on the eight Upaniṣads.[3] T.S. Rukmani endorses this view saying that "all the *upaniṣadbhāṣyas* are *Vedāntālokas* in this sense and it appears that Aufrecht mistook *Vedāntāloka* for a separate work".[4]

Vijñānabhikṣu's authorship of *Sāṃkhyakārikābhāṣya* is controversial. Ram Shankar Bhattacharya's view that it is a work by Vijñānabhikṣu is based on a hearsay.[5] Disagreeing with Bhattacharya and supporting Suresh Chandra Śrīvāstavya's contention[6] that it is not Vijñānabhikṣu's work, T.S. Rukmani says that "one strong argument against Vijñānabhikṣu's authorship of this work is that there is no reference to it in any of the other works written by him."[7] Suresh Chandra, too, points out that the copier wrote[8] '*Vijñānabhikṣuviracitasāṅkhyabhāṣyam'* wrongly at the end whereas the last *śloka* of the manuscript attributes the commentary to Gauḍapāda.[9]

That *Pāṣaṇḍamatakhaṇḍana* is another work by Vijñānabhikṣu

1. YV in *SYD,* p. 111.
2. *Ibid.,* p. 351.
3. *A Study of Vijñānabhikṣu and His Place in Indian Philosophy,* p. 49.
4. T.S. Rukmani, *Yogavārttika,* Vol. I, Introduction, p. 7.
5. *SPB,* Introduction, p. 6.
6. Suresh Chandra, *Vijñānabhikṣu and His Place,* p. 50.
7. T.S. Rukmani, *Yogavārttika,* Vol. I, p. 7.
8. Suresh Chandra, *op. cit.,* p. 50.
9. भाष्यञ्चात्र गौडपादकृतम् । Suresh Chandra, *op. cit.,* p. 50.

which was not listed in Aufrecht's catalogue has been brought to light by Gopīnātha Kavirāja. He informs us that it is a work in which Vijñānabhikṣu criticized the followers of Śaṅkarācārya.[1] But T.S. Rukmani[2] does not subscribe to this view. She says that there is no such manuscript as would suggest that *Pāṣaṇḍamatakhaṇḍana* was written by Vijñānabhikṣu.

So far as Vijñānabhikṣu's authorship of the other sixteen works listed in Aufrecht's catalogue is concerned, there is no difference of opinion. These works are:

Upadeśaratnamālā
Brahmasūtrabhāṣya
Kaṭhavallyupaniṣadāloka
Kaivalyopaniṣadāloka
Maitreyyupaniṣadāloka
Māṇḍūkyopaniṣadāloka
Muṇḍakopaniṣadāloka
Praśnopaniṣadāloka
Taittirīyopaniṣadāloka
Śvetāśvataropaniṣadāloka
Īśvaragītābhāṣya
Brahmādarśa
Yogavārttika
Sāṅkhyapravacanabhāṣya
Sāṅkhyasāra
Yogasārasaṃgraha.

The chronological order mentioned here is generally accepted except that on the basis of mutual references, as T.S. Rukmani holds, *Yogavārttika* and *Sāṅkhyapravacanabhāṣya* were written simultaneously.[3] But Narayan Kumar Chattopadhyay has something slightly different to say in this regard. He takes into consideration the nature of the published works and views that since *Vijñānāmṛtabhāṣya* does not evince maturity, it should be the maiden work of Vijñānabhikṣu.

1. स्वकृते पाषण्डमतखण्डननामके ग्रन्थे श्रीशङ्कराचार्यानुयायिनः संन्यासिनो दूषयामासायं भिक्षुरिति विज्ञायते । *Kāśī kī Sārasvata Sādhanā*, quoted in *SPB*, Introduction, p. 5.
2. T.S. Rukmani, *Yogavārttika*, Introduction, p. 8.
3. T.S. Rukmani, *Yogavārttika*, Vol. I, Introduction, p. 6. Also cf. *Encyclopedia of Indian Philosophies* , Vol. IV, p. 376.

Yogavārttika is a better written work but lacks the maturity and precision of *Sāṅkhyasāra* and *Sāṅkhyapravacanabhāṣya*. It, therefore, seems proper to assume that *Yogavārttika* followed *Vijñānāmṛtabhāṣya* and preceded *Sāṅkhyapravacanabhāṣya*. The fourth in order should be *Sāṅkhyasāra* in which he is at his best since the arguments which he puts forward in this work are precise and convincing. *Yogasārasaṃgraha* contains no serious reasoning but makes references to all the four works referred to above. This means that it is the last in order and also perhaps bears testimony to his declining age.[1]

Leaving aside the still controversial *Pāṣaṇḍamatakhaṇḍana*, which, nevertheless, is also a work concerning Vedānta as implied by a passage in Gopīnātha Kavirāja's *Kāśī kī Sārasvata Sādhanā*,[2] we find that out of the sixteen works written by Vijñānabhikṣu there are eight works which he wrote on the philosophy of Vedānta. The magnitude of his writings on the Upaniṣadic philosophy shows his predilection for Vedānta. Keeping this in view, we should consider it understandable that he has preference for the Vedāntic liberation.[3] It ensues when the individual self discriminates itself from Brahman, whereas the *Sāṅkhyan* liberation in his view is brought about by the discriminating knowledge between the self and the intellect and its cause, i.e. *mahat* and *prakṛti*. Nonetheless after studying *Vijñānāmṛtabhāṣya* we gather the impression that it lacks the rigour that we find in *Sāṅkhyasāra* and *Sāṃkhyapravacanabhāṣya*. However, it cannot be gainsaid that it is the *Brahmamīmāṃsābhāṣya* (*Vijñānāmṛtabhāṣya*) which presents a somewhat coherent system of his philosophy, the indications of which are found scattered in other works written by him.

The present attempt is mainly based upon *Vijñānāmṛtabhāṣya*. Other works have also been drawn upon insofar as they help present a coherent picture of his philosophical system named by him as *avibhāgādvaita* (Integral Non-dualism). It is mainly this work in which *Vijñānabhikṣu* is seen to launch a vehement attack on Śaṅkara and his followers as if he were rescuing Vedānta from their clutches.

---

1. N.K. Chattopadhyay, *Indian Philosophy—Its Exposition in the Light of Vijñānabhikṣu's Bhāṣya and Yogavārttika: A Modern Approach*, Introduction, p. iii.
2. Quoted in *SPB*, Introduction, p. 5 fn.
3. Vijñānabhikṣu's view on the Vedāntic liberation is different from that conceived by Śaṅkara.

But it is a necessary exercise on his behalf to justify his endeavour to provide a 'genuine' metaphysics and ethics based on it so that it might 'really' help the aspirants to attain liberation.

Śaṅkara appears to follow a tradition when he outlines the philosophy of Advaita in the first four *sūtras.*[1] He interprets the *sūtra* (BS 1-1-5)[2] in a way that *prakṛti* is not accepted as a cause of the universe. Vijñānabhikṣu does not accept this view. He holds that *prakṛti* being a power of the Absolute (Brahman) is a cause of this universe and that it does not go uncorroborated from the Śrutis.[3] *Prakṛti,* in its pure *sattva* form, is the Eternal Adjunct of the Absolute and accounts for Its meaningful activity, which, according to Vijñānabhikṣu, is the defining characteristic of existence and reality.[4] It is perhaps this necessity that he made the first five *sūtras* a basis to explain his philosophy in a nutshell. Secondly, it is the Advaitin's theory of the unreality and inexpressibility of the world which was treated by him with as much significance.[5]

In this context it may be pointed out that Suresh Chandra Śrīvāstavya's observation that Vijñānabhikṣu's severe criticism of Śaṅkara and his followers bears testimony to his innate self-confidence, is not correct for the following reasons:

1. Though he endeavours to propound an altogether new system of philosophy, he does not seem to possess the matching competence. It is clear from the fact that his main work, *Vijñānāmṛtabhāṣya,* lacks the rigour of *Sāṅkhyasāra* and *Sāṃkhyapravacanabhāṣya* whereas it should have been interpreted in a more precise and convincing manner since his Integral Non-dualism is mainly based on this text. It has been discussed in more detail in the last chapter of this work that it is an instance of misplaced emphasis.

---

1. अथातो ब्रह्मजिज्ञासा, जन्माद्यस्य यत:, शास्त्रयोनित्वात्, तत्तु समन्वयात् । *BS,* 1-1-1 to 4.
2. ईक्षतेर्नाशब्दम् ।
3. प्रधानक्षेत्रज्ञपतिर्गुणेश:, अजामेकाम्, यस्तु तन्तुनाभ इव तन्तुभि: प्रधानजै: स्वभावत:, मायां तु प्रकृतिं विद्यादित्यादिश्रुतिभि: प्रधानस्यापि श्रौतत्वात् शक्तिविधया प्रधानस्य जगत्कारणत्वश्रवणाच्च 'बह्वी: प्रजा: सृजमानां सरूपा:' इत्यादिश्रुतिष्विति ।

   Vijñānāmṛtabhāṣyam ed. Pt. Kedāranātha Tripāṭhī, Banaras Hindu University, 1979, p. 67. (Hereinafter referred to as *VAB*).
4. For more details see chapters on the Absolute and self.
5. Suresh Chandra Śrīvāstavya's *Vijñānabhikṣu and His Place in Indian Philosophy,* p. 61.

2. The exaggerated references such as by hundreds of Śrutis and Smṛtis, his dubbing the Advaitin as *vedāntibruva*, *pracchannabauddha*, *vaināśika*, *mūḍha*, *digbhrānta* and calling the philosophy of Advaita as *kalikṛta-apasiddhānta* do not at all prove that he had the requisite confidence. They rather indicate that he was not adequately equipped to propound an independent system of thought.
3. It seems that he was greatly influenced by the compulsions of his time. His syncretic attitude is a case in point. Or, his syncretism might have been a reaction to Akbar's concept of '*tauhid*' or unity of all religions.

2

CONCEPT OF THE ABSOLUTE

Vijñānabhikṣu's Absolute is an integral whole in Which selves and *prakṛti* inhere as Its powers. He has described It as *avibhāgādvaita.* It means that the reals like selves and *prakṛti* remain non-separate from the Absolute distinguishably during creation and indistinguishably at the time of dissolution or before creation. *Sat* and *cit,* according to him, constitute Its nature. So far as Its *ānanda* (bliss) aspect, as given in the Upaniṣads, is concerned, he attributes it to the *sattva* constituent of the Eternal Adjunct of the Absolute. In contrast, Śaṅkara, for example, includes bliss in the defining characteristics of the Ultimate Reality. Vijñānabhikṣu also differs with Śaṅkara on the question of the self-luminosity of the Absolute. The former holds that the Absolute being of the nature of illumination does become an object of experience though in the highest state of contemplation.

Before the nature of Absolute is taken up for detailed discussion, it seems proper to consider the syllogistic evidence Vijñānabhikṣu adduces for the proof of the existence of Absolute.

It reads :

1. Effects like intellect, etc. are created by the perceptual mode reflecting their material cause.
2. Because they are products.
3. Such as a pitcher, etc.

It is a given fact that the knowledge in the form of perceptual mode having as its object the material cause of each and every product precedes the manifestation of the product. It means that among other factors the perceptual mode is also the cause of every effect. Vijñānabhikṣu proceeds to point out that the intellectual mode perceiving the material cause of the effects like intellect, ego, subtle elements, etc. cannot belong to the likes of us, the human beings. The production of a pitcher is obviously preceded by the intellectual mode (knowledge) of the potter reflecting its material cause—the clay. The knowledge of the material cause of the pitcher is a modification of the intellect, the supervisor of which is the individual self. Similarly the perception of the material cause of the world is a mode of the Eternal Adjunct comprising pure *sattva.* This pure *sattva* is the *Upādhi* of the Absolute as in the case of a pitcher the intellect is the *upādhi* of the individual self. So far as the creation of the world is concerned, the perception of the material cause cannot but belong to the Absolute.[1] To ward off the contingency of *prakṛti* itself assuming the status of the causality of the world he takes help from the scriptures. The scriptural statement 'He willed to be many' implies that the ultimate cause is of conscious nature. Besides, it takes care of the fact that the psychological phenomenon such as willing does not solely belong to *prakṛti* which is unconscious. Even if 'willing' be taken to mean a mode of the intellect without involving consciousness, the advocates of the view that the independent *prakṛti* is the cause do not accept that the impulse of *pradhāna* or *prakṛti* is preceded by the act of 'willing'. Neither can this act of willing which precedes the creation be assigned to the individual self as according to Vijñānabhikṣu it is not supposed to possess consciousness before the creation of *mahat,* etc. It is all the more undesirable to hold the view that this creation is preceded by the act of willing after *mahat* has come into existence,[2] for creatorship could, then, belong to the individual self rather than God. So the act

1. तत्र ब्रह्मानुमानस्यायं प्रकारः—बुद्धिप्रभृतिकार्यम् उपादानगोचरप्रत्यक्षजन्यम्, कार्यत्वाद्, घटादिवदिति । अत्र चोपादानगोचरप्रत्यक्षवृत्तेरेव कार्ये हेतुत्वं लाघवात् न तु चैतन्यस्यापि गौरवात् । तदा बुद्ध्यादीनामुपादानगोचरवृत्तीच्छाकृतिमज्जन्यत्वेन कारणसत्त्वस्य सिद्ध्यनन्तरं, तत्कारणसत्त्वं परस्य भोग्यम् इच्छादिमत्त्वाज्जीवोपाधिवदिति कारणसत्त्वभोक्तृतयेश्वरोऽनुमेय इति ।

VAB (under *BS,* I-1-3), p. 37.

2. जगत्कारणस्येक्षणे श्रुतयश्च "तदैक्षत बहु स्यां प्रजायेये"त्याद्याः ।. . . .न हीदमीक्षणं प्रधानादीनामचेतनानां संभवति, ईक्षणध्यानचिन्तनादिशब्देषु चैतन्यस्य विशेषत्वात् । ईक्षणादिशब्दस्योपाधिवृत्तिमात्रवाचकत्वेऽपि प्रकृतिस्वातन्त्र्यवादिभिस्तत्पूर्विका प्रधानप्रवृत्तिर्नाभ्युपगम्यत एव । नापि जीवानां, महदादिसृष्टेः पूर्वं कारणाभावेन जीवानां चैतन्यफलोपधानाभावात् । न चेयमीक्षणपूर्विका सृष्टिर्महत्तत्त्वसृष्टेः पश्चादिति वक्तुं शक्यते । *Ibid.,* p. 66. See also *ibid.,* p. 65.

of willing preceding the setting forth of creation does presuppose as creator the Absolute of the nature of consciousness Which is eternally invested with the Pure-*Sattva*-Adjunct.

The Absolute is defined by Vijñānabhikṣu as pure consciousness eternally invested with the Pure-*Sattva*-Adjunct. All powers in the form of *prakṛti* and *puruṣas* exist in It by the relation of non-separation. It remains untainted by affliction, *karma,* fruition and latent deposits and is a special kind of consciousness. The world manifested as name and form, comprising conscious and unconscious categories of objects and having a definite spatial arrangement and temporal sequence is liable to six-fold transformation—birth, existence, expansion, modification, degeneration and destruction. Such a world, the creation and design of which are beyond comprehension, surges forth from It as *mahāvāyu* from *ākāśa,* the earth from *mahājala* and the sentient and non-sentient entities from earth. In other words,[1] it is the all-encompassing locative cause of all.

The concept of locative causality is peculiar to Vijñānabhikṣu. It is indispensable so far as understanding his conception of the Absolute is concerned. According to him, the Locative Cause is a substratum cause or a receptacle cause unseparated from, and aided by, which the material cause gets transformed into effects. To illustrate, water is the locative cause of earth at the time of its creation, since the subtle essences (*tanmātras*) of earth unseparated from and aided by it are transformed into earth.[2] Vijñānabhikṣu's postulation of the Locative Cause helps him tide over the dilemma, namely, how does the Absolute not undergo any transformation even as *prakṛti* inhering in It does? The presupposition of Brahman as the Locative Cause makes It free from the contingency of being liable to change. Vijñānabhikṣu clarifies that Brahman as the Locus remains unaffected by change, while *prakṛti* existing in It as material cause does undergo change and is transformed as this world. Given

---

1. अस्य जगतो नामरूपाभ्यां व्याकृतस्य चेतनाचेतनरूपस्य प्रतिनियतदेशकालसंस्थानव्यापारादिमतोऽचिन्त्यरचनात्मकस्य जायतेऽस्ति वर्धते विपरिणमतेऽपक्षीयते विनश्यतीत्येवंरूपं जन्मादिषट्कं यत: परमेश्वरादन्तर्लीनप्रकृतिपुरुषाद्यखिलशक्तिकात् स्वतश्चिन्मात्राद् विशुद्धसत्त्वाख्यमायोपाधिकात् क्लेशकर्मविपाकाशयैरपरामृष्टाच्चेतनविशेषाद् भवति, आकाशादिव महावायुर्महाजलादिव च पृथिवी पृथिव्या इव च स्थावरजङ्गमादिकं, तद्ब्रह्मेति वाक्यशेष: । *VAB,* p. 17.
2. तदेवाधिष्ठानकारणं यत्राविभक्तं येनोपष्टब्धं च सदुपादानकारणं कार्याकारेण परिणमते । यथा सर्गादौ जलाविभक्ता: पार्थिवसूक्ष्मांशा: तन्मात्राख्या: जलेनैवोपष्टम्भात् पृथिव्याकारेण परिणमन्त इत्यतो जलं महापृथिव्या अधिष्ठानकारणमिति । *Ibid.,* p. 17.

this concept of the Locative Cause, Vijñānabhikṣu points out that the prevalent idea or view that Brahman is also the material cause is substantiated in the process. For the locative cause is also conventionally called the material cause like *prakṛti.* As such it is appropriate to say that Brahman is the material cause of the world and the latter is non-separate from the former.[1] The illustration given to exemplify the concept of Locative Cause renders the view much clearer.

That Brahman is the Ultimate Cause[2] of all is an alternative definition of the Absolute offered by Vijñānabhikṣu. He makes it clear by giving an example of eyes, etc. which individually are the causes of acts of seeing, etc. All these individual causes of different acts of cognition belong to the individual self because they are superintended by it. Being the superintendent of cognition the individual self may be called the all-comprehensive cause. In a similar manner Brahman superintends all the functions of Its powers the instrumentality of which is determined individually in each case in the form of material cause, etc. The omnipotent Absolute is the cause of all by virtue of Its being superintendent of all the powers (adjuncts). Thus the Absolute can be called the non-separate material as well as efficient cause of the universe,[3] the creatorship and material causality respectively being due to Its Pure-*Sattva*-Adjunct and *prakṛti* along with its effects.

The Locative Causality as defined by Vijñānabhikṣu suffers from the defect of overpervasion; the definition apparently extends to

---

1. अत एवाविकारिचिन्मात्रत्वेऽपि ब्रह्मणो जगदुपादानत्वं जगदभेदश्चोपपद्यते । विकारिकारणवदधिष्ठानकारणस्यापि उपादानत्वव्यवहारात् । *VAB*, p. 19.
2. Brahman as the Ultimate Cause cannot be identical with *jīva* as the Śaṃkarites hold, saying that the primary meaning of 'Brahman' is '*jīva*'. Maintaining the distinction between the Absolute and individual selves Vijñānabhikṣu asserts that 'Brahman' connotes 'capacity of infinite expansion'. This characteristic of infinite expansiveness belongs to the Ultimate Cause and not to *jīva.* Brahman in this sense is derivative-conventional (*yogarūḍha*) like '*paṅkaja*'. So identity between Brahman and *jīva* is untenable.
   Cf. एतच्च जगज्जन्मादिकारणत्वं ब्रह्मशब्दप्रवृत्तिनिमित्तमपि बोध्यम् । मूलकारणस्यैव निरतिशयबृहत्त्वात् । ब्रह्मशब्दश्च पङ्कजादिवद् योगरूढः । अतो न जीवादिर्मुख्यो ब्रह्मशब्दार्थः । *Ibid.*, p. 18.
3. एवञ्च जगतः सर्वप्रकारकारणत्वमपि ब्रह्मलक्षणं कर्तुं शक्यते । प्रकृतिपुरुषादिषु शक्तिषु प्रत्येकमुपादानत्वादिरूपेण प्रतिनियतमेव कारणत्वम् । ब्रह्मणस्तु सर्वशक्तिकत्वात् तत्तदुपाधिभिः सर्वकारणत्वम् । यथा चक्षुरादीनां दर्शनादिकारणत्वं यत्प्रत्येकमस्ति तत्सर्वं सर्वाध्यक्षस्य जीवस्य भवतीति । एतेन जगतोऽभिन्ननिमित्तोपादानत्वं व्याख्यातम् । *Ibid.*, p. 18.

ākāśa, mahāvāyu, etc. To ward off this defect, he amends the definition by introducing into it an addition in the form of 'witnesshood'. The amended definition of the Absolute comes to mean that by being their witness It aids the unseparated *prakṛti,* etc. to be transformed into the present creation. The inclusion of the word 'witnesshood'[1] in the definition of Locative Causality also does away with the contingency of the modifiability of Brahman. Besides, witnesshood is a quality which belongs neither to *prakṛti* nor to the self before creation.[2]

Śaṅkara holds that Brahman does not undergo any change. The change is only apparent. It is against the *Vivartavāda* of Śaṅkara that Vijñānabhikṣu postulates the concept of Locative Causality, which is a separate kind of causality in addition to the three others obtaining in the Nyāya system of Philosophy. Nyāya holds that God is the efficient cause only.[3]

The Advaitins hold that the world is superimposed on the Absolute due to *māyā* as the snake is superimposed upon, since illusorily perceived in, the rope due to darkness. No sooner is the darkness dispelled than the illusory appearance of the snake disappears and the rope is seen in its true form. Likewise when *ajñāna* is destroyed the phenomenal world is sublated and the Supreme Reality shines in Its real form. The Advaitic system compares the world to the illusory snake and so regards it as unreal. But Vijñānabhikṣu avers that the objects are perceived by the self in the form of reflections cast in it. If the reflections of the mental modes reflecting the objects cease to be cast in it, it does not at all imply that the original ones are also blotted out of existence.[4] They cease to matter for the liberated self, but they do continue to enjoy the status of reality.

---

1. Vijñānabhikṣu has discussed this aspect in the context of self at several places. Commenting on the *Sāṅkhyasūtra* VI.2, he says that the self is immutable (eternal) since it always witnesses the mental states. For details see *infra* pp. 48f, 72ff.
2. ब्रह्मणश्च स्वाविभक्तप्रकृत्याद्युपष्टम्भकत्वं साक्षितामात्रेणेति जगत्कारणत्वेऽपि न ब्रह्मणो विकारित्वं न वा प्रकृतिपुरुषादिष्वतिप्रसङ्गः, सर्गात्पूर्वमन्येषां साक्षित्वासम्भवात् । *VAB*, p. 17.
3. वैशेषिकादिभिरपीदृशं ब्रह्मण कारणत्वमिष्यत एव । परन्तु तैरिदमपि निमित्तकारणतेति परिभाष्यते । अस्माभिस्तु समवाय्यसमवायिभ्यामुदासीनं निमित्तकारणेभ्यश्च विलक्षणतया चतुर्थमाधार-कारणत्वमिति । *Ibid.*, pp. 17-18.
4. यत्तु अनयैव रीत्या चैतन्येऽध्यस्ततया जगतः प्रकृतिपर्यन्तस्य सिद्धत्वाच्चिदेवैकं तत्त्वम्, अन्यत् सर्वं दृश्यजातं मरीच्युदकादिवत्तुच्छमित्याधुनिका विवर्तवादिनोऽभ्युपगच्छन्ति, तन्न, तथापि बिम्बरूपाणां विषयाणामेव प्रतिबिम्बरूपेणैव भानात् प्रतिबिम्बरूपतया चैतन्ये बाधेऽपि स्वतो बाधाभावादिति । *Ibid.*, p. 41.

Vijñānabhikṣu, an upholder of the 'reality' of the world, argues out why he rejects Śaṅkara's view of the unreality of the world. He points out that the states of bondage and liberation[1] would be rendered insignificant, if the world were to be taken as unreal. For it loses its significance for the man aspiring after liberation, when he is enjoined upon to strive for achievement simply because the very scriptures which tell about the freedom from bondage fall within the domain of unreality. Liberation, the means to it and the (nature of the) Ultimate Reality would all become inauthentic because they are preached by the 'unreal' scriptures. Total unbelief will be the result. It is, therefore, necessary to give a different meaning to the word 'Advaita' so that the reality of the world may be preserved and inauthenticity of the scriptures, avoided. The presupposition of the Locative Causality helps Vijñānabhikṣu to maintain his realistic stance in the sense that the selves and the products of *prakṛti* are real and not mere appearance as Śaṅkara holds.

Unlike Śaṅkara, Vijñānabhikṣu holds that the relationship of non-separateness subsists between the Absolute and the world. It is real since it is natural, eternal and existent in the beginning and in the end.[2] He likens this relationship to the mixture of milk and sugar, and the unity of the individual self and the intellect to the inseparable relationship of the principal and its subsidiary. He indicates clearly that this relationship of intense mixing up may be a form of either conjunction or 'identity'. Even the men endowed with discrimination-knowledge say that sugar and milk are one, after the sugar has been dissolved in the milk. This eternal and seeming identity of the phenomenal world with the Absolute is held by Vijñānabhikṣu to be in the form of the relation of non-separateness.[3] The Advaitins say that, with deference to the scriptural statements conveying identity, the Absolute should be taken to be one undivided whole and the statements of difference could be satisfactorily explained with the help of the theory of *māyā*. Vijñānabhikṣu rebuts

---

1. किं च बन्धमोक्षादिकं सर्वं मिथ्येति वेदान्ता आहुरिति गुरुमुखादापातत: श्रवणादेवाकृतसाक्षात्कारस्यापि शिष्यस्य सर्वत्रैवानाश्वासात् श्रवणमननादौ साक्षात्काराय प्रवृत्तिरेव न स्यान् महानास्तिकत्वसंपादनात्, बह्वायाससाध्ये फलनिश्चयस्यैव प्रवृत्तिहेतुत्वादिति । *Ibid.*, p. 56. See also *SPB*, p. 96.
2. तत्राप्यविभाग एव आद्यन्तयोरनुगतत्वात् स्वाभाविकत्वात् नित्यत्वाच्च सत्य: । *VAB*, p. 32.
3. अयं च सार्वकालो ब्रह्मणि प्रपञ्चाभेदो बुद्धिपुरुषयोरिव गुणप्रधानभावेनात्यन्तसंमिश्रणरूप: संयोगादिविशेष: स्वरूपसम्बन्धविशेषो वाऽस्तु, विवेकिनामपि शर्करादुग्धयोरेकीभावव्यवहारात् । *Ibid.*, p. 59. See also *ibid.*, p. 26 for *vibhāga* and *avibhāga*.

it and says that the same argument of compliance with the scriptural statements also holds good for his view about the Absolute. He maintains that identity can be satisfactorily explained in terms of non-separateness and the scriptural statements about the notion of difference would be appreciated more appropriately even without invoking the theory of illusion. When compliance with the scriptures is possible both ways it is better to subscribe to the latter view. Moreover, the view on non-separateness does not go unillustrated in the scriptures. Just as pure water poured into pure water turns into one indistinguishable whole, similarly the soul of the saint enters into an indistinguishable union with the Absolute. There remains nothing else which is separate from It. The Absolute is non-separate but seems to be stationed separately distinguishable in the creatures. It is both manifest and unmanifest and never parts with Its powers. It is in this sense that Vijñānabhikṣu considers the relationship of non-separateness to be real in the ultimate sense.[1] He does not consider separation or *vibhāga* to be real because it is caused and exists only in the middle, i.e. during creation only.[2] According to Vijñānabhikṣu it is *ajñāna* which through *dharma* and *adharma* is responsible for the separation of the self from the Absolute.[3] The separation or *vibhāga* is defined by him as the state of having different and manifest characteristics[4] with which the individual selves and the effects of *prakṛti* are endowed during creation. When *ajñāna* is absolutely destroyed by the knowledge of discrimination, there is nothing left which causes this contingent or accidental separation to come into existence. To understand Vijñānabhikṣu adequately, let's take into account the Advaitin's objection. The Advaitin says that if *abheda* be taken to mean *avibhāga*, Vijñānabhikṣu

---

1. तत्रोच्यते–अभेदवाक्यानुरोधेन भेदवाक्यानामौपाधिकभेदपरत्वं यथा कल्प्यते, तथा भेदवाक्यानुरोधेना-भेदवाक्यानामविभागादिलक्षणाभेदपरत्वं कथं न कल्प्यते ? अविरोधस्योभयथैव सम्भवात् । श्रूयते चाविभागादिरूपाभेदोऽपि "यथोदकं शुद्धे शुद्धमाक्षिप्तं तादृगेव भवति एवं मुनेर्विजानत आत्मा भवति गौतम, न तु तद्द्वितीयमस्ति ततोऽन्यद् विभक्तमि " त्यादिश्रुतिषु ।
   स्मृतिषु च–
   अविभक्तं च भूतेषु विभक्तमिव च स्थितम् ।
   व्यक्तं स एव वाऽव्यक्तं स एव पुरुषः परः ।। इत्यादिषु । प्रत्युताविभागादिलक्षणाभेदस्य पारमार्थिकतया तत्परत्वमेवोचितम् । *VAB*, p. 21.
2. विभागस्तु मध्ये स्वल्पावच्छेदेन नैमित्तिको विकारान्तरवद् वाचारम्भणमात्रमिति विशेषः । *Ibid.*, p. 32.
3. धर्माधर्मादिद्वारा विभागजनके ज्ञाने. . . . *Ibid.*, p. 31.
4. विभागश्च लक्षणान्यत्वम् अभिव्यक्तधर्मभेद इति यावत् । *Ibid.*, p. 26.

would have to take recourse to *lakṣaṇā*. The latter replies that there is no need to resort to *lakṣaṇā* in this case since the root √ *bhid* meaning 'to cleave', i.e. 'to separate', from which the word *abheda* is derived would serve the purpose. Both the words *abheda* and *avibhāga* would thus become synonymous.[1]

The Advaitin invokes the theories of reflection and limitation to prove the illusory nature of the plurality of selves and the consequent undivided oneness of the Absolute. The former theory explains how the qualityless Absolute appears as many selves and objects. To illustrate, the sun appears to be as many as there are receptacles of water in which it is reflected. It also seems to be affected when the nature of the reflecting medium changes. For example, when the receptacle is full of dirty water, the sun appears to be dirty, though in reality it remains unsullied. Similarly the Absolute does become, though only seemingly, affected by the intellects in which It is reflected. This theory reduces the individual selves to mere images. This is why the alternative theory of limitation is preferred by some Advaitins to secure some status of reality for the individual selves. Śaṅkara makes use of the latter theory on the analogy of pot and space to explain that the Absolute seems to assume differentiations on account of Its being limited by the intellects, sense-organs, bodies, etc. The limitation which causes differentiation is due to *ajñāna*, 'primal ignorance'. The Absolute in reality remains one undivided whole like space.[2] The principle of *ajñāna* which generates the illusion of distinctions is also sought to resolve the contradictions among scriptural statements which declare the individual self to be both identical with, and different from, the Absolute.

Vijñānabhikṣu does not accept the view of Advaitins. He says that so far as the resolution of the contradictory scriptural statements is concerned, it can be achieved if the identity conveyed by them is taken to mean non-separateness. He asserts that his view seems to be more consistent with the spirit of the scriptures for several reasons: The scriptural statements expressing non-separate nature of the Absolute are not wanting; the principle of non-separateness confers the status of reality on the variegated existence; both the theories of limitation and reflection do not satisfactorily explain the

---

1. न चाविभागपरत्वे सत्यभेदशब्दे लक्षणाऽस्ति, भिदिर्विदारणे इति विभागेऽपि भिदिधातोरनुशासनात् । *VAB*, p. 21.
2. *Encyclopedia of Indian Philosophies*, ed. Karl H. Potter, Vol. III, Delhi, 1981, pp. 84-85.

phenomenon of liberation of the individual self as according to these theories its release means its destruction; these theories imply that the difference between the Absolute and individual selves is illusory, but the states of bondage and release of individual selves presuppose a real difference between them; moreover identity cannot subsist between an unreal entity (individual self) and a real one (Absolute); in the case of the individual selves being accepted as real, the undivided oneness of the Absolute is abandoned[1] and the integral nature of Brahman containing several reals gets strengthened.

Unlike Advaitins, Vijñānabhikṣu says that the word '*bheda*' means 'separation' also. He, therefore, explains somewhat differently the Upaniṣadic statement '*ekamevādvitīyam*'. The three words making up the statement mean the absence of homogeneous, heterogeneous and internal 'separations'[2], while the Śaṃkarites interpret the same as signifying the absence of homogeneous, heterogeneous and internal 'differences' in the Absolute.[3] Vijñānabhikṣu further clarifies that by '*bheda*' he means duality, too, by virtue of its being characterized by the form of manifest effects. He considers this manifest state to be *māyā* which is apparently located in the Supreme Soul.[4] The manifest nature is as illusory or fleeting as that of the objects projected by magic. On the other hand, '*abheda*' or '*avibhāga*' meaning non-separateness after dissolution is of ultimate reality as it is the eternal nature of the Absolute. Compared with it, separation, that is, manifest creation, is unreal as it is only an object of speech.[5]

Vijñānabhikṣu describes the state of non-separateness of the Absolute as a merger of *prakṛti* and *puruṣas* in It. They remain in It indistinguishably in the form of knowledge and not as manifest

---

1. *VAB*, pp. 20-23. See also J.N. Sinha, *The Philosophy of Vijñānabhikṣu*, Calcutta, 1976, pp. 30-35.
2. एवं च सति सदेवेत्यादिवाक्यस्थमेवकारादिपदत्रयं सजातीयविजातीयस्वगतविभागशून्यपरत्वमिति मन्तव्यम् । *VAB*, p. 58.
3. सजातीयविजातीयस्वगतभेदनिरासार्थम् एकमेवाद्वितीयमिति पदत्रयम् ।
Ratnaprabhā on Brahmasūtra Śāṅkarabhāṣya on *BS*, I-1-4 ed. J.L. Shastri, Delhi, 1980, p. 62.
4. भेदो विभागलक्षणद्वैतं तु व्यक्तकार्यरूपेण । सा च व्यक्तावस्था आत्माधिष्ठाना मायैव मायाकार्यत्वात् इन्द्रजालवत् क्षणभङ्गुरत्वादिति । *VAB*, p. 58.
5. यदेतत् प्रलयाद्वैतमुक्तम्, एतदेव विभागस्य वाचारम्भणत्वेनाव्यक्तावस्थायाश्च स्वाभाविकतया नित्यत्वेन च पारमार्थिकमित्युक्तं कौर्मादिषु । *Ibid.*, p. 58.

objects because the characteristics and conditions responsible for their manifestation during creation cease to exist during dissolution. He clarifies it by giving an illustration pertaining to cosmology.

Earth before its own creation is manifested as water and not as earth since smell, hardness and other such characteristics as are capable of manifesting it, are absent at that particular time. Consequently having no manifesting characteristics, *prakṛti* and *puruṣas* exist in the Absolute in the form of knowledge which is Its nature in the same manner as earth exists as having the form of water on account of the absence of its manifestors at the beginning of its own creation.[1]

We become more familiar with Vijñānabhikṣu's view on non-separateness, when we come to know his interpretation of quietude preceding creation. He interprets it as absence of desires and activity belonging to the adjunct, and not as absence of cognition of the objects as happens in the case of a person who is fast asleep. If the latter interpretation were to be accepted, the Absolute's omniscience would be compromised[2] and Its omniscience consists in Its comprehensive mode reflecting all without any mediation.

That there exists mutual difference (*anyo'nyābhāva*) between the Absolute and selves at the ontological level provides sufficient justification for presupposing a relation of the controller and the controlled between the Absolute and the selves even before the latter enter into union with their *upādhis.*[3] The Mahābhārata tells us explicitly that there is One Ultimate over and above the group of twenty-five elements, that is, the unconscious principle *prakṛti* along with its twenty-three evolutes and *puruṣa,* the principle of consciousness.[4] According to Vijñānabhikṣu it implies that the non-separateness being a characteristic of oneness has been emphasized after

1. ज्ञानस्वरूपे परमात्मनि प्रलीनतया तदविभक्तत्वमेव तत्स्वरूपत्वं बोध्यम् । प्रलये हि पुंप्रकृत्यादिकं ज्ञानस्वरूपेणैव रूप्यते न त्वर्थरूपेण, अर्थतो व्यञ्जकव्यापाराभावात् । यथा स्वसर्गादौ पृथिवी जलरूपेणैव व्यज्यते न तु पृथिवीरूपेण गन्धकाठिन्यादीनां व्यञ्जकानामभावादिति । *VAB.*, p. 59.
2. शान्तम् रागादिरहितम् औपाधिकव्यापारशून्यं च न तु सुषुप्तवद् विषयसंवेदनरहितम्, सर्वज्ञमित्युत्तरात् । *Ibid.*, p. 19.
3. न चायमुपाधिसंबन्धात् पूर्वमधिष्ठेयाधिष्ठातृभावो निरंशस्यात्मनः स्वरूपभेदं विनोपपद्यत इति । *Ibid.*, p. 25.
4. अन्यश्च राजन् प्रवरस्तथान्यः पञ्चविंशकः ।
तच्छ्रुत्वा चानुपश्यन्ति एक एवेति साधवः ।। *MBH, Mokṣaparva,* Ch. 318, śl. 78, quoted in *VAB*, p. 25.

pointing out clearly the ontological distinction between the Absolute and the individual selves on the one hand, and between the Absolute and *prakṛti* on the other.[1] Consistency, therefore, demands that every Non-dualistic enunciation is to be construed as depicting the non-separate nature of the Absolute.

In this context it would not be out of place to discuss the part-and-whole relationship between the selves and the Absolute. Vijñānabhikṣu does not subscribe to the view that the Absolute and the individual selves are in relation with each other as the original (archetype) and its reflection are; that in his view would render the status of the self absolutely unreal. To confer on it a status of 'reality', he invokes the relationship of *aṃśa* and *aṃśī* between the selves and the Absolute. All the more so, because the theories of reflection and limitation are not compatible with each other. Undivided (indivisible) oneness of the Absolute, too, does not find mention in the *Brahmasūtras,* whereas *aṃśavāda* is clearly mentioned.[2]

As such the relation between the Absolute and selves should be one of identity-in-difference which, according to him, is the true meaning as propounded in the *Brahmasūtras*. Though they are ontologically different, the postulation of identity (in the sense of non-separateness) between them is perfectly conceivable when temporal manifestations are taken into consideration. Selves though different from the Absolute, remain eternally inseparable from It as the innate power of its possessor can't be separated from him.[3]

Vijñānabhikṣu makes a clear distinction between *avayava* and *aṃśa* when he avers that though the self is not an *avayava* of the Absolute yet it can be called Its *aṃśa* in the sense that it is an adjunct of non-separateness from a homogeneous whole.[4] As a consequence *aṃśī* has been defined as a subjunct of non-separateness from a homogeneous whole[5] the adjunct rests upon. Thus according to Vijñānabhikṣu *aṃśatva* has the true implication of the homogeneity

---

1. इति मोक्षधर्मादौ स्वरूपभेदमुक्त्वाऽधिष्ठेयाधिष्ठात्रोरविभागलक्षणमैक्यमुक्तम् । *VAB*, p. 25.
2. प्रतिबिम्बावच्छेदांशादिवादाः परस्परविरोधेन सर्वे न सम्भवन्तीत्येक एव वाद आश्रयणीयः ।. . . . तथा च सति अंशवाद एवाश्रयितुं युक्तः "अंशो नानाव्यपदेशादि"त्यादिसूत्रेणाचार्यैरंशत्वस्यैव न्यायतो मीमांस्यत्वात् । प्रतिबिम्बादिभावेनाखण्डत्वे स्पष्टसूत्राभावात् । *Ibid.*, p. 26.
3. अंशांशिनोश्च भेदाभेदौ विभागाविभागरूपौ कालभेदेनाविरुद्धौ ।अन्योऽन्याभावश्च जीवब्रह्मणोरात्यन्तिक एव, तथा शक्तिशक्तिमदविभागोऽपि नित्य एवेति मन्तव्यम् । *Ibid.*, p. 26.
4. अंशत्वं च सजातीयत्वे सति अविभागप्रतियोगित्वम् । *Ibid.*, p. 26.
5. तदनुयोगित्वं चांशित्वम् । *Ibid.*, p. 26.

of the Absolute with the selves and also inseparableness of the latter from the former. Unlike Advaitins, he insists that the self is primarily a part (*aṃśa*) of the Absolute as hair forms a part of the body and as son is considered to be a part of his father.[1] All the selves relinquishing their individual characteristics of manifesting objects submerge indistinguishably in the Absolute manifesting all, as the consciousness of the son remains without apparent distinction from that of his father before he sees the light of the day.[2] Likewise the selves being endowed with consciousness by virtue of the volition and desire of the Absolute manifest themselves. They, therefore, can be duly called *aṃśas* of the Absolute.[3]

Besides being *aṃśī*, the Absolute is also invested with the property of ultimate agency. Vijñānabhikṣu elucidates it by describing the agency of the self in respect of its acts of seeing, hearing, intellection and intimately knowing through the sense-organs and mind. He states that the apparent agency of these psychic processes is said to belong to the individual self, though these take place in the sense-organs and in turn in the mind. But according to him these psychic processes, in reality, belong to the Absolute as these take place under the latter's control or supervision. This act of supervision implies that both ownership and doership accrue to It as the selves have been relegated to the status of instruments. He further elaborates that as the self assumes the role of directing the senses to various stimuli, so does the Absolute when the selves have become Its instruments.[4]

The non-separate nature of the Absolute having been dwelt upon, it, now, looks proper to discuss Vijñānabhikṣu's view regarding Its existence-aspect.

---

1. ननु निरवयवस्य ब्रह्मणः कथं मुख्योंऽशः स्यादिति चेन्न, यथोक्तलक्षणांशत्वस्यावयवत्वाभावेऽपि दर्शनात् । यथा शरीरस्य केशादिरंशो. . . . पितुश्च पुत्र इति । *VAB*, p. 27.
2. सर्वे च जीवाः पितरि पुत्रचेतना इव चिन्मात्रे ब्रह्मणि नित्यसर्वावभासके विषयभासनरूपं स्वलक्षणं विहाय प्रलये लक्षणानन्यत्वं गच्छन्ति । *Ibid.*, p. 27.
3. सर्गकाले च तदिच्छया तत एव लब्धचैतन्यफलोपधाना आविर्भवन्ति पितुरिव पुत्राः ।अतो जीवा ब्रह्मांशा भवन्ति ।. . . . अतो जीवा ब्रह्मांशा मुख्या एव भवन्ति । *Ibid.*, p. 27.
4. किं च जीवदर्शनश्रवणमननविज्ञानानामप्यन्तर्याम्यायत्ततया अन्तर्यामिण एव तानि भवन्ति तत्स्वामिकत्वात् तत्कर्तृकत्वाद् येन तु करणस्थानीयस्य जीवस्येति महिमोत्कीर्तनादिति । *Ibid.*, p. 273.
   And also cf. न चेश्वरस्य सम्बोध्यत्वप्रयोक्तृत्वाभावात् कथं त्वमहंशब्दार्थता स्यादिति वाच्यम्, वागिन्द्रियद्वारा जीवस्य प्रयोक्तृत्ववज्जीवाख्यकरणद्वारा ब्रह्मण एव संबोध्यत्वादिसकलव्यवहारप्रतिपादनायैव तत्त्वमसीत्युपदेशादिति ।तथा च श्रुत्यन्तरम्–"नान्योऽतोऽस्ति द्रष्टा श्रोता मन्ता बोद्धे"त्यादिना परमात्मन एव दर्शनश्रवणादिसर्वव्यवहारकर्तृत्वमाह । *Ibid*, p. 31.

He defines existence as the state of having a property contributing to the emergence of meaningful activity directed towards some goal.[1] Interpreting the quotes from the *Narasiṃhapurāṇa* in consonance with his metaphysical view of the Absolute, Vijñānabhikṣu defines non-existence as submergence like that of a dead snake in a ditch. Had non-existence been taken to mean absolute absence, it would have contradicted the word *antarlīnavikāram* occurring in the quotes and the *Brahmasūtra* II-1-16,[2] which speaks about the existence of the individual selves and unconscious effects at the time of dissolution. The interpretation that non-existence is nothing but locus is not acceptable to him since resort to the secondary meaning in this case is without justification when *abheda* of cause and effect can satisfactorily be explained as non-separateness. This has been further substantiated by Vijñānabhikṣu in his commentary on the *Brahmasūtra* II-1-15 where he adduces arguments concerning the pre-existence of effect in the cause.[3]

To describe the Absolute in terms of existence, he postulates Its Eternal Pure-*Sattva*-Adjunct. It is because of this Adjunct that perception visualizing the whole world exists in the Absolute even at the time of dissolution just as it exists in It during creation, the only difference being that *prakṛti* and *puruṣas* having ceased to perform such functions as are performed by them during creation lie in It as if fast asleep.[4] The postulate of the Eternal Adjunct serves two purposes. One, it helps him to explain the scriptural cosmogonical statements fairly consistently. Two, the existence of Absolute becomes definable in terms of the meaningful activity, produced by Pure-*Sattva*-Adjunct. It would not have been possible in the absence of the Adjunct which contributes to the emergence of meaningful activity in the form of the eternal mode of the Absolute.

Vijñānabhikṣu asserts that the Absolute endowed with the existence as defined by him remains one inseparable and integral whole

---

1. पुरुषार्थक्रियाकारित्वमेव च लोके सत्त्वमिति व्यवह्रियते । *VAB*, p. 58.
2. नासीदिति विरतव्यापारतया कारणरूपेण गर्तस्थमृतसर्पवद् विलीनमासीदित्यर्थः । अन्यथाऽन्तर्लीनविकारं चेत्युत्तरासंगतेः, अत्यन्तासत्त्वे "सत्त्वाच्चावरस्ये" त्यागामिसूत्रविरोधापत्तेश्च । *Ibid.*, p. 19.
3. अवरस्य चेतनाचेतनरूपकार्यजातस्य "सदेव सौम्येदमग्र आसीत्. . . ." इत्यादिश्रुतिभिः प्रलये सत्त्वसिद्धेरित्यर्थः । न चेदमासीदित्यस्य एतदधिष्ठानकारणमेतदभिन्नं वासीदित्यर्थ इति वाच्यम्, लक्षणाया अन्याय्यत्वात् कार्यकारणाभेदस्याविभागमात्ररूपत्वाच्च, अन्यस्य वक्तुमशक्यत्वात् । *Ibid.*, p. 153.
4. प्रलयेऽपीदानीमिवैव कुर्वदास्ते प्रकृतिपुरुषादयस्तु सृष्ट्यादिलक्षणस्वकार्येभ्य उपरता एव सुषुप्तास्तिष्ठन्ति इति । *Ibid.*, pp. 57-58.

comprising *puruṣas* whom he likens to the rays of the sun. In other words, the Absolute and selves are inseparably related to each other in the manner of *aṃśa* and *aṃśī.*[1] This analogy he further explains thus. The sun endowed with many lights in the form of its rays is one and non-separate from them. Similarly the Absolute comprising several individual consciousnesses can be one and non-separate from them. The many *puruṣas* being Its parts (*aṃśas*) are described to be Its manifold divisions by the example of rays in that the selves are in conjunction with their *upādhis.* Just as the rays of the sun are inseparable from it, likewise the individual selves are inseparable from the Absolute and the divisions exist in speech only. It does not at all mean that the Absolute is one undivided whole.[2]

The implication of Vijñānabhikṣu's view of selves as the instruments of the Absolute becomes explicitly clear when we come to his conception of the degrees of soulhood (*ātmatva*) and reality (*sattva*). He defines *ātman* as a category from which the creation issues forth and wherein, located and having lived, it again submerges.[3] In this regard he offers an illustration of the sea and its waves. The waves emerge in the sea; they are sustained in it and after having lived they just disappear in it. As per the definition given above, the sea can be called the 'soul' of the waves. Similarly the self can also be said to possess *ātmatva,* for it is responsible for the emergence, sustenance and submergence of the intellect and other sense-organs. The individual self is also described *ātman* in the sense of assuming superintendence over the functions of other faculties as is the case with the life-breath *prāṇa* vis-a-vis sense-organs, but he hastens to add that the individual self endowed with the power of consciousness is *ātman* only in a secondary sense.[4]

The individual self does not possess *ātmatva* for two reasons: First, if the individual self were called *ātman* in the sense mentioned

1. सूर्यकिरणवदंशानामंशिन्यविभागादित्यर्थः । *VAB*, p. 58. See also *ibid.*, pp. 19-20.
2. अनेकतेजोमयादित्यमण्डलवद् अनेकात्ममयमपि चिदादित्यमण्डलमेकरसमविभक्तमेकपिण्डीकृत्य तस्य किरणवत् स्वांशभूतैरसङ्ख्यपुरुषैरसङ्ख्योपाधिष्वसङ्ख्यविभाग एव प्रतिबिम्बादिदृष्टान्तैः प्रतिपाद्यते, विभागलक्षणान्यत्वस्य वाचारम्भणमात्रत्वं बोधयितुं न पुनरखण्डत्वम् । *SPB* (under *sūtra* I-154), p. 95.
3. यो यत आगत्य यदधिष्ठितं यत्र जीवित्वा यत्र लीयते समुद्रतरंगादिवत् जीवात् तद्बुद्ध्यादिवच्च स तस्यात्मा भवति । *VAB*, p. 28.
4. जीवाश्चिच्छक्तिगुणयोगाद् गौणात्मान एव, यथाऽध्यक्षत्वगुणयोगेन प्राणः करणानामात्मा तद्वत् । *Ibid.*, p. 29.

above, the *BS* III-3-40[1] would be contradicted and the state of self's experiencing pleasure and pain would become untenable. The positing of consciousness in the individual selves, according to Vijñānabhikṣu is only confined to speech because it is contingent.[2] The acquisition of consciousness by the selves becomes possible because they possess the capacity to acquire it.

As such both consciousness and *ātmatva* belong to the Absolute in the primary sense. The Absolute is an abode of the manifestation, sustenance and submergence of all the *jīvas* along with their paraphernalia in the same manner as the *jīva* is assumed to be the locus of the emergence, sustenance and submergence of the intellect, sense-organs, etc., to be their controller and witness so that it may be called *ātman,* though secondarily. The Absolute is the controller and witness of all the *jīvas.* Hence it is proper that It may be called the *ātman* of all the selves.[3] More so, because the Absolute is eternally omniscient and absolutely independent.[4] To substantiate this, Vijñānabhikṣu quotes from the *Nārada Purāṇa* a *śloka* which states that the selves (souls) are of two kinds: primary and secondary. The former is said to be devoid of qualities while the latter is invested with egoity.[5]

Vijñānabhikṣu's over-all view on the concept of Absolute vis-a-vis individual selves may be appreciated better when understood in

---

1. तस्मादन्तर्यामिणोऽधिको द्रष्टा नास्तीति श्रुत्या तस्यैव पारमार्थिकात्मत्वमित्येव दर्शितम् न तु व्यावहारिकमप्यात्मान्तरं निषिद्धम् । अतो भक्तिश्रद्धोत्पादनार्थ एव चेतनान्तरप्रतिषेध इति सिद्धम् । . . .व्यावहारिकपारमार्थिकभेदेन सत्ताद्वैविध्यात् आत्मनो द्वैविध्यस्यापि श्रुतिस्मृत्यभिप्रेतत्वादिति । *VAB,* p. 274.
Vijñānabhikṣu says that the *Brahmasūtra* III-3-40 does not indicate the absence of other empirical selves but it aims at arousing faith and devotion for the Absolute, Which is endowed with the ultimate *ātmatva* as against the empirical (secondary) *ātmatva* of the individual selves.
2. *Ibid.,* p. 29.
3. यथा हि देहेन्द्रियादीनां बुद्धिपर्यन्तानामुत्पत्तिलयाधारतया तत्साक्षित्वेनाधिष्ठातृत्वादिना च जीवस्तेषामात्मा.... तथैव जीवानां चिन्मात्रस्वरूपाणामप्युत्पत्तिलयाधारतया तत्साक्षित्वेन तदधिष्ठातृत्वादिना चेश्वरस्तेषामप्यात्मा । *Ibid.,* p. 29.
4. मुख्यस्त्वात्मेश्वर एव, सदा सर्वज्ञत्वादपरतन्त्रत्वाच्च । *Ibid.,* pp. 29-30.
And also एकस्यैव ब्रह्मण: पारमार्थिकात्मत्वमुक्तम् । *Ibid.,* p. 28.
5. तथा च नारदीये गौणमुख्यभेदेनात्मद्वयमुक्तम्–
आत्मानं द्विविधं प्राहु: परापरविभेदत: ।
परस्तु निर्गुण: प्रोक्तो ह्यहङ्कारयुतोऽपर: ।।
परापरौ श्रेष्ठाश्रेष्ठौ मुख्यगौणत्वाभ्यामिति भाव: । *Ibid.,* p. 30.

comparison with that of Śaṅkara. Śaṅkara draws a clear distinction between the status of dream objects and that of the waking life objects.[1] It may lead to the impression that he acquiesces in accepting the degrees of reality. But this is not the case, obviously because he maintains that only the Absolute is ontologically real and the individual self is in a relation of identity with It. In other words, only the Absolute continues to exist ultimately. Unlike it, the Absolute of Vijñānabhikṣu is all-inclusive and all-comprehensive. Śaṅkara can hardly afford to hold this view as it would render his postulation of *māyā* redundant, which is clearly meant to draw an inviolable distinction between real and unreal. Nevertheless Vijñānabhikṣu shows no hesitation in accepting the degrees of reality, even holding that the Absolute is ultimately real since It is eternal and always remains bereft of unreality, which is not the case with the empirical objects which become unreal both at the time of dissolution and at the ultimate plane.[2]

Vijñānabhikṣu defines reality as a state of having practical efficiency or a state producing an effective action. The individual selves in conjunction with their *upādhis,* and *prakṛti* and its effects do possess distinctly manifest characteristics by which they, though inseparable from the Absolute, can be distinguished from the latter. As such, being in possession of the property of having practical efficiency or of producing an effective action, they are accepted as endowed with reality during creation. In this context the difference between Vijñānabhikṣu and Śaṅkara lies in the fact that the latter holds the world to be on a par with the illusory objects whereas the former maintains that the illustrations of silver in the conch-shell and dream objects concern the aspect of relative unreality and not that of absolute unreality. The dream objects, he holds, are also not totally devoid of reality, even if they differ from those of the waking life in the sense that the latter exist externally whereas the former do not.[3] They can be described as unreal from the ontological point of

1. *BSS* on "वैधर्म्याच्च न स्वप्नादिवत्", *BS,* II-2-29.
2. यत्तावद् विकारासत्यत्वमुक्तं तदस्माभिरप्यभ्युपगम्यते, कूटस्थनित्यस्यैव पारमार्थिकसत्त्वात् सर्वथैवासत्ताविरहात्, न तु प्रकृतितद्विकारयो: । *VAB*, p. 55.
3. विशेषस्त्वयान्, यद् भवद्भिर्विकाराणां शुक्तिरजततुल्यत्वमिष्यतेऽस्माभिस्तु असत्तामात्रांशे शुक्तिरजतस्वप्नादेर्दृष्टान्तत्वमिष्यते न त्वत्यन्तासत्त्वेऽपि, "वैधर्म्याच्च न स्वप्नादिवदि" त्यागामिसूत्रात्, स्वाप्नवस्तूनामपि कनककुण्डलवन्मन:परिणामतया तुच्छत्वस्य निराकरिष्यमाणत्वाच्च । बाह्यविषयसत्त्वासत्त्वाभ्यामेव च जाग्रत्स्वप्नयोर्वैधर्म्यमिति । *Ibid.*, p. 55.

view, because absolute unreality, in the primary sense, belongs to things like the hare's horn only.[1]

Vijñānabhikṣu's definition of empirical reality seems to be a corollary of what has just been discussed above, namely, that empirical reality is constituted by both existence and non-existence.[2] To explain, the selves and the empirical objects have both real and unreal aspects. The significance of their real aspect lies in the latter serving the purpose of the former, i.e. both have the state of practical efficiency. Their unreal aspect consists in their being submerged, at the time of dissolution, in the Absolute indistinguishably and their being divested of such characteristics as are responsible for making them possess a state of practical efficiency during creation.

The position that effects are both real and unreal presents something of a contradiction which cries for resolution. Vijñānabhikṣu seeks to resolve it by invoking the states of manifest and unmanifest characteristics which, according to him, should be understood as reality and unreality respectively. To illustrate it, he states that a pitcher having a manifest characteristic during the present moment is said to be real, but in respect of the characteristics during the preceding and succeeding moments it descends to the status of unreality.[3] It results in the statement by him that the phenomenal existence is indescribable as compared to the Absolute on the one hand and to the hare's horn on the other; it falls under neither category. In other words, the creation is unique insofar as its characterization as existence or non-existence is concerned.[4]

To substantiate his view about the nature of empirical reality, Vijñānabhikṣu quotes *Nyāyasūtra* IV-2-37 and interprets it thus:[5] From the ontological point of view the knowledge of the effect is false as it (effect), though real on the empirical plane, is ultimately unreal.

---

1. तत्त्वतो मिथ्याबुद्धिः कार्येषु, कार्याणां व्यावहारिकसत्त्वेऽपि परमार्थतोऽसत्त्वात् । प्रधानतो मुख्यतस्तु मिथ्याबुद्धिः शशश्रृंगादिषु तेषां सर्वथैवासत्त्वादिति विभाग इत्यर्थः । *VAB*, p. 54.
2. सदसद्रूपत्वमेव च व्यावहारिकसत्त्वम् । *Ibid.*, p. 55.
3. ननु विरुद्धं सदसत्त्वं कथमेकत्रोपपद्येतेति चेन्न, एकधर्मेण सत्त्वदशायां परिणामिवस्तूनामतीतानागत-धर्मेणासत्त्वात् । *Ibid.*, p. 55.
4. प्रपञ्चस्यानिर्वचनीयत्वं तु पारमार्थिकसदसद्भ्यां कूटस्थशशश्रृंगाभ्यां विलक्षणत्वमिति । *Ibid.*, p. 55.
5. न्यायाचार्यैरपि विकारमिथ्यात्वं विचारतः प्रतिपादितम्. . . . तत्त्वप्रधानभेदाच्च मिथ्याबुद्धेर्द्वैविध्यो-पपत्तिरित्यादिसूत्रैरिति । तत्त्वतो मिथ्याबुद्धिः कार्येषु, कार्याणां व्यावहारिकसत्त्वेऽपि परमार्थतोऽसत्त्वात् । प्रधानतो मुख्यतस्तु मिथ्याबुद्धिशशश्रृंगादिषु, तेषां सर्वथैवासत्त्वादिति विभाग इत्यर्थः । *Ibid.*, p. 54.

The knowledge of the hare's horn is false in the primary sense as it is absolutely unreal. The scriptural statement of *vācārambhaṇa* also endorses this view saying that the effect exists only in speech since its parts are destined to disintegrate. After disintegration what remains is only the material cause, which obviously seems to be more real than the product.[1] In case it is not accepted, the illustrations of clay and its effects would be rendered meaningless, as they would cease to serve any purpose other than their expressing the degrees of reality. He discusses this problem at length in his commentary on *Brahmasūtra* I-1-1.[2]

In the foregoing Vijñānabhikṣu has adduced arguments to conclude that the empirical and dream objects are less real. Similarly the individual selves are understood to be both real and unreal, i.e. less real in comparison with the Absolute. Besides, their soulhood exists not in the primary sense as is the case with the Absolute. He adds one more argument to endorse his own view about the status of reality and soulhood of the individual self. It runs: The individual self submerges in the Absolute at one or the other time and assumes the state of potentiality in it.[3] Its submergence means that it becomes one with the knowledge of the Absolute. It is because of this submergence of the individual self along with its *upādhi* that it is unreal in relation to the Absolute. On the contrary the Pure-*Sattva*-Adjunct of the Absolute, being eternal, does not get separated from It and remains operative in performing Its function of producing the mode reflecting the world even after the dissolution has taken place.[4] As a consequence the Absolute is real ontologically, while the individual selves, both real and unreal, are on a par with the empirical objects only.

The bliss aspect of the Absolute, though generally accepted, has been viewed differently by different Vedānta teachers; compare, for example, Śaṅkara and Rāmānuja. While the former says that Bliss is

---

1. या च वाचारम्भणश्रुतिः सा अवयवविभागे सति विकाराणां नाममात्रत्वं वदति, उपादानस्यैव च तदपेक्षया तदानीं सत्यत्वं वदति । अन्यथा मृद्विकारादिदृष्टान्तासिद्धिदोषात् । *VAB*, p. 55.
2. *Ibid.*, p. 12.
3. ज्ञानं ज्ञानस्वरूपः परमात्मा, स एव सत्यः जीवाश्चांशतया अंशिन्येकीभूताः । अथवा लयवत्त्वेन परमात्मापेक्षया तेऽप्यसन्तः । *Ibid.*, p. 56.
4. ब्रह्मचैतन्यं हि विश्वावभासनरूपं स्वकार्यं प्रलयेऽपि इदानीमिवैव कुर्वदास्ते प्रकृतिपुरुषादयस्तु सृष्ट्यादिलक्षणस्वकार्येभ्य उपरता एव सुषुप्तास्तिष्ठन्तीति । पुरुषार्थक्रियाकारित्वमेव च लोके सत्त्वमिति व्यवह्रियते । *Ibid.*, pp. 57-58.

itself the Absolute, that it is free from subject-object-relationship and is natural, eternal and indivisible,[1] the latter holds that it is an attribute of the Absolute, though the term, at times, is used as a synonym of the Absolute.[2] It seems from what Śaṅkara says about bliss that he keeps Bliss at par with Existence and Consciousness. In other words, all the three positive properties exist in a relationship of identity with one another.[3] They all belong to the transcendental realm. Rāmānuja on the other hand holds that the highest form of bliss, which sometimes indicates its own substratum, is possessed by God, that is, it is related to God as possession is related to the possessor.

Vijñānabhikṣu rejects both the views and holds that bliss is confined to the realm of *prakṛti* or the Pure-*Sattva*-Adjunct of the Absolute, and that it is neither the nature nor possession of the Absolute. He regards himself consistent in holding this view, saying that, when the phenomenon of bliss can be satisfactorily explained as belonging to *prakṛti*, it is against the law of parsimony to extend it to the Absolute. In case it is said that bliss as different from pleasure which belongs to the *sattva* aspect of *prakṛti* has to be postulated to explain the event of the experience of bliss, it can be rebutted by exposing the redundance of such a presupposition. The experience of bliss, like that of pleasure, is adequately accounted for in terms of the modification of the *sattva* aspect of *prakṛti*.[4]

That the Absolute always witnesses the modes of Its own *Upādhi* necessitates the postulation of knowledge which is different from the knowledge of the form of adjunctival mode. In case knowledge is not separately postulated, the event of witnessing the adjunctival mode would become untenable.[5] This is why Vijñānabhikṣu maintains that knowledge is an indispensable defining characteristic of the Absolute. So far as the property of bliss is concerned, it can be

1. तं ब्रह्मण आनन्दं. . . . आत्मभूतं विषयविषयिसम्बन्धविनिर्मुक्तं स्वाभाविकं नित्यमविभक्तं परमानन्दं ब्रह्मणो विद्वान्. . . . । *Śāṅkara-bhāṣya* on *TaittUp*, II-9.
2. आनन्दः स्वाश्रयमावेदयति । *Śrībhāṣya* on I-1-13. See also *ibid.*, I-1-1.
3. Kalidas Bhattacharyya, *A Modern Understanding of Advaita Vedānta*, L.D. Series 47; 1975, p. 41 fn. 3, para II.
4. न च प्रकृतावपि पृथक् सुखान्तरं कल्प्यं तथा सति तेनैव सुखानुभवोपपत्तौ सत्यामात्मसुखान्तरकल्पनावैयर्थ्यात् । *VAB*, p. 34.
5. बुद्धिवृत्तिरूपज्ञानादतिरिक्तं पुनरात्मस्वरूपं ज्ञानं कल्प्यमेव, अन्यथा बुद्धिवृत्तेः साक्ष्यत्वासम्भवादिति । *Ibid.*, p. 34.

explained by referring to the *sattva* aspect of the *upādhi.*

So far as the scriptural sentences conveying the blissful nature of the Absolute are concerned, they may be construed as referring to the Absolute in a secondary sense. To explain, the modes of the intellect are understood to be belonging to the self, whereas in reality they do not. In a similar manner, the transformation (mode) of the Eternal Pure-*Sattva*-Adjunct of the Absolute may be said to be belonging to It. To substantiate it, Vijñānabhikṣu offers the following syllogism:

1. Bliss has the form of unmanifestness.
2. Because it possesses objectivity
   (state of becoming an object of experience) even without a mental mode reflecting it.
3. Such as sorrow.[1]

In this syllogism, Vijñānabhikṣu's thrust seems to be on maintaining a distinction between the status of consciousness and that of bliss,[2] since if a distinction between the statuses of bliss and consciousness is proved, bliss automatically ceases to characterize the Absolute, there being no difference of opinion between him and Śaṃkara so far as the consciousness aspect of the Absolute is concerned. This is exactly what he seeks to achieve by the syllogism given above. Bliss is of the form of unmanifestness. Consciousness on the other hand is nothing if not manifest. It is proved by means of valid knowledge which proves, too, that manifestness constitutes consciousness, the nature of the individual self.[3] How can consciousness possess the contradictory characteristics of manifestness and blissfulness?

Consciousness perceives itself through a mental mode of its *upādhi* reflecting it. If it is said to perceive itself without the mediation of a mode, it would incur the subject-object-contradiction. Further if consciousness other than the consciousness which is being perceived is presupposed, it would lead to infinite regress. This argument can also be extended to the problem of bliss. Like consciousness, it may be experienced through a mental mode and

1. आनन्दो दुःखवत् स्वगोचरवृत्तिं विनाऽपि दृश्यत्वादप्रकाशरूपः । *VAB*, p. 33.
2. *Loc. cit.*
3. चैतन्यं तु धर्मिग्राहकमानेन प्रकाशरूपतयैव सिद्धमिति प्रकाशाप्रकाशरूपतयोभयोर्विरोधः । *Ibid.*, p. 33.

thus the subject-object-contradiction may find resolution as both are being perceived through the mediation of mind. Vijñānabhikṣu replies that the problem is unlikely to end here as the resolution of the subject-object-contradiction with respect to pleasure or bliss leads to yet another contradiction in the form of one being known and the other being unknown. During reflection over sorrow, pleasure does remain unknown and during the meditation accompanied by bliss, consciousness, too, remains unknown. How can two contradictory properties constitute the Absolute, bliss being known and consciousness being unknown during the meditation of bliss?[1]

The scriptural passages delineating the identity of bliss and Brahman do not render Vijñānabhikṣu's argument conducive to the conclusion that bliss is a mode of *prakṛti.* To this rejoinder he replies that there are also such passages in the Śruti-literature as give an account of the difference between bliss and Brahman. They also inform that bliss is not the nature of Brahman.[2] In consonance with this analysis of the nature of bliss, Vijñānabhikṣu interprets both 'not bliss = *na ānandam*' and 'not devoid of bliss = *na nirānandam*' respectively as 'Brahman is not bliss' and 'bliss as a modification of the Pure-*Sattva*-Adjunct is attributed to Brahman.[3] And consequently the scriptural mention about bliss as being experienced during the state of liberation must be construed as 'absolute absence of all sorrows'. He adds that it is even conventional to use 'pleasure or bliss' when 'absence of sorrow' is sought to be implied.[4] It may be concluded from the foregoing discussion that bliss as a mode may be attributed to the Absolute, but it is definitely not Its nature.

Vijñānabhikṣu further differs with the Advaitin on the latter's conception of self-luminosity of the Absolute. For the proper assessment of Vijñānabhikṣu's views on the subject, it seems necessary to

---

1. चैतन्यस्य तु बुद्धिवृत्तिद्वारैव स्वविषयत्वं चैतन्यगोचरचैतन्यान्तराङ्गीकारे ऽनवस्थानात्, साक्षात् स्वविषयत्वे च कर्मकर्तृविरोधादतश्चैतन्यस्य प्रकाशकत्वमुपपन्नमिति । यदि वा चैतन्यवत् सुखस्यापि वृत्तिद्वारैव मानमभ्युपगम्यायं विरोध: परिह्रियते तथाऽपि एकज्ञानेऽन्याज्ञानाद् विरोध: स्यात् ज्ञातत्वाज्ञातत्वयोरेकदा विरोधात्, दु:खानुव्यवसायकाले सुखाज्ञानात् सानन्दसमाध्यादौ च चैतन्याज्ञानात् । *VAB*, p. 33.
2. *Ibid.*, p. 33.
3. अत्र नानन्दमित्यानन्दरूपताप्रतिषेध:, न निरानन्दमिति चौपाधिकानन्दधर्मकत्वानुमति: । *Ibid.*, p. 34.
4. एतेन आत्मन आनन्दरूपताप्रतिषेधान्मोक्षकाले सुखप्रतिपादकं वाक्यजातं दु:खनिवृत्तौ गौणं बोध्यम्, ''तृष्णाक्षयसुखस्यैते नार्हत: षोडशीं कलामि'' त्यादिप्रयोगदर्शनेन दु:खनिवृत्तौ सुखशब्दस्य निरूढलक्षणासिद्धे: । *Ibid.*, p. 34.

know what the Advaitin has to say in this regard. The latter considers the Absolute to be self-luminous, for It does not require a mental mode for Its revelation in the sense in which the empirical objects do. To clarify, the Advaitic perception of empirical objects results when the object of perception is pervaded by both the mental mode (*vṛtti*) and the consciousness reflected in the mind (*phala*). But it is a different case with Brahman as an 'object of perception'. In case Brahman too is accepted to be pervaded in the manner in which the empirical objects are, the former would be on a par with the latter in all respects. In order to avoid this undesirable consequence, Advaitins describe the experience of Brahman (*Brahmasākṣātkāra*) differently. They admit that the Absolute is pervaded by the mental mode reflecting Its undivided form in deep meditation. As such, the statement *manasaivānudraṣṭavyam* finds itself adequately accounted for since pervasion of the Absolute by the mental mode is needed to annihilate *ajñāna*. On the other hand, the Upaniṣadic statement *yato vāco nivartante* implies that the Absolute cannot be pervaded by the '*phala*', the reflection of consciousness in the intellect, for it is not possible for the reflected consciousness to illuminate its own archetype, the Absolute.[1] In other words, It cannot become an object of experience in the sense in which other empirical objects assume objectivity as they do get pervaded by the '*phala*' also or are illuminated by the reflected consciousness.

Vijñānabhikṣu rejects the Advaitin's view of self-luminosity because such a presupposition, in the first place, suffers from lack of evidence.[2] He goes on to criticize the Advaitin, asserting that the linguistic usage of Brahman implies that It does become an object of experience, though during the highest state of meditation. In case the usage is attributed to the mental mode only, as the Advaitin would certainly desire, infinite regress would result. Therefore, the Absolute's being pervaded by the mental mode only does not conduce towards the occurrence of the usage conveying It. The necessity of postulating a mental mode may be explained by the fact that it makes the objects revealed to the self. It is not meant to

1. आधुनिकास्तु ''यतो वाचो निवर्तन्त'' इत्यादिवाक्यैरनुभवाख्यफलव्याप्यत्वं प्रतिषिध्यते, मनसैवानुद्रष्टव्यमित्यादिभिश्चाज्ञाननाशाय ब्रह्मणि वृत्तिव्याप्यत्वं स्वीक्रियत इत्यविरोध इत्याहुः । *VAB*, p. 38.
2. तत्र, एतादृशकल्पनायां प्रमाणादर्शनात् । *Ibid.*, p. 38.

account for their usage as otherwise it would involve cumbrousness. Moreover, the pitcher and the mode of the mind do not differ in respect of their essences since both of them are unconscious. Consequently, the usage of Brahman by Its knowers would become impossible, if It is not accepted as an object of their experience.[1]

The Advaitin joins issue with Vijñānabhikṣu averring that he does not envisage any problem of usage as the self-luminosity of the Absolute is a sufficient ground for Its usage in the scriptural passages. On the contrary the alleged defect of cumbrousness, the Advaitin adds, would actually be involved, if Its becoming an object of experience is accepted as a reason for Its occurrence in the usage. Vijñānabhikṣu retorts by saying that the Advaitin's view is untenable for the following reason: The property of knowledge is common to both the intellectual mode and perception and hence it should be responsible for the object being in linguistic usage. This happens only when both the intellectual mode and perception have a common content. It is not warranted, Vijñānabhikṣu points out, to presuppose an unseen category at the cost of an accepted one. He points towards one more defect in the Advaitin's view, that is, the justification for the usage of Brahman in the Upaniṣadic passages by Its self-luminosity leads him to postulate darkness named *ajñāna* to explain the absence of Its usage, whereas it can be accounted for simply by the absence of knowledge without invoking darkness of the form of *ajñāna* for this purpose. Vijñānabhikṣu adds that it is nevertheless necessary to accept darkness for the sake of withholding mental modes during sleep. To press darkness into the service of justifying one more purpose of withholding the usage is to become liable to being cumbersome.[2]

---

1. किं च व्यवहारत्वावच्छेदेनैवानुभवविषयकत्वमेव प्रयोजकं, बुद्धिवृत्तिगोचरव्यवहारेऽनवस्थाभयेन वृत्तिविषयत्वस्याप्रयोजकत्वात् ।घटादिभानार्थं चेतने तत्सम्बन्धायैव वृत्तिसिद्धेः न तु घटादिव्यवहारार्थमपि । तस्या अपि बाह्यव्यवहाराजनकत्वकल्पनेन च गौरवात्, जडत्वेन घटाविशेषाच्च । तथा च ब्रह्मणोऽनुभवव्याप्यत्वानङ्गीकारे विदुषां ब्रह्मणि व्यवहारो न स्यादिति । *VAB*, p. 38.
2. यत्तु स्वप्रकाशत्वादेव ब्रह्मणि व्यवहारो भवति तद्विषयकज्ञानस्य तद्व्यवहारहेतुत्वकल्पने गौरवात् । वृत्तिव्याप्यत्वन्तु व्यवहारप्रतिबन्धकाज्ञाननिवृत्त्यर्थमपेक्ष्यत इत्युच्यते, तदप्यसारम्, समानविषयकत्वप्रत्यासत्त्या ज्ञानत्वेनैव व्यवहारत्वावच्छिन्नं प्रति कारणत्वात् । दृष्टं विहायात्मव्यवहारे अदृष्टकल्पनानौचित्याच्च । अज्ञानाख्यतमसो व्यवहारप्रतिबन्धकल्पने प्रमाणाभावाच्च, ज्ञानाभावादेव व्यवहाराभावसंभवात् ।सुषुप्त्यादौ ज्ञानानुत्पत्त्यर्थं तमसो वृत्तिप्रतिबन्धकत्वस्यावश्यकल्प्यतया पुनर्व्यवहारप्रतिबन्धकत्वकल्पनावैयर्थ्याच्चेति । *Ibid.*, pp. 38-39.

When the Advaitin defends his position by stating that the occurrence of usage should be explained by the self-luminosity of the Absolute to avoid the subject-object-contradiction, Vijñānabhikṣu replies back that the contradiction mentioned above would be incurred only in the Advaitic system which emphasizes the undivided oneness of the Absolute, and not in his system according to which the individual self is not identical with but different, though non-separate, from the Absolute. Even when the individual self perceives itself in the discriminative meditation (*vivekakhyāti*), there is no incurrence of the subject-object-contradiction because the individual self becomes an object of its own perception in the form of its own reflection in the intellect but as the archetype of its reflection, it does remain the subject. He gives an illustration to clarify it. The sun, as the original (archetype) assumes subjectivity but as reflection, it becomes an object of its manifestation.[1] When the original and the reflection differ from each other in a sense, he asserts that there is no subject-object-contradiction involved.

In this context Vijñānabhikṣu also analyzes Citsukha's definition of the self-luminosity of Brahman and rejects it. Citsukha in *Tattvapradīpikā* defines self-luminosity as 'the capability of being called immediately known without being an object of cognition'.[2] He says that the definition is not acceptable because it suffers from the following defects: (1) The scriptures do not lend authenticity to it as it does not find mention there. (2) The etymological meaning of '*svaprakāśa*' does not seem to corroborate what is implied by the definition. The etymology of '*svaprakāśa*' yields only one sense, that is, 'knowable by itself'. (3) It is only knowledge or cognition which is the foundation of all linguistic usage. When the objectivity of cognition or experience is denied in the case of Absolute's self-luminosity, It ceases to be operative in usage.[3] Moreover, all the obvious scriptural references to Brahman will be rendered invalid.[4] Vijñānabhikṣu continues to differ with the Advaitin even if the latter

---

1. सूर्यो बिम्बरूपेण प्रकाशकः प्रतिबिम्बरूपेण च प्रकाश्य इति न कर्मकर्तृविरोधः । *VAB*, p. 42.
2. V.A. Sharma, *Citsukha's Contribution to Advaita*, Mysore, 1974, p. 44.
3. आधुनिकास्तु स्वकल्पितमात्मारोपत्वं सिद्धान्तीकृत्य स्वप्रकाशलक्षणं रचयन्ति "अवेद्यत्वे सत्यपरोक्षव्यवहारयोग्यत्वमि" ति । तत्रेदमुच्यते – एवं स्वप्रकाशत्वमात्मनः श्रुत्यादिष्वदर्शनादसिद्धमिदं लक्षणम् । स्वप्रकाशशब्दस्यास्मिन्नर्थे यौगिकत्वमपि न संभवति, स्वज्ञेयत्वस्यैव योगतो लाभात् । अपि च वेदनस्य सर्वव्यवहारकारणतया वेद्यत्वाभावे व्यवहारासंभवादप्यसिद्धं लक्षणम् । *VAB*, p. 43.
4. *Ibid.*, p. 43.

maintains that the intellectual mode reflecting Brahman does lead to freedom from ignorance and that this mode does not give rise to any resultant state in the self. He asks the Advaitin why he substitutes 'freedom from ignorance' for 'valid cognition', when the word *pramāṇa* appropriately connotes 'a means to valid cognition'[1]. So the propriety of the mental mode of the Absolute lies in the fact that it brings about Its perception. To put it differently, though Vijñānabhikṣu admits the luminosity of the Absolute, he affirms that It admits of knowability, that is, It can know Itself or be known to the individual self through Its Pure-*Sattva*-Adjunct or through the *upādhi* of the self respectively.

According to Vijñānabhikṣu, Absolute's unknowability or inaccessibility to experience means that It does not become an object of an ordinary perception.[2] Known from the scriptures in a general way,[3] It can be experienced in all Its particulars by the yogin as his mind acquires a special and inconceivable capacity through yoga.[4] It may be mentioned here that he concedes that a characteristic which is beyond speech and senses may be regarded as residing in the Absolute. But the opponent proceeds to argue with him asking how the incomprehensible and unknowable Absolute becomes knowable to the yogin.[5] He adds that the distant objects which are not in contact with the senses do not come within the reach of layman's experience. In a similar manner, the Absolute Which is said to be beyond the approach of senses cannot be grasped by the yogin's internal sense, there being no contact between the two. Vijñānabhikṣu offers two solutions to the dilemma posed by the opponent. First, accept the mind as all-pervading and yogic capacity, then, will dispel the darkness which obstructs the emergence of the mental mode reflecting the Absolute or a distant object, as the all-pervasive mind is already in contact with everything everywhere, Brahman too. In case mind's all-pervasiveness is not acceptable, its

---

1. स्यादेतद्, ब्रह्माकारवृत्तेरनुभवाख्यफलाभावेऽपि पुरुषनिष्ठाया अविद्याया निवृत्तिरेव पुरुषनिष्ठं फलं स्यादिति । अत्रोच्यते प्रमाकरणस्यैव प्रमाणशब्दार्थतया अविद्यानिवृत्तिरूपफलेन प्रमाणत्वासंभवः। *VAB*, p. 43.
2. ब्रह्मणोऽतीन्द्रियत्वं लौकिकप्रत्यक्षाविषयत्वमेव । *Ibid.*, pp. 61-62.
3. तस्मात् शब्दतः सामान्यतो ज्ञातेऽपि ब्रह्मणि विशेषज्ञानरूपसाक्षात्काराय विधिर्युक्त इति । *Ibid.*, p. 62.
4. अपि च ब्रह्मणोऽतीन्द्रियतया न तत्र योगजधर्मं विना साक्षात्कारः संभवति । *Ibid.*, p. 61.
5. नन्वस्तु विशेषस्तथापि स विशेषः शब्दागोचरोऽतीन्द्रियश्च कथं योगिमनसाऽपि गृह्येत । *Ibid.*, p. 38.

capacity acquired through yoga may be construed as 'contact'[1]. He maintains that it does not violate the qualityless nature of Brahman, as he explains the word 'qualityless' in a different way. According to him the Absolute is called so because It does not suffer from egoity—It is eternally free from egoity, impurity, etc. unlike the individual self which suffers from egoity, etc. on account of its association with its adjunct—and in turn qualities do not affect It the least. Or, It may be called qualityless as all the qualities get submerged in It indistinguishably and become inoperative at the time of dissolution.[2]

1. योगजधर्माणां शास्त्रसिद्धाचिन्त्यशक्तित्वात्. . . . ननु संयोगादिप्रत्यासत्त्यभावात् कथं व्यवहितादिज्ञानं योगिनां स्यादिति चेन्न, मनोवैभवमते सर्वत्रैव मनःसंयोगसत्त्वात् योगजधर्मस्य च वृत्तिप्रतिबन्धकतमोमात्रनाशकत्वात्. । मनःपरिच्छिन्नतामते च योगजधर्मस्यैव प्रत्यासत्तित्वकल्पनादिति ।
VAB, p. 38. See also *ibid.*, p. 61.
2. निर्गुणं नित्यमेव गुणानभिमानेन गुणासङ्गेन च गुणातीतं, गुणानां विलयाद्वा निर्गुणत्वम् । नित्यनिर्मलमिति जीवव्यावृत्तिर्जीवानामौपाधिककादाचित्कमालिन्यात् । *Ibid.*, p. 19.

3

CONCEPT OF SELF

I

Proof and Definition

Self may be conceived as a metaphysical principle of unity underlying subjective experience. It is an epistemological necessity and a priori principle involved in all forms of human knowledge.[1] It is postulated to account for the intelligent order of manifested entities and also for the subjective aspect[2] of reality. This subjective aspect is made more explicit by K.C. Bhattacharyya when he points out that there is immediate introspective consciousness of the object being other than the self and of the self as feeling or experiencing.[3] Differently put, the proposition would be: The self is different and so opposed to the object or to the totality of the objects called world and as such it may be distinguished from 'not-me' as conceived by William James.[4]

Vijñānabhikṣu on the other hand does not subscribe to the view that the self never enters the plane of objectivity. It means that in his view pure subjectivity, which does not at all admit of knowability, cannot be the essential nature of self.[5] In this respect he is opposed

1. Anima Sen Gupta, *Classical Sāṃkhya: A Critical Study*, Delhi, 1982, p. 80.
2. Pulinbihari Chakravarti, *Origin and Development of the Sāṁkhya System of Thought*, 1975, p. 315.
3. *Studies in Philosophy*, p. 193, section 117.
4. "One great splitting of the whole universe into two halves is made by each of us, and for each of us almost all of the interest attaches to one of the halves; but we all draw the line of division between them in a different place. When I say that we all call the two halves by the same name, and that those names are 'me' and 'not-me' respectively, it will at once be seen what I mean."

   Principles of Psychology, I, 289.
5. अज्ञेयत्वरूपं तावत्स्वप्रकाशत्वमस्माभिर्नाभ्युपगम्यते । *VAB*, p. 39.

to the Advaita view of self-luminosity. Nevertheless he admits that there is difference between subject and object. This point is brought out more fully in the elucidation of the syllogistic argument which he uses to refute that self cannot be distinguished from the infinite number of objects, and to demonstrate that self exists as an entity distinct from all objects and their collocation. Here is the syllogistic argument:

1. The seer is distinct from the objects (mental modes[1]) which are immediately illuminated by it.
2. Because it is the illuminator.
3. Whatever illuminates is different from the illuminated.

For example, the light which illuminates (manifests) a pitcher is different from it.

The example in the syllogism belongs to the objective world, yet it can be extended to the subjective plane where the intellectual modes reflecting the objects are illuminated by the luminous self. The latter being the illuminator is inferred to exist as an entity distinct from the modes. Vijñānabhikṣu here emphasizes that if self as a distinct entity witnessing the intellectual modes is not admitted, then either alternative, viz. the self invested with the properties in the form of mental modes or the intellect equipped with the characteristic of consciousness, will entail subject-object-contradiction. This would mean that the principle that the subject (self) cannot become immediately an object of its own cognition would be violated. And thus the argument[2] to dispel the doubt about the existence of self

---

1. See *Vyāsabhāṣya* on *Yogasūtra,* II-17.
2. तथा हि द्रष्टा साक्षात्स्वप्रकाश्येभ्यो भिन्नः प्रकाशकत्वात्, यो यस्य प्रकाशकः स तस्माद् भिन्नः यथा घटादालोको वृत्तिप्रकाश्याच्च वृत्तिरित्यनुमानेनादावन्तर्दृश्येभ्यो बुद्धिवृत्तितदारूढार्थेभ्यो विवेकतो बुद्धिसाक्षी सिध्यति कर्मकर्तृविरोधश्चानुकूलतर्कः:* अत्रात्मनि व्यभिचारवारणाय साक्षात्पदम्, वृत्तिद्वारैवात्मनः स्वविषयत्वात् । *SSR,* 1978, pp. 8-9.

* The argument used to dispel ambiguity about the inferable property is known as *anukūla tarka.* Vijñānabhikṣu uses here the argument of the subject-object-contradiction to dispel the doubt about the existence of self as a distinct entity in the same manner as that about the concomitance of cause and effect is used to remove doubt about the existence of fire on the mountain in the following manner:
If there were no fire on the mountain, there would be no smoke on it since fire is the cause of smoke. But smoke is visibly perceived, which makes absurd the objection of the opponent doubting the existence of fire on the mountain. Thus the incurrence of absurdity removes the very doubt about the inferable property.

also being taken cognizance of, the syllogistic argument that self exists as an entity distinct from the cognizable phenomena stands corroborated.

Vijñānabhikṣu further brings out the significance of the use of the word '*sākṣāt*' (immediately given) in the statement of the thesis (*pratijñā-vākya*). He points out that the word '*sākṣāt*' restricts the inference to the inferable property since the statement of the thesis without the word '*sākṣāt*' could lead to the undesirable conclusion that self is distinct from itself, which is absurd. It is Vijñānabhikṣu's view that the self does not manifest itself immediately but by means of the mental mode[1] reflecting the self. In this light only can it be said that he too believes in the dichotomy between the self as subject and the collocation (*saṅghāta*) including intellectual modes (*buddhi-vṛttis*) as objects. Unlike Advaitins he holds the view that the self, though luminous, does become an object of cognition through a mental mode. In other words, he subscribes to the view that the self being self-luminous—not knowable with the aid of any other light except its own—admits of knowability.[2]

Besides the syllogistic argument that has just been elucidated, Vijñānabhikṣu marshalls several other none-too-unfamiliar ones to demonstrate that the self exists as an independent entity distinct from the collection of objects including material and mental bodies (*sthūla* and *sūkṣma śarīras*). These arguments should also be taken as an implicit criticism of the view of Cārvākas who believe that there is no self other than the material body composed of four elements (excluding *ākāśa*), and of that of Vijñānavādins who hold the view that self is nothing but a stream of fleeting ideas or awarenesses (*citta-santāna*). The first of these arguments resembles Descartes' *cogito ergo sum.* Descartes says that the cognitive experience 'I know', is an infallible psychological proof that the knower, that is, the self exists, and particularly so when there is no other evidence to the contrary.[3] Even if someone insists on holding that the self does not exist, it may

1. See fn. 2 on previous page.
2. *VAB*, p. 43.
3. जानामीत्येवं प्रतीयमानतया पुरुषः सामान्यतः सिद्ध एवास्ति बाधकप्रमाणाभावात् । *SPB* (under *sūtra* VI-1), p. 219. तत्र सामान्यतः सिद्धो जानेऽहमिति धीबलात् । *SSR*, p. 26 and अस्मन्मते ज्ञातृतया पुरुषसिद्ध्यनन्तरम् । *SPB* (under *sūtra* I-99), p. 64.

be argued with advantage in Śaṅkara's manner that the one who denies is none but one's own self.[1]

According to Vijñānabhikṣu, the self is inferred on three grounds, namely, (1) *saṃhataparārthatvāt,* that the composite objects exist for the sake of someone other than themselves, (2) *triguṇādiviparyayāt,* that the self is opposite to what is constituted by the three *guṇas,* (3) *adhiṣṭhānāt,* that the inanimate objects stand in need of being controlled by some conscious principle. The other two arguments given in the *Sāṅkhyasūtras* to this effect are not taken by him as grounds proper for the inference of self, but are treated as *anukūla-tarka.* They are: (1) *bhoktṛbhāvāt,* that there should be someone to enjoy the products of *prakṛti,* and (2) *kaivalyārthapravṛtteḥ,* that it is evident that man tries to attain absolute freedom from pain. These two arguments help dispel any doubt which might arise with regard to the existence of self in the same manner as the argument of cause-effect-relationship removes the doubt about fire to be inferred on the mountain.

It may be mentioned in passing that K.C. Bhattacharyya interprets these arguments somewhat differently. He thinks that *saṃghātaparārthatvāt* and *adhiṣṭhānāt* are the main inferential grounds whereas the others, namely, *triguṇādiviparyayāt, bhoktṛbhāvāt* and *kaivalyārthapravṛtteḥ* are only aspects of self immediately revealed by reflection.[2] Before the inferential arguments are taken up for discussion, it may be noted that according to Vijñānabhikṣu the inference based on the first ground that the collocation of objects is meant for someone else is to indicate that it is possible for the self to discriminate itself from the collocation of objects. He further points out that it is not at all intended in the inferential statement that the self is absolutely unperceived and hence is going to be established afresh by the inferential arguments to be elaborated in

---

1. न ह्याकाशादयः पदार्था प्रमाणनिरपेक्षाः स्वयंसिद्धा केनचिदभ्युपगम्यन्ते । आत्मा तु प्रमाणादिव्यवहाराश्रयत्वात् सिध्यति । न चेदृशस्य निराकरणं संभवति । आगन्तुकं वस्तु निराक्रियते न स्वरूपम् । य एव हि निराकर्ता तदेव तस्य स्वरूपम् । न ह्यग्नेरौष्ण्यमग्निना निराक्रियते ।

Brahmasūtraśāṅkarabhāṣya (under *sūtra* II.3.7), ed. J.L. Shastri, Motilal Banarsidass, 1980, pp. 508-9.

For proofs for the non-existence of self, see *Nyāyavārttika,* ed. Pt. Vidhyesvari Prasad Dvivedin, Delhi, 1986, pp. 338-50 and for a similar and fuller treatment of the problem, see *Pañcadaśī,* chapter III, *Pañcakośa-viveka,* particularly the verses, 13, 18, 20, 21, 22, and 23.

2. *SP*, p. 193, section 117.

the following.[1] K.C. Bhattacharyya appears to favour Vijñānabhikṣu's viewpoint when he says that the self is known immediately in reflection and is not really inferred and that the inferential arguments are indeed used to help in rising to and clarifying the reflection.[2]

The syllogistic formulation based on the first ground may be presented like this:

1. *Prakṛti, mahat* and the rest which are under dispute are for the enjoyment (*bhoga*) and liberation of someone other than themselves.
2. Because they are of the nature of collocation. Whatever is of the nature of collocation is meant for the other.
3. A bed and a seat are of such nature and hence are obviously meant for someone else to sleep and sit on respectively.

This formulation demonstrates that the objects of composite nature exist for the sake of someone else who does not possess such nature. In a similar manner, *prakṛti* and its evolutes composed of the three constituents (*triguṇa*) interpenetrating one another are evidently of composite nature and as such they are necessarily to be meant for someone else who is by nature different from a collocation. And this someone else should be none but self.[3]

While commenting on *Vyāsabhāṣya* on *Yogasūtra* IV-24, Vijñānabhikṣu criticizes and refutes the Buddhists' view that mind is the sole reality and that it may be in a state of continuous flux under the impact of its own innumerable latent impressions. He emphasizes the point that the mind which is not the sole reality is teleologically conditioned to exist for someone other than itself as it has just been pointed out in the inferential formulation. Vijñānabhikṣu holds the view that *prakṛti* would neither exist nor undergo any mutation unless it had the teleological motive of offering the self opportunities for enjoyment and liberation. It may also be men-

---

1. संहतपरार्थत्वात् पुरुषस्येत्युक्तसूत्रेणापि विवेकानुमानमेवाभिप्रेतं न तु तत्र पुरुषस्य सर्वथैवा-प्रत्यक्षत्वमभिप्रेतमिति । *SPB* (introduction to *sūtra* I-139), p. 82.
2. *SP*, p. 192, section 117.
3. संहतानां प्रकृतितत्कार्याणां परार्थत्वानुमानेन पुरुषस्य बोध इत्यर्थः । तद् यथा विवादास्पदं प्रकृतिमहदादिकं परार्थं स्वेतरस्य भोगापवर्गफलकं संहतत्वात् शय्यासनवदित्यनुमानेन प्रकृतेः परोऽसंहत एव पुरुषः सिध्यति । *SPB*, p. 45. Also see *ibid.*, p. 32 and *YV* in *SYD*, p. 440.

tioned here that it is in consonance with this view of Vijñānabhikṣu that when the mind merges into *prakṛti* after having performed its function for the self, the latter is said to have attained liberation. He further elucidates it by pointing out that it is also the nature of a composite object that when it is aided by another object of the same nature it serves the purpose of some conscious being. To illustrate, the home helps someone to enjoy sleep as and when the body and the bed come in contact with each other. But such is not the case with the conscious self as it does not stand in need of something else for the act of being aware since it is itself of the nature of eternal consciousness. In other words the self, not being a collocation, does not have to serve some ulterior purpose.[1] In case self were taken to be a collocation, it would incur infinite regress.[2] Moreover, should any member of the collocation of *prakṛti* and its evolutes having the property of pleasure, pain, etc. be understood to exist for its own sake, it is very likely that it also would be rendered knowable by itself. Consequently the principle that the subject cannot become an object of its own cognition (activity) would be violated since it is just not possible that the experience of pleasure, etc. should occur without the experience of pleasure, etc. being apprehended. Resultantly the collocation of *prakṛti, mahat,* etc. has to be invested with subjectivity in order to account for the incidence of experience, should the conscious self be not postulated as a separate entity. And as such the incurrence of subject-object-contradiction cannot be avoided.[3]

Further, if each member of the collocation of the transformative constituents of *prakṛti* were assumed to possess the property of consciousness, it would involve cumbersomeness. On the other hand, postulating the conscious self over and above the collocation

---

1. यदुक्तं चित्तस्य सर्वात्मकत्वाङ्गीकारेऽसंख्यवासनावशात् स्वत एव चित्तस्य परिणामोऽस्तु किं पुरुषेणेति, तन्न–यतस्तच्चित्तमसंख्येयवासनाभिश्चित्रितमपि परार्थं परस्यान्यस्य भोगापवर्गायैव विना तौ न स्थातुं परिणन्तुं वा क्षमते संहत्यकारिपदार्थानां लोके परमात्रार्थत्वदर्शनादित्यर्थः, तथा च पुरुषार्थसमाप्तौ चित्तविलयेन मोक्षोपपत्तिरिति. . . .संहत्यकारित्वाद् इतरसाहाय्येनार्थक्रियाकारित्वात् गृहवदिति, गृहं हि शयनादिकार्यमास्तरणशरीरादिसाहाय्येनैव करोति पुरुषस्तु नित्यचैतन्यरूपतया चैतन्यार्थं नान्यमपेक्षते । अन्या चार्थक्रिया पुरुषस्य नास्ति स न संहत्यकारीत्याशयः । *YV* in *SYD,* pp. 439-40.
2. तस्यापि संहतत्वेऽनवस्थापत्तेः। *SPB,* p. 45. Also see *ibid.*, p. 32 and *YV* in *SYD*, p. 440.
3. अन्यच्च सुखादिमत् प्रधानादिकं यदि स्वस्य सुखादिभोगार्थं स्यात् तदा तस्य साक्षात्स्वज्ञेयत्वे कर्मकर्तृ-विरोधः, न हि धर्मिभानं विना सुखस्य भानं सम्भवति । अहं सुखीत्येवं सुखानुभवादिति ।
SPB (under *sūtra* I-66), pp. 45-46.

would be in consonance with the law of parsimony[1]. Besides, it would help tide over the incurrence of subject-object-contradiction.

It may be noted here with advantage that Vijñānabhikṣu draws our attention to an important point that it is not serving the purpose in general of the other, which proves the existence of self. Should it be admitted so, it would pose no problem in naming the purpose of anything. To illustrate, the coming of anything into existence may have destruction as its purpose. If so, the syllogism meant to prove the entity of self may end up proving something other than the self. As a result, the syllogism would be rendered untenable. To avoid this contingency Vijñānabhikṣu takes recourse to *Vyāsabhāṣya* to specify the nature of the purpose used as probans (*hetu*) in the syllogism which proves the existence of self. It is serving the purpose of someone else in a particular, and not in a general, sense that has to be taken into account in arriving at the conclusion. To put it differently, when the other is to be proved, it is to be proved as having the purpose of enjoyment and liberation only. The purpose being thus qualified, another fault, *siddhasādhana* attributed to Vijñānabhikṣu by the Buddhists is also avoided. They point out that the purpose in general as probans in the syllogism could also prove the existence of momentary consciousness since it may be postulated to exist for the sake of the succeeding emergent consciousness. Vijñānabhikṣu says that it is not by virtue of the preceding consciousness that the succeeding momentary consciousness experiences abidingness but it is self's being eternally conscious that it naturally does so[2] since an unconscious entity (inanimate object) cannot be admitted to experience pleasure, pain, etc. This is why he maintains that it is the eternally immutable conscious self which is not a collocation and which is the other to be proved, and not the momentary consciousness held by Vijñānavādins as the sole metaphysical reality.

---

1. अपि च संहन्यमानानां बहूनां गुणानां तत्कार्याणां चानेकविकाराणामनेकचैतन्यगुणकल्पनायां गौरवेण लाघवादेक एव चित्प्रकाशकः पुरुषः सर्वसंहतेभ्यः परः कल्पयितुं युज्यत इति ।
SPB (under *sūtra* I-66), p. 46.
2. ननु परार्थतामात्रेण न पुरुषसिद्धिः विनाशादीनामपि परार्थत्वसंभवाद् विनाशार्थमेवोत्पत्तेः पैरभ्युपगमादित्याशङ्कायामाह यश्चेति भोगापवर्गार्थवानेवात्र परः साध्ये प्रविष्टोऽतो न सामान्येन येन केनचित्परेण सिद्धसाधनमर्थान्तरं चेत्यर्थः स्वोत्तरोत्पन्नक्षणिकचित्तस्य भोगार्थकतया पराभिप्रेतं सिद्धसाधनमपाकरोति–यत्तु किंचिदिति स्वरूपेणात्मरूपेण भोक्तृतयेति यावत् यस्त्विति यस्त्वसौ विशेषः पुरुषाख्यः परः स कूटस्थनित्यत्वाद् न संहत्यकारीति । *YV* in *SYD*, pp. 440-41.

The second argument that the characteristics in the form of pleasure, pain, etc. cannot be assumed to belong to, or inhere in, the experiencer in order to avoid the subject-object-contradiction is taken on by the opponent. He points out that Vijñānabhikṣu accepts in principle that the self as the archetype or original (*bimba*) cognizes itself as reflected in the intellect to avoid the fault just mentioned. Is it not arbitrary on his part not to follow the same line of argument in the present context also? It may be put like this: Let pleasure, pain, etc., be admitted as the properties of the self. Then the properties may be assumed to be cognized by the self when they are reflected in the intellect along with it. It is in conformity with the theory of knowledge held by him. Vijñānabhikṣu does not agree with the opponent and says that though it is in consonance with his line of argument, yet to avoid the subject-object-contradiction, it is necessary to assume that pleasure, pain, etc. are the properties of the intellect. Otherwise, it would be cumbersome to postulate that they are self's properties and are reflected in the intellect to be intuited by the self. He gives two reasons to endorse his view: (1) The assumption that pleasure and pain are the properties of the self would render the latter subject to change. (2) The experiential intuitions, 'I feel pleasure', 'I feel pain', etc. could hardly be taken as an evidence to prove that pleasure, pain, etc. are its properties. They can be explained to be belonging to the self in the sense in which a thing is said to belong to its owner. Self's ownership of pleasure, pain, etc. is further substantiated when it is assumed that pleasure, pain, etc. are the properties of the intellect and that they are reflected in the self to account for their being apprehended by it.[1]

It has already been shown that the knower exists in an immutable form over and above the collocation that undergoes continuous change. The immutability of self can also be accounted for by the psychological fact that the self always keeps knowing all the modes

1. शरीरादीनां हि यः सुखाद्यात्मकत्वं धर्मः स सुखादिभोक्तरि न सम्भवति स्वयं सुखादिग्रहणे कर्मकर्तृविरोधात् । धर्मिपुरस्कारेणैव सुखाद्यनुभवादिति । ननु बुद्धिवृत्तिप्रतिबिम्बितं स्वसुखादिकं पुरुषेण गृह्यतां स्ववदिति चेन्न । एवं सति बुद्धेरेव सुखादिकल्पनौचित्यात् पुरुषगतसुखादेः बुद्धौ प्रतिबिम्बकल्पने गौरवात् । अहं सुखी, अहं दुःखी मूढ इत्यादिप्रत्ययास्तु न पुरुषे सुखादिसाधकाः तत्स्वामित्वेनाप्युपपत्तेः । बुद्धेः सुखादिमत्त्वेनाप्युपपत्तेश्च । *SPB* (under *sūtra* I-141), pp. 82-83.

of the mind related to it.[1] It is this point which dispenses with the undesirable entailment that everything irrespective of its belonging to self or not is always known to the self. To clarify, an object is said to be known to the self only when it has taken the form of intellect and not otherwise. It means that, even if the self, being all-pervasive is in contact with all, it immediately knows only the modes of the intellect it is in contact with. Vijñānabhikṣu has said more than once that the mental modes do not remain unknown to the self. Should it be admitted that there are mental modes which may not be known to the self, then one may doubt one's own experiential intuitions as in the case of any other object in the world. But such is never the case with one's own intuitions. There is a possibility that one may have doubt about the reality of a pitcher, a rope, etc. but it is psychologically impossible that one should doubt one's own intellectual modes called knowledge, pleasure, etc. In other words, nobody says 'Maybe I know or not', and 'Maybe I am happy or not'. It means that, since the self always knows all the modes of the intellect, it is unchanging and a distinct entity over and above the collocation of the changing things which also include the intellectual modes.[2]

The third logical ground to prove self is the postulation of the principle of consciousness for the control over the inanimate and composite objects. The conscious self being an experiencer may legitimately assume the role of the controller of composite entities. It is inferred thereby that the self is other than the composite entities which are controlled by it. Vijñānabhikṣu here points out that control or supervision consists in the contact of experiencer with the collocation. This contact impels *prakṛti* to undergo change and, then, gives rise to the incidence of experience. He further clarifies that the contact is possible only when the entities that enter into it

---

1. प्रकृत्यादयस्तावत्प्रत्यक्षागमानुमानैः परिणामितयैव सिद्धाः, पुरुषस्यापरिणामित्वं तु सदाज्ञात-विषयत्वादनुमीयते । *SPB* (under *sūtra* VI-2), p. 220.

   And also cf. विकारं प्रकृतिं चैव पुरुषं च सनातनम् ।
   यो यथावद् विजानाति स वितृष्णो विमुच्यते ।।

   MBH, Śānti-parva, 217.37, quoted *ibid.*, p. 100.

2. बुद्धिवृत्त्यारूढतयैव त्वन्यद् भोग्यं भवति पुरुषस्य न स्वतः सर्वदा सर्वभानापत्तेः । ताश्च बुद्धिवृत्तयो नाज्ञातास्तिष्ठन्ति । ज्ञानेच्छासुखादीनामज्ञातसत्तास्वीकारे तेष्वपि घटादाविव संशयादिप्रसंगादहं जानामि न वा सुखी न वेत्यादिरूपेण । अतः तेषां सदाज्ञातत्वात् तद्द्रष्टा चेतनोऽपरिणामीत्यायातम् ।

   Ibid. (under *sūtra* VI-2), p. 220.

are different.[1] According to him the individual self takes the help of the supervising function of the vital force to bring the body[2] into existence in order to reap the fruits of actions.

Besides, there are two other arguments which Vijñānabhikṣu does not use as grounds proper but as *anukūlatarka* to remove the doubt about the subject of the syllogism discussed above. (1) In his view it is difficult to account for the teleology of the collocation, unless it is accepted as being experienced, witnessed and supervised by the individual self. And the event of experiencing the collocation beginning with body and ending with *prakṛti* would find itself justified only if someone other than the collocation is postulated. And it cannot be anything but self. Its postulation will also dispense with the subject-object-contradiction.[3] (2) In case someone maintains that it is the body accompanied by the senses, mind, etc. which strives to attain liberation, and that there is no need for the postulation of self, Vijñānabhikṣu would meet the objection like this: If it were so, nobody would be seen trying for liberation, since nobody does that for a perishable entity, which body is. Moreover, should *prakṛti, mahat,* etc. be assumed to strive for absolute release from pain, it will not be feasible as it has been established elsewhere[4] that it has the natural properties of pain, pleasure, etc. and as such absolute freedom from them cannot be attained. Thus in both the cases, the phenomenon of striving for liberation from pain defies justification. But it is evident that man puts in effort to attain absolute freedom from the experience of pain. Vijñānabhikṣu concludes that the very fact that man tries to attain liberation[5] should dispel doubt about the existence of self over and above the collocation (*saṃghāta*).

---

1. भोक्तुरधिष्ठातृत्वाच्चाधिष्ठेयेभ्य: प्रकृत्यन्तेभ्योऽतिरिक्ततेत्यर्थ: । अधिष्ठानं हि भोक्तु: संयोग:, स च प्रकृत्यादीनां भोगहेतुपरिणामेषु कारणम् । भोक्तुरधिष्ठानाद् भोगायतननिर्माणमिति वक्ष्यमाणसूत्रात् (V-114) संयोगश्च भेदे सत्येव भवतीति भाव: । *SPB* (under *sūtra* I-142), p. 83.
2. भोक्तु: प्राणिनोऽधिष्ठानाद् व्यापारादेव भोगायतनस्य शरीरस्य निर्माणं भवति ।
   And also—देहनिर्माणे व्यापाररूपाधिष्ठानं स्वामिनश्चेतनस्यैकान्तात् साक्षान्नास्ति किन्तु प्राणरूपभृत्यद्वारा । *Ibid.* (under *sūtra* V-115), p. 211.
3. यदि हि शरीरादिस्वरूप एव भोक्ता स्यात् तदा भोक्तृत्वमेव व्याहन्येत कर्मकर्तृविरोधात् । स्वस्य साक्षात्स्वभोक्तृत्वानुपपत्तेरित्यर्थ: । *Ibid.* (under *sūtra* I-143), pp. 83-84.
4. Chapter 4 "*Concept of Prakṛti*".
5. शरीरादिकमेव चेद् भोक्तृ स्यात् तथा भोक्तु: कैवल्यार्थं दु:खात्यन्तोच्छेदार्थं कस्यापि प्रवृत्तिर्नोपपद्येत । शरीरादीनां विनाशित्वात् प्रकृतेश्च धर्मिग्राहकमानेन दु:खस्वाभाव्यसिद्ध्या कैवल्यासंभवात् । न हि स्वभावस्यात्यन्तोच्छेदो घटत इत्यर्थ: । *SPB* (under *sūtra* I-144), p. 84.

II
Plurality of Selves

It is in consonance with Vijñānabhikṣu's view of *avibhāgādvaita* that he admits the plurality of selves. To hold the view that selves are many and that they are different from the Absolute logically entails that the relation which subsists between them is real. It is this view which pits him against the Advaitic view that the relation between the Absolute and the selves is not real. In this regard K.C. Bhattacharyya's observation is worth noting. He says that the Advaitins (Non-dualists) seek to show that the datum (phenomenal reality of the world and the individual selves) is due to illusion in order to demonstrate that the view about the plurality of selves is invalid.[1] The Non-dualists claim to be in agreement with the scriptural statements in holding the view that the Self is one undivided whole. But there is also difference of opinion among them about the nature of relation between the Absolute and the selves. Since it is they who hold that the Ultimate Reality is one undivided whole, it naturally falls upon them to explain this relation in a manner that their view about the Absolute and Its relation with the empirical reality does not find itself violated. In view of this, the Advaitins postulate the principle of illusion (*ajñāna*) to account for the difference and plurality at the empirical plane. Despite this being the fact that they are unanimous on the postulation of *ajñāna*, they are divided so far as the nature of relation between Brahman and *jīvas* is concerned. The difference in their approach to the problem of relation between the two is brought out clearly in the form of theories popularly known as *pratibimbavāda* and *avacchedavāda* propounded by them to establish the identity of self.

The theory of reflection (*pratibimbavāda*) seeks to establish the undivided oneness of the Absolute by showing that the relation between the Absolute and the selves is like that of the original (archetype, *bimba*) and its reflection. To put it in other words, just as the original appears as separate and distinct from itself by way of reflection, in the same way the Absolute when reflected in the numerous adjuncts (*upādhis*) in the form of intellects, said to be the modifications of *ajñāna* (*avidyā*), appears as many individual selves. Madhusūdana Sarasvatī drives this point home more effectively

1. *SP*, p. 194, section 120.

when he enjoins upon us to clearly understand, by the example of face and its reflection in the mirror, that self and Brahman are identical. Those who admit that there is difference between the face and its reflection in the mirror explain their point of view with the example of Caitra and his shadow. They further clarify that it is evident to the person who is sitting near that his face and its reflection in the mirror are distinct. Moreover, even in the absence of any other person sitting near, the distinction between the original and its reflection becomes evident to the person himself when he takes into consideration his own hand and its reflection in the mirror. Madhusūdana Sarasvatī does not accept it and points out that the difference between the original and its reflection is apparent, and not real. He further points out that, if it were scrutinized closely, it would become absolutely clear that it is due to the mirror that the face is superimposed on it or that the face occasions its own reflection in the mirror. It is the experience of one and all that everybody understands and says that it (reflection) is the same as the original (face in the present case). In this way when the point at issue is investigated properly, it becomes crystal clear that the original and its reflection are not essentially different and it is on this basis that the analogy of the original and its reflection is offered to establish the identity of the self with the Absolute.[1] The view about identity becomes clearer and more definite when the example of one and the same person seen at two different places and times[2] is given to prove the point.

The limitation-theory (*avacchedavāda*) as propounded by Vācaspati Miśra[3] is also an attempt to establish that self is none but the Absolute. As per this view, the one undivided and unlimited

---

1. तथा जीवब्रह्मणोः मुखप्रतिमुखवत् बिम्बप्रतिबिम्बरूपत्वादप्यभेदोऽवगन्तव्यः । ननु दृष्टान्ते नाभेदः संप्रतिपन्नः चैत्रतच्छाये भिन्ने इतिवत् चैत्रतत्प्रतिबिम्बे भिन्ने इत्येव पार्श्वस्थितेन ग्रहणात्, स्वेनापि स्वकरतत्प्रतिबिम्बे भिन्ने इति ग्रहणाच्चेति चेन्न; आपाततो भेदप्रतीतावपि सयुक्तिकप्रत्यक्षेण बिम्बप्रतिबिम्बयोरैक्यसिद्ध्या दृष्टान्तत्वोपपत्तेः. . . . ग्रीवास्थं मुखं यत्स्वलक्षणकं प्रतिपन्नं दर्पणस्थमपि तथेत्यवधार्य तथैवेदं मुखमिति स एवायं कर इति च स्वपरसाधारणप्रतीतिरप्यनुभवसिद्धा ।
Madhusūdana Sarasvatī, *Advaitasiddhi*, edited by Ananta Krishna Śāstrī, Parimal Publications, Delhi, 1982, p. 847.
Also cf. V.P. Upādhyāya, *Lights on Vedānta*, Varanasi, 1959, pp. 33-38.
2. सोऽयं देवदत्तः ।
3. न जीव आत्मनोऽन्यः । नापि तद्विकारः किन्त्वात्मैवाविद्योपधानकल्पितावच्छेदः । आकाश इव घटमणिकादिकल्पितावच्छेदो घटाकाशो मणिकाकाशो न तु परमाकाशादन्यस्तद्विकारो वा । *Bhāmatī* on *Brahmasūtra*, I-IV-22.

Ultimate Reality comes to be viewed as limited on account of different limiting adjuncts (*upādhis*). It is based on the pot-space analogy. The space in a pot and space are interlocked in a relation of identity with each other. In a similar way the relation between self and the Absolute is that of identity. Self is not a part or modification of the Ultimate (Self) just as the pot-space cannot be termed as a part or modification of space. The individual self gets its name because of the body in the same manner as the pot-space gets its name on account of the pot. Śaṅkara uses this analogy as if to clarify the point at issue. He says that it is due to adjuncts that the Absolute is said to give rise to the emergence of many individual selves just as different parts of space are apparently perceived to arise when space is limited by pots, etc. and dissolved back into space when pots, etc. disappear. What is worth noticing in the illustration is that space is held to be the cause in both the situations.[1] In this way *avacchedavāda*, too, seeks to demonstrate that the Absolute is one undivided whole and the apparent emergence of many selves is due to numerous limitors in the form of *upādhis* which are said to be the modifications of *avidyā*.

Vijñānabhikṣu analyzes the arguments advanced by Advaitins in support of the theories of reflection and limitation and concludes that Advaitins' attempt to establish the undivided oneness of the Absolute is both inadequate and wrong. It is wrong in the sense that the arguments put forward to corroborate *pratibimbavāda* and *avacchedavāda* do not represent the true spirit of scriptures. It is also inadequate since objections raised against the theories do not find themselves adequately answered and convincingly refuted. Both these points will be made clear in the following discussion about the plurality of selves, the view held by Vijñānabhikṣu. Though both Advaitins and Vijñānabhikṣu proclaim that their standpoints are consonant with the scriptural statements, yet the point at issue has to be decided on the basis of logical propriety coupled with scriptural uniformity. It may, however, be mentioned, before we start discussing the problem, that both believe in the oneness of the Absolute. The Advaitins hold that It is both one and undivided, whereas Vijñānabhikṣu bases his concept of oneness on the universal characteristic of consciousness which belongs to both the Absolute

1. यथा आकाशस्य सुषिरभेदोत्पत्तिप्रलयनिमित्तत्वं घटाद्युपाधिकृतमेव, तद्वदक्षरस्यापि नामरूपकृत-देहोपाधिनिमित्तमेव जीवोत्पत्तिप्रलयनिमित्तत्वम् ।

Śāṅkarabhāṣya on *Muṇḍaka Upaniṣad*, II-1-i.

and the individual self.[1]

In this context Vijñānabhikṣu refers to the view of the modern exponents of Non-dualism that Brahman means *jīva* too, since both Brahman and *jīva* are one and the same. They elucidate it with the help of an illustration of space meaning primarily also the space in a pot. What they want to convey is that it is due to ignorance that the individual self is not understood to be the same as Brahman. There exist several statements in the scriptures that show that there is identity between the Absolute and the individual self. They are nothing but consciousness. So far as the scriptural statements about the difference between the Ultimate Reality and the empirical selves are concerned, they are to be understood to be based on the adjunctival difference (*aupādhika bheda*). To illustrate, Brahman is said to be different from the individual self which is nothing but consciousness limited by the intellect just as the great space is understood to be different from the space limited by the pot. The Advaitins seek to explain the difference in another way:

The magician sitting on the ground is different from the one equipped with a sword, a shield, etc. who climbs along with a rope into the sky. The latter appears to be so under the impact of his magical power. In a similar manner Brahman is considered to be distinct from the individual self having the characteristics of agency and experiencership brought into existence because of *avidyā*. Vijñānabhikṣu points out here that the Advaitins press into service the two theories of reflection and limitation to explain away the difference between the Supreme Lord and the empirical self.[2]

It will not be out of place to refer to the view of Advaitins that it is the knowledge of identity between the Absolute and the individual self that annihilates *ajñāna*, the cause of bondage. In this way there

---

1. आत्मैक्यश्रुतीनां विरोधस्तु नास्ति तासां जातिपरत्वात् । जातिः सामान्यमेकरूपत्वं तत्रैवाद्वैतश्रुतीनां तात्पर्यात् न तु अखण्डत्वे प्रयोजनाभावादित्यर्थः । *SPB* (under *sūtra* I-154 नाद्वैतश्रुतिविरोधो जातिपरत्वात्), p. 93.
2. आधुनिकास्तु जीवब्रह्मणोरखण्डतया जीवेऽपि ब्रह्मशब्दो मुख्य एव आकाशशब्द इव घटाकाशे । जीवस्याब्रह्मत्वं त्वज्ञानकल्पितम् । तथाहि 'तत्त्वमसि. . .' इत्याद्यभेदश्रुतिशतेभ्यो जीवोऽपि ब्रह्मैव चिन्मात्रत्वाविशेषात् । ऐश्वर्यबन्धयोश्चोपाधिद्वयधर्मत्वात् । न च 'द्वा सुपर्णा. . .' इत्यादिभेदश्रुतिशतानुपपत्तिरिति वाच्यम्, औपाधिकभेदानुवादकत्वेन तादृशवाक्योपपत्तेः । यथाहि घटाकाशादुपाधिपरिच्छिन्नान्महाकाशोऽन्य इति व्यवह्रियते तथैव बुद्ध्यवच्छिन्नचैतन्याज्जीवादन्यः परमेश्वर इति श्रुतिषु व्यवह्रियते । अथवा मायाविनः खड्गचर्मधरात् सूत्रेणाकाशमधिरोहतः सकाशात् स एव मायावी परमार्थभूतो भूमिष्ठोऽन्यस्तथैवाविद्याकल्पितात् कर्तृभोक्तृलक्षणाज्जीवादन्य परमेश्वरोऽस्तु । तदेवमवच्छेदभेदेन प्रतिबिम्बरूपेण वा जीवेश्वरयोर्भेदः । *VAB*, p. 20.

arises no need to restrict the import of the identity-statements, as the Advaitic scheme of things seems to be perfectly in consonance with their view on the Ontological Reality. Contrary to this, Vijñānabhikṣu holds the view that it is the knowledge of discrimination which brings the cause of bondage to an end. He adds further that the statements to this effect do occur in the scriptures more frequently. In reality, it is the discriminatory knowledge which constitutes the right knowledge immediately leading to liberation.[1]

Vijñānabhikṣu continues his tirade against the Advaitins by pointing out that it is beyond the capacity brought about by the knowledge of identity to immediately terminate the ignorance characterized by the experience of pain, etc. The reason he gives is that when the individual self has been postulated as one undivided whole, both pain and its absence will have to be accepted as residing in it, though they are different: one being the cause and the other being the effect. He elucidates it with the example of sound and its absence which are admitted to be coexisting in *ākāśa* owing to the difference in limitors. Vijñānabhikṣu further exposes the absurdity of the Advaitic view of the undivided oneness of the Absolute. He points out that in that case inanimate objects will have to be assumed to be identical with Brahman and that it is utterly absurd to talk of pain and its absence with reference to these lifeless objects. The illogicality of the principle of identity thus renders impossible the attainment of emancipation which is supposed to result from it. But on the other hand there is ample evidence to establish that the knowledge of discrimination between individual self and *prakṛti* on the one hand and between the former and the Absolute on the other gives rise to the state of liberation. It is in this sense, Vijñānabhikṣu concludes, that the statements conveying difference carry more weight than those of identity. And consequently the scriptural statements of the latter kind should be construed as depicting the non-separate nature of the Absolute[2].

1. ननु मोक्षफलश्रवणादभेदवाक्यानामेव सम्यग्ज्ञानपरत्वमसंकोचश्चेति युक्तमिति चेन्न 'पृथगात्मानं प्रेरितारञ्च मत्वा जुष्टस्ततस्तेनामृतत्वमेती' त्यादिश्रुतिभिर्भेदज्ञानस्यापि मोक्षहेतुत्वश्रवणात् । भेदज्ञानस्य विवेकज्ञानतया अविद्यानिवर्तकस्यैव 'तमेव विदित्वाऽतिमृत्युमेती 'त्यादिभेदवाक्येष्वाधिक्येन मोक्षफलश्रवणात् । किं च सम्यग्ज्ञानत्वेन हेतुना भेदाख्यविवेकज्ञानस्यैव साक्षान्मोक्षहेतुत्वं श्रुतिसिद्धम् । *VAB*, p. 21.
2. न ह्यभेदज्ञानं साक्षादेवाहं दुःखीत्यादिलक्षणामविद्यामुच्छेत्तुमर्हति । एकस्मिन्नेवाकाशेऽवच्छेदभेदेन शब्दतदभाववदेकस्मिन्नेवात्मनि कार्यकारणलक्षणावच्छेदभेदेन दुःखादितदभावसंभवादिति । किं च ब्रह्माभेदस्य जडेष्वपि श्रवणान्न तेन दुःखादिशून्यतासिद्धिः । तस्माद् विवेकवाक्यरूपतया भेदवाक्यान्येव बलवन्ति, तद्विरोधेन चाभेदवाक्यान्यविभागपरतयैव संकोच्यानि । *Ibid.*, pp. 21-22.

Vijñānabhikṣu attaches great significance to the part-whole analogy since it is, he thinks, conducive to the authentic interpretation of the scriptures. In pursuance of this standpoint, he considers the relation of identity-cum-difference to be really subsisting between the Absolute and the individual self and suggests that the pot-space and reflection analogies should be interpreted in such a manner that they may conform to the primary sense borne out by the part-whole analogy. The basic difference in his approach from that of the Advaitins comes down to a comparison between the part-whole analogy on the one hand and both the reflection and limitation models on the other. The limitation and reflection theories are used by the Advaitins to demonstrate the Non-dualistic nature (undivided oneness) of the Absolute, while Vijñānabhikṣu's part-and-whole view subscribes to the ontological difference between the Absolute and the individual selves, though they remain inseparable all through. It is precisely the reason why Vijñānabhikṣu holds the view that it is the knowledge of discrimination which actually terminates bondage. As a result the scriptural statements of discrimination ought to be construed as primary and the ones expressing identity should be taken as conveying identity as non-separateness. Vijñānabhikṣu performs this philosophical feat fairly successfully by saying that non-separateness is the true import of identity as it is less cumbersome a philosophical postulate and as it occurs in the scriptures more frequently.[1]

Unlike Vijñānabhikṣu, the Advaitins debunk difference and maintain that it is the knowledge of identity between the Absolute and the individual self that brings about the release of the latter. It is in this light that the Non-dualist accords primary importance to the statements expressing identity and consequently observes that the statements of difference are to be taken as really explanatory.[2]

Further examining the Advaitic view on the undivided oneness of *ātman* vis-a-vis the part-whole relationship between Īśvara and *jīva*, Vijñānabhikṣu points out that if the part-whole-relationship between Īśvara and *jīva* be construed as that between the pervader and the pervaded, it would have to be conceded that the place of *ātman* which is limited by *jīva* is also limited by Īśvara. It would entail the

1. *YV* in *SYD*, p. 73.
2. भेदाभेदोभयश्रुतिस्मृतिमध्ये भेदनिन्दयाऽभेदज्ञानस्य मोक्षफलकत्वकथनेन चाभेदवाक्यानि एव स्वार्थपराणि भेदवाक्यानि त्वनुवादमात्राणि । *YV* in *SYD*, p. 72.

contingency of Īśvara being subject to birth, death, etc., as It is limited by the Causal *Sattva*. He explains this with the help of two examples: (i) Bad sound would become liable to being possessed by the universal space on account of the latter's being limited by the mouth of a donkey. (ii) The same universal space would also have to be taken as possessing bad smell since it is limited by the anus too.[1]

To escape this contingency should the Advaitin propose that Īśvara and *jīva* be the parts of *ātman* (consciousness) and that *jīva* be not primarily a part of the former, they would exclude each other as is the case with the pot-space and the bowl-space which exclude each other. Consequently Īśvara's being the inner controller of all *jīvas* would be rendered incongruous, for on acceptance of this proposition Īśvara would cease to exist where *jīvas* do.[2]

The Non-dualist nevertheless attempts to make his view on the unity of the Absolute clear by pointing out that the individual self and Īśvara are called so since they are qualified by different adjuncts and as such the nature of the Absolute remains unaffected. But Vijñānabhikṣu rebuts it drawing his (Advaitin's) attention to the fact that the Advaitic view does not succeed in adequately solving the problems raised in this context: In case both the qualified ones (Īśvara and *jīva*) were assumed to be one and the same, the characteristics of the individual self such as being subject to birth, death, etc., would also apply to Īśvara. Moreover, the phenomenon of bondage and liberation will defy explanation, since its incidence gets mixed up in the event of the nature of self being admitted as non-dual.[3]

Were it admitted that there is no difference between Īśvara and the individual self, two alternative situations about the nature of difference would arise: If the difference is accepted to be temporary, bondage and liberation will cease to bear any significance, as it is no

---

1. जीवेश्वरयोरंशांशिनोस्तावद् व्याप्यव्यापकभावस्वीकारेण जीवोपाधिनाऽवच्छेद्यस्यात्मप्रदेशस्येश्वरोपाध्यवच्छिन्नत्वं वक्तव्यम् । तथा च यथा ब्रह्माण्डाकाशस्य गर्दभमुखावच्छेदेन दुःस्वरत्वं पाय्ववच्छेदेनौपाधिकं दुर्गन्धित्वमेवं कारणसत्त्वावच्छिन्नचिदाकाशस्यापीश्वरस्य जीवोपाध्यवच्छेदेन संसारित्वं स्यात् । *YV* in *SYD*, pp. 72-73.
2. यदि च जीवेश्वरौ चैतन्यस्यैवांशौ न तु जीव ईश्वरस्य साक्षादंशोऽतो घटकुण्डाकाशवदेवान्योऽन्यव्यावृत्तौ जीवेश्वरौ स्वीक्रियेतां तदापीश्वरस्य जीवान्तर्यामित्वानुपपत्तिः, जीवप्रदेशेऽपीश्वरासत्त्वादिति । *Ibid.*, p. 73.
3. ननूपाधिविशिष्टयोरेव जीवेश्वरत्वे वक्तव्ये इति चेत् ? न विकल्पासहत्वात् । विशिष्टानतिरेके जीवेश्वरत्वबन्धमोक्षादिसांकर्यतादवस्थ्यात् । *Ibid.*, p. 73.

use discussing bondage and liberation with reference to the non-eternal entities. And in order to avoid redundance, if it is admitted that the difference is eternal and, therefore, both Īśvara and the individual self are also eternal, it will be like the act of falling into the mouth of a poisonous snake while running away from a scorpion out of fear. It would be so because if many a qualified self is to be postulated to escape the cumbersomeness involved in assuming many independent selves, the same fault would fall to the lot of the Advaitin who postulates many qualified selves.[1] Besides, the assumption of a single *ātman* over and above its qualified versions will add to the cumbersomeness already involved. Should the Advaitin still hold that such a postulation of a common single *ātman* is in conformity with the Non-dualistic scriptural statements, it would nevertheless become difficult for him to explain the scriptural statements about identity such as 'Thou art that', etc. when the distinction between the *ātman* and the qualified one is real. The manifold nature of self would also remain absolutely unaccountable in the face of total identity between the Absolute and the individual self, or between the common single *ātman* and the qualified one. If the solution of the problem is sought in the device of postulating a relation of identity-cum-difference it would, says Vijñānabhikṣu, amount to accepting the position held by him.[2]

Vijñānabhikṣu further has a poser for the Advaitin. The latter resolves the contradiction between the scriptural statements of identity and difference by explaining the difference expressed in them in terms of adjunctival (*aupādhika*) differentiations (*bheda*). This the Advaitin does in deference to the identity propositions. But if, Vijñānabhikṣu tells the Advaitin, the statements conveying difference are given due weightage, the identity expressed in scriptures can satisfactorily be explained in terms of non-separateness (*avibhāga*). When the resolution of the contradiction between the statements of identity and those of difference is possible both ways why does the Advaitin unduly prefer the identity statements and

1. अतिरेके तु तदनित्यं नित्यं वा ? आद्ये विनाशितया तस्य बन्धमोक्षाद्यनुपपत्तिः, अन्त्ये वृश्चिकभिया पलायमानस्याशीविषमुखनिपातः । यदि हि विशिष्टा अनेके आत्मानः कल्पनीयास्तर्हि अस्मासूपन्यस्तं गौरवं भवतामप्यापतितम् । *YV* in *SYD*, p. 73.
2. अधिकं तु सामान्यैकात्मकल्पनमिति । न चात्माद्वैतश्रुत्यनुरोधेन तदप्युचितमिति वाच्यम्, विशिष्टात्मभ्यः सामान्यात्मनोऽत्यन्तभेदे तत्त्वमस्याद्यभेदवाक्यानुपपत्तितादवस्थ्यात्, अत्यन्तमभेदे च विशिष्टातिरिक्तता-विरोधात्, भेदाभेदे चास्मन्मतप्रवेशादिति । *Ibid.*, p. 73.

disregard the real status of the world?[1]

It is in this context that Vijñānabhikṣu cites such illustrations as bear upon the relationship of part and whole, that is, one of identity-cum-difference. He thinks that the illustrations of fire and its sparks bear more significance than those of space, the sun and so on. It is, therefore, appropriate to hold that the illustrations pertaining to space, the sun and the like cannot alone establish that the Absolute by nature is one undivided whole.

Preferring the illustrations about the relationship of identity-cum-difference and explaining the difference as extremely ephemeral like bubbles, Vijñānabhikṣu maintains that the difference expressed in the scriptures should be taken as separateness or as division and that is opposite to the real nature of the Absolute. As such his view that the individual selves eternally reside in Brahman non-separately as Its *aṃśas* makes better sense and also conforms to the true spirit of the scriptures.[2]

The theory of reflection too fails to meet the objections raised against itself. The reflection being devoid of substance is insignificant. It, therefore, cannot be taken to be identical with Brahman, the Ultimate Substance. It is irrational to hold that the real and the unreal are identical. In case selves are assumed to be substantially significant, it will be tantamount to accepting the plurality of selves and this in turn would render the Non-dualistic position untenable.[3]

It may be mentioned in this context that Vijñānabhikṣu does not accept Madhusūdana Sarasvatī's view that there is no difference between the original and its reflection. But if it is proposed by the latter that the discernible difference is merely due to illusion as the sighting of two moons in lieu of a single one, it also does not sound logical. For bondage and liberation will still be entailed in the case

---

1. तत्रोच्यते-अभेदवाक्यानुरोधेन भेदवाक्यानामौपाधिकभेदपरत्वं यथा कल्प्यते तथा भेदवाक्यानुरोधेना-भेदेवाक्यानामविभागादिलक्षणाभेदपरत्वं कथं न कल्प्यते ? अविरोधस्योभयथैव सम्भवात् । *VAB*, p. 21.
2. न्यायानुग्रहेण बलवद्‌भिरग्निविस्फुल्लिङ्गादिभिः सांशदृष्टान्तैः विरोधादाकाशसूर्यादिदृष्टान्ता अखण्डतापरा न भवन्ति, किन्तु ब्रह्मणि सर्वजीवानामविभागलक्षणाभेदस्य सर्वकालस्थायितया पारमार्थिकत्वेऽपि यत्किञ्चिदवच्छेदेन फेनबुद्‌बुदादिवद् अतिभंगुरस्य विभागलक्षणभेदस्यापारमार्थिकस्यौपाधिकत्वमात्रं प्रतिपादयन्तीति । एतेन भेदनिन्दावाक्यानि प्रकरणभेदैः विभागवैधर्म्यादिभेदपराण्येव । *YV* in *SYD*, p. 73.
3. प्रतिबिम्बवादस्त्वत्यन्तं विकल्पासहः ।प्रतिबिम्बस्य तुच्छत्वे प्रतिबिम्बरूपजीवस्य ब्रह्मणा सहाभेदानुपपत्तिः, सदसतोरभेदानुपपत्तेः, अतुच्छत्वे चात्मनानात्वस्य शब्दभेदेन स्वीकारापत्तिरद्वैतानुपपत्तिश्चेति । *Ibid.*, p. 73.

of the Absolute. In order to lend logical propriety to the Advaitic point of view, should the scripture and the order defined in them be assumed to be a product of *ajñāna*, it would strike at the very root of the means of knowledge. And as such the scriptural evidence that negates everything other than Brahman will be rendered inauthentic. It may be elucidated with the help of an example. The linguistic expression that has taken place in a dream stands contradicted in the waking state. As such the meaning of the linguistic expression of the dream does become subject to doubt. In a similar manner when it is learnt that the phenomenon of bondage and liberation does not exist at all, nobody will feel like paying attention to the practice of meditation, etc. The reason is obviously the scriptural ordaining that there is no bondage and liberation in reality, which implies that there is no pursuit worth the name for human beings.[1]

If the Advaitin still insists on maintaining that the phenomenon of bondage and liberation can be accounted for by postulating reflection and limitation models, Vijñānabhikṣu does not entertain it and points out that such an attempt to explain the phenomenon of bondage and liberation is merely an exercise in rationalization to beguile the disciples. For it is absurd to talk of bondage and liberation with respect to the individual self if it is merely a reflection as already pointed out. So far as the limitation model is concerned it will result in the destruction of the individual self itself when the adjunct or *upādhi* ceases to operate at the rise of knowledge. It would also contradict the non-relational (*akhaṇḍa*) meaning of the identity-propositions such as 'Thou art that', and the like since a relation of identity cannot subsist between what is and what is not. To avoid the anomaly, if the original itself is assumed to be the individual self when in contact with the adjunct (*upādhi*), the Advaitin should be asked to explain why he uses the reflection model whereas this view seems to be an aspect of the limitation model. Vijñānabhikṣu charges the Advaitin with the unnecessary postulation of two

1. अथैवमुच्यते बिम्बप्रतिबिम्बयो: परमार्थतो नास्ति भेद: किन्तुद्विचन्द्रदर्शनवदेकस्मिन्नेव वस्तुनि भेदमात्रमिति, तदपि न विचारसहम्, बन्धमोक्षानुपपत्तितादवस्थ्यात् । व्यवस्थातत्प्रतिपादकश्रुत्यादिकं च सर्वमेवात्मातिरिक्तम् अज्ञानकल्पितमेव वक्तव्यमिति चेन्न, एवमपि प्रमाणस्यापि बाधेन ब्रह्मातिरिक्तनिषेधस्य श्रुतस्यापि पुन: संशयापत्ते:, स्वाप्नशब्दस्य जाग्रति बाधे पुनस्तच्छब्दबोधितार्थसंशयवत् । तथा बन्धमोक्षादिकं सर्वथा नास्ति इति श्रवणानन्तरं मननादिषु प्रवृत्त्यनुपपत्तेश्च, आप्तवाक्यत: पुरुषार्थाभावनिर्णयादित्यादीनि अनेकानि दूषणानि । *VAB*, p. 22.

different models.[1]

Moreover, the scriptural statements conveying the part-whole-relationship between the Absolute and the individual self run counter to the theory of reflection. It is absurd to consider reflection as a part of the original. Vijñānabhikṣu here cautions that the word *ābhāsa* occurring in *Brahmasūtra* II-4-50 cannot be taken as an evidence to prove the theory of reflection, as it does not even connote reflection. He further adds that this aspect is brought out more clearly when the overall view of the author of *Brahmasūtra* that the individual self is a part of the Absolute, is taken into consideration. Both the 'part-whole' and 'reflection' views cannot go together as they are mutually exclusive. Regarding the word *ābhāsa* interpreted as reflection by most of Advaitins, Vijñānabhikṣu offers two probable meanings: (1) Illumination and (2) Appearance. In the latter sense like the word *hetvābhāsa*, it may mean '*ātmābhāsa*' and in that case soulhood is denied to the individual self in the ultimate sense as true sense is denied to the term '*hetu*' understood as '*hetvābhāsa*'. So far as the first meaning of *ābhāsa* is concerned, it may be said that the individual self derives its illumination from the Absolute. The illustrations regarding the reflection model are interpreted in a manner that Īśvara, an aggregate of selves may be said to illuminate them by His reflection in them just as the sun being a composite whole of its rays illuminates the receptacles when the rays are reflected in them.[2]

To remove the defect of the incurrence of the phenomenon of birth, death, bondage, liberation, etc. in the case of Īśvara on the theory of reflection, the Advaitin offers this explanation. The reflections of the Single Self cast in the individual and universal

---

1. या च प्रतिबिम्बावच्छेदरूपाभ्यां बन्धमोक्षादिव्यवस्था रचिता सा स्वशिष्यमोहनमात्रं प्रतिबिम्बस्य तुच्छतया बन्धमोक्षानौचित्यात् । ज्ञानेनोपाधिवियोगे जीवनाशप्रसङ्गात्, तत्त्वमसीत्यादिवाक्यार्थतयाभ्युपगतस्याखण्डत्वस्य विरोधाच्च सदसतोरभेदानुपपत्तेः। न च प्रतिबिम्बोपाधिना बिम्बस्यैव जीवत्वं वाच्यं तथा सति अवच्छेदभेद एव पर्यवसानात् किमिति प्रतिबिम्बवादः पृथङ् निर्मीयते । *VAB*, p. 22.
2. किं च प्रतिबिम्बवादे अंशश्रुतिस्मृतिसूत्राणां विरोधः प्रतिबिम्बेऽशव्यवहाराभावात् । यत्त्वाभास एवेति जीवप्रकरणस्थसूत्रं तत्राभासशब्दो न प्रतिबिम्बवाची तथा 'प्रयोगादर्शनात्', 'अंशो नानाव्यपदेशादि' ति सूत्रेणांशत्वमुक्त्वा पुनः सूत्रान्तरेण तद्विरुद्धप्रतिबिम्बतायाः सूत्रणानौचित्याच्च । किन्तु प्रकाशवाची 'सर्वेन्द्रियगुणाभासमिति' । अस्तु वा हेत्वाभासवदात्माभासवाची जीवस्यापि पारमार्थिकात्मत्वस्य प्रतिषेध्यमानत्वात् प्रकाशे प्रयोगदर्शनाद् इति, न तत्स्वाभासं दृश्यत्वादिति च । अथैवं प्रतिबिम्बदृष्टान्तः कथमुपपद्येतेति चेत्, अंशांश्यविभागेन किरणसूर्ययोरिव जीवब्रह्मणोरेकपिण्डीभावेन जीवेन अंशैः नानाबुद्धिप्रतिबिम्बनादित्यवेहि । *Ibid.*, p. 23.

adjuncts (*upādhis*) may be called *jīvas* and Īśvara respectively. These reflections are mutually distinct, and as such the defect just mentioned does not become applicable in the case of Īśvara and the theory of reflection ceases to be untenable as pointed out by Vijñānabhikṣu. The latter, however, rejects such a position for the following reasons:

If the original as self and its reflection is assumed to be different, experiencership, bondage, etc. will be rendered incongruous because the reflection being inanimate (unsubstantial) cannot have such states predicated of it and in the process the established Advaitic principle of identity between Brahman and *jīva* would be jeopardized. Moreover, the postulation of soul over and above both *jīva* and Īśvara is not acceptable as it has no logical support.

If the reflection and its original be admitted to be identical, it would be extremely difficult to escape ambiguity about the phenomenon of bondage and liberation. To get rid of such an anomalous situation, if the Advaitin condescends to accept the view of identity-cum-difference between Brahman and *jīva*, he will have to relinquish his position as an exponent of absolute identity, i.e. Non-dualism.[1]

After refuting the Advaitic theory of reflection, Vijñānabhikṣu addresses himself to analyzing the limitation theory, lays bare its hollowness and avers that it, too, fails to explain the distinction between the Absolute and the individual self, which the scriptural statements acclaim to be a reality. Should Īśvara and the individual self be assumed to be different on account of the adjunctival difference, in other words, if the distinction be sought to be explained by the difference in their qualifications, it would be difficult to convincingly explain whether the qualified is the same or a different entity. If the qualified were distinct, it would contradict the undivided nature of the Absolute as shown by the identity propositions.[2] There is one more flaw in accepting this alternative;

1. यद्यपि केचिन्नवीना वेदान्तिब्रुवा आहु:– एकस्यैवात्मन: कार्यकारणोपाधिषु प्रतिबिम्बानि जीवेश्वरा:, प्रतिबिम्बानां चान्योऽन्यं भेदाज्जन्माद्यखिलव्यवस्थोपपत्तिरिति । तदप्यसत्, भेदाभेदविकल्पासहत्वात् । बिम्बप्रतिबिम्बयो: भेदे प्रतिबिम्बस्याचेतनतया भोक्तृत्वबन्धमोक्षाद्यनुपपत्ति:, जीवब्रह्माभेदरूपतत्सिद्धान्तक्षतिश्च । जीवेश्वरभिन्नस्यात्मनोऽप्रामाणिकत्वं च । अभेदे तु साङ्कर्यापरिहार: । भेदाभेदाम्युपगमे तु तत्सिद्धान्तहानि: । *SPB* (under *sūtra* I-151), p. 90.
2. अवच्छेदवादेऽपि 'तयोरन्य: पिप्पलं....' इत्यादिविभागानुपपत्ते:, धर्मिण: एकत्वात् । अथोपाधिविशिष्टयोरेव जीवेश्वरत्वे वाच्ये, तथा विशेषणभेदाद् भेद:स्यादिति चेन्न विशिष्टस्यातिरेकानतिरेकयोरुभयत:पाशात् । विशिष्टस्यातिरेके भवदभिमतस्य तत्त्वमसीत्यादिवाक्यार्थस्याखण्डत्वस्यानुपपत्ते: । *VAB*, p. 23.

that is that the individual self is rendered liable to annihilation when at the attainment of liberation the adjunct is discarded.[1] And on the presumption that the qualified does not distinguish itself from the unqualified (Pure Self), the phenomenon of bondage, liberation, etc. would become applicable even in the case of Pure Self. Thus, it would render inexplicable the scriptural statements indicating distinction between the two. Nor would the wise venture to hold that the same self can be described both as liberated and bound at the same time because the limitors are different. Vijñānabhikṣu explains this point with the help of a stock example of Nyāya: If a monkey sits on the top (branch) of a tree—and not on its stump—the tree is said to have both monkey and its absence since contact is assumed to be a relation of non-pervasion (*avyāpya-vṛtti*). But no sensible person will say in this context that a tree has a monkey on it and another does not have on account of difference in the limitors (*avacchedakas*). (In this case the branch and the stump are two different limitors.) Nevertheless the scriptural statements which convey distinction are not amenable to such interpretation as is generally done in the example of tree and monkey. Moreover, both the result of knowledge and the defect of ignorance are unsubstantial as difference is assumed to be illusory and as such they fail to inspire man to seek freedom from ignorance and attain liberation. On the contrary it is better to say, Vijñānabhikṣu observes, that the individual self experiences pain at one time and does not do so at another time and that this diversity may be attributed to the difference in time. As such the incidence of non-discrimination and its termination can be accorded a status of reality.[2] That man exerts to liberate himself from *avidyā* also assumes significance in that case.

Another difficulty which crops up on the view about the undivided oneness of self is that the liberated individual self becomes subject to bondage again, since the self which has attained liberation after having been freed of its mind, may again come in contact with

---

1. किं च मोक्षावस्थायां विशेषणनाशेन जीवनाशप्रसङ्गः । *VAB*, p. 23.
2. यदि च विशिष्टमनतिरिक्तमुच्यते तदा एकस्मिन्नेवात्मन्यवच्छेदभेदेन बन्धमोक्षैश्वर्यादिप्रसक्त्या 'ये तद् विदुरमृतास्ते भवन्त्यथेतरे दुःखमेवापियन्ति. . . .' इत्यादि विभागानुपपत्तिः न ह्येकस्मिन्नेव वृक्षेऽवच्छेद-भेदेन कपिसंयोगतदभाववति एको वृक्षः कपिसंयोगवानन्यश्च नेत्यमूढैः प्रयुज्यते न लौकिकभेदानुवादेन तादृशवाक्यान्युपपादयितुं शक्यन्ते, ज्ञानफलस्य अज्ञानदोषस्य चापारमार्थिकत्वे तदर्थकप्रवृत्त्याद्यनौचित्यात् अस्मन्मते चात्मनि दुःखभोगतदभावयोः कालभेदेन पारमार्थिकत्वस्योपपाद्यत्वात् ।

Ibid., p. 23. Cf. also *SPB*, pp. 89-90.

some mind or the other. It is like the pot-space which having been freed from its limitor in the form of a pot when it is destroyed, may again come in contact with another pot. It would not be proper to hold the view that the same part of the self which has been freed from the mind does not come into contact with another mind, since in that case the yogi's capacity to be omnipresent would become suspect.[1]

The Advaitin takes recourse to the indicative power of word (*jahadajahallakṣaṇā*) to find a solution to the problem referred to above and comes to the conclusion that the words 'Thou' and 'That' would mean pure consciousness after relinquishing their incompatible qualifications. But Vijñānabhikṣu does not come round to this interpretation and points out that the qualified words mean distinct entities, and with the help of *jahadajahallakṣaṇā* they will be taken to mean a separate entity (pure consciousness in the present case). In that case, Vijñānabhikṣu points out, it will not be possible for the individual self to give up its sense of identity, since it is real in some respect. But on his view which says that there is distinction between Brahman and *jīva*, the identity-propositions like 'Thou art that' can be explained satisfactorily by taking recourse to *jahallakṣaṇā*.[2]

After having made a thorough examination of the limitation and reflection theories and having found them not worthy of acceptance, Vijñānabhikṣu now attacks the very concept of *ajñāna* which the Advaitin postulates to explain the phenomenon of diversity and which is also responsible for the views mentioned above. He raises a question about the very locus of *ajñāna* and critically evaluates the possible alternative replies to be offered by the Advaitin. He observes that if the Advaitin holds the view that Brahman is the locus of *ajñāna*, the scriptural statements denying any such characteristic in

---

1. किं चाखण्डैकात्म्ये सति मुक्तस्य पुनर्बन्धापत्तिः, एकान्तःकरणवियोगेऽपि मुक्तांश एकान्तःकरणान्तर-संभवात् । यथैकघटावच्छिन्नाकाशस्य तद्घटभङ्गेऽपि घटान्तरेण पुनः सम्बन्धो भवति तद्वत् । न च तेनावच्छेदेनान्तःकरणसम्बन्ध एव न भवतीति वाच्यम्, तथा सति योगिनां सर्वगतत्वानुपपत्तेरिति । *VAB*, p. 23.
For details on *manovaibhava* cf. *Yogasārasaṅgraha*, ed. Ram Shankar Bhattacharyya and Goswami Prahlad Giri Vedantakeshari, Bharatiya Vidya Prakashan, Delhi, 1989, pp. 160-61.
2. न च लक्षणया विशेषणद्वयं परित्यज्य केवलचैतन्यपरत्वं तत्त्वंपदयोर्वक्तव्यमिति वाच्यम्, वाक्यार्थयोर्विशिष्टयोरतिरिक्ततया केवलचैतन्ये तटस्थलक्षणापत्तौ जीवस्य देहाद्यभिमाननिवृत्त्यसंभवात्, सर्वपदार्थपरित्यागेन लक्षणया तत्त्वमसीत्यभेदवाक्यस्य जीवब्रह्मभेदवादिनाप्युपपादयितुं शक्यत्वाच्च । *VAB*, p. 23.

Brahman stand contradicted. He further views that if it is assumed that the state of illusion belongs to the individual self, it will expose the Advaitin to the charge of the logical fallacy of circularity inasmuch as the existence of the individual self is established only when the difference between the original and its reflection has been brought about by *ajñāna*. Thus both the individual self and *ajñāna* depend on each other for their conception to be possible.[1]

After refuting the theory of *ajñāna* which the Advaitin uses to establish the undivided oneness of the Self, Vijñānabhikṣu proceeds to establish the plurality of selves. The first argument he offers is that the scriptures themselves allot manifold loci to account for the incidence of birth, death, bondage, etc. The distributive nature of the incidence of birth and death is brought into light by such statements as 'He is born and another is dead' and the like. It is precisely for this reason that it should be conceded that the selves are many. So the view on the undivided oneness of the Self for which the Advaitin invokes the space-analogy should not be given undue importance.

Moreover, the scriptures depict both the unity and the plurality of self. In such a situation due weightage should be given to the logical arguments to decide the point at issue. Vijñānabhikṣu adds that Kapila also enjoins such a course of action. He cautions that the scriptural statements about the distribution of bondage, liberation, birth, death, etc. should not be understood as merely explanatory ones (*anuvādas*) and hence as bearing no primary significance. What Vijñānabhikṣu wants to say here is that it is proper to postulate many selves in deference to the scriptural statements of birth, death, liberation, bondage, etc. rather than take these statements as *anuvādas* and consider the plurality of selves as illusory.[2] Besides, by establishing a false object of pursuit—which is the case when *ajñāna* is taken recourse to to explain the plurality of selves—the scriptures would

---

1. किं चात्मभेदादिकमज्ञानकल्पितं चेत्तदज्ञानं कस्येत्युच्यताम् । ब्रह्मणो भ्रान्तत्वे "ज्ञाज्ञौ द्वावजावीशानीशौ नाविद्यानुभवात्मनि स्वप्रकाशे, अभयं भ्रान्तिरहितमनिद्रमजरामरम्, पर: पराणां सकला न यत्र क्लेशादय: सन्ति परावरेशे" इत्यादिवाक्यै: ब्रह्मण्यज्ञानप्रतिषेधस्य विरोधात् । जीवस्य भ्रान्तत्वे चान्योऽन्याश्रयात् भ्रमेण बिम्बप्रतिबिम्बभेदसिद्धौ जीवसिद्धि: जीवसिद्धौ च तदाश्रयस्य भ्रमस्य सिद्धिरिति । *VAB*, p. 22.
2. आत्मैक्ये सत्यौपाधिकानां जन्ममरणादीनामौपाधिकानां च भोगादीनां श्रुतिस्मृतिसिद्धा आश्रयविभागव्यवस्था न स्याद् अयं जातोऽयं मृत: इत्यादिरूपा अतश्च चेतना बहव एव न तु लाघवादाकाशवदेकत्वमित्याद्यसूत्रार्थ: । श्रुतौ च भेदवदभेदस्याप्यवगमात् तर्केणैव व्यवस्थेत्याशय: कपिलाचार्याणाम् । *VAB*, p. 24. See also *SPB*, p. 89 (under *sūtra* I-149).

become subject to doubt and suspicion. However there does not exist even the slightest justification for such an eventuality.[1]

The Advaitin tries to stop Vijñānabhikṣu from establishing the plurality of selves by pointing out that even on Vijñānabhikṣu's view that the self is devoid of characteristics, it is not perfectly in order to demonstrate that the opposing characteristics such as birth, death, etc. exist in the self, as according to the latter all the characteristics are postulated to be existing in the adjuncts. Upon this Vijñānabhikṣu clarifies his viewpoint. He says that he has denied that the transformative characteristics exist in the self; he nevertheless concedes that conjunction, disjunction and experience belong to the self. Pleasure, pain, etc. which are in reality the modifications of the intellect and Brāhmaṇahood, warriorhood, etc. which are characteristics of the body can be said to be belonging to the self just as the redness and blueness of the flowers lying in the proximity of the crystal are attributed to the latter.[2] Vijñānabhikṣu does not accept the Advaitic view that soulhood, jīvahood, etc. consist in consciousness which is limited by the adjuncts. He scrutinizes closely the problem involved in this conception and points out that it would entail the destruction of the self just as the pot-space which terminates when the pot is destroyed.[3] It will contradict the scriptures which proclaim that the self does not perish even when the adjunct ceases to function. This is why it is held that it is pure consciousness which constitutes the self and not the consciousness limited by the adjuncts.[4] Consequently the Advaitic postulation of *ajñāna* and the resultant different adjuncts having been refuted, Vijñānabhikṣu establishes the view on the Sāṅkhya lines that selves are many and diverse.

---

1. न च बन्धमोक्षव्यवस्थाश्रुतिरपि लौकिकभ्रमानुवादमात्रमिति वाच्यम्, मोक्षस्यालौकिकत्वात् । मिथ्यापुरुषार्थप्रतिपादनेन श्रुतेः प्रतारकत्वाद्यापत्तेश्च । *SPB* (under *sūtra* I-150), p. 90.
2. ननु पुरुषो निर्धर्मकस्तत्र कथं जन्ममरणबन्धमोक्षादिविरुद्धधर्मसाङ्कर्यमापद्यते भवद्भिरपि सर्वेषां धर्माणामुपाधिनिष्ठत्वाभ्युपगमादिति चेन्न । उक्तधर्माणां संयोगवियोगभोगाभोगरूपतया पुरुषे स्वीकारात् परिणामरूपधर्माणामेव पुरुषे प्रतिषेधस्योक्तत्वादिति । यथा स्फटिकेषु लौहित्यनीलिमादिधर्माणामारोपितानामपि व्यवस्थास्ति तथा पुरुषेष्वपि बुद्धिधर्माणां सुखादीनां शरीरधर्माणां च ब्राह्मणक्षत्रियत्वादीनामारोपितानामपि व्यवस्थास्ति । *SPB* (under *sūtra* I-152), p. 91.
3. See *supra,* discussion on the limitation theory.
4. आत्मत्वजीवत्वादिकन्तु नोपाध्यवच्छिन्नस्य । उपाधिवियोगे घटाकाशनाशवत् तन्नाशेन जीवो न म्रियते इत्यादिश्रुतिविरोधप्रसङ्गात्, किन्तु केवलचैतन्यस्येति । *Ibid.* (under *sūtra* I-153), p. 92.

III
Nature of Self

It has been made clear in the preceding section that Vijñānabhikṣu is an advocate of the view that selves are many and inhere in the Absolute inseparably. It now appears to be proper to discuss the nature of self. But before we embark upon discussing it, it seems necessary to define clearly the terms, *puruṣa, ātman* and *jīva* which frequently occur in the works of Vijñānabhikṣu, and which have a direct bearing on the question concerning the nature of self.

Vijñānabhikṣu defines *puruṣa* as pure consciousness. It is totally devoid of mutability, etc.[1] This aspect becomes more lucid when he says that *puruṣa* is distinct from the collocation of *prakṛti* and its effects. The meaning is that the nature of *puruṣa* is opposite to that of *prakṛti* and its evolutes.[2] Vijñānabhikṣu does not subscribe to the Vaiśeṣika view that the self remains devoid of consciousness before it enters into relationship with the mind. For on the Vaiśeṣika view it is this relation which causes knowledge to emerge in the self which, then, can be said to be conscious. Vijñānabhikṣu further adds that the self cannot be classified along with other unconscious inanimate objects which are never seen to acquire knowledge[3] in the sense in which self in union with the mind does. This he clarifies by drawing our attention to the distinction which according to him exists between the light of consciousness and that of fire (*tejas*). The fire even without its form (light) having been cognized is experienced through touch whereas consciousness (self) cannot be experienced in any case if the light in the form of knowledge is not comprehended. So brevity, Vijñānabhikṣu asserts, demands that self should be postulated as a substance which is of the nature of consciousness. But consciousness should not be considered as a property of the self.

---

१. पुरुषस्वरूपे चैतन्ये। *SPB* (under *sūtra* I-104), p. 66 and also चित: परिणामित्वस-धर्मत्वादिशंकानिरासायावसानपदम् । *Ibid.*, p. 66. Also compare चैतन्यं नात्मनो गुण:, किन्तु द्रव्यविशेष एव धर्मधर्मिभागशून्यश्चेतन इति । *VAB*, p. 33 and चेतने प्रकाशरूपधर्म: सूर्यादिष्विव नास्ति किन्तु चित्स्वरूप एव पदार्थो जडं प्रकाशयति । यतो जडव्यावृत्तिमात्रेण चिदित्युच्यते, न तु जडविलक्षणधर्मवत्तयेत्यर्थ:। अत एष निर्धर्मतया स एव नेति नेतीत्येव श्रुत्योपदिश्यते न तु विधिमुखतया ।

2. शरीरादिप्रकृत्यन्तं यच्चतुर्विंशतितत्त्वात्मकं वस्तु ततोऽतिरिक्त: पुमान् । *SPB* (under *sūtra* VI-50), p. 236.

3. वैशेषिका आहु: प्रागप्रकाशरूपस्य जडस्यात्मनो मन:संयोगाज्ज्ञानाख्य: प्रकाशो जायते इति तन्न । लोके जडस्याप्रकाशस्य लोष्टादे: प्रकाशोत्पत्त्यदर्शनेन तदयोगात् । *Ibid.* (under *sūtra* I-145), p. 85.

He puts forth the following arguments in support of his view: (1) Consciousness should not be understood as a property since it does possess other properties. And according to the Nyāya view also a property is not assumed to have another property. (2) Consciousness on the other hand does not inhere in something else but has other properties like conjunction, etc. Both these arguments show that consciousness is not a property but constitutes the very nature of self.[1]

So far as the term *ātman* is concerned, Vijñānabhikṣu defines it as an entity from which effect issues forth and wherein located and having lived, it (the effect) again submerges. As per this definition, the sea can be termed as *ātman* with respect to its waves since they emerge in the sea, they are sustained in it and after having lived in it, they just disappear therein. In a similar manner *jīva* (the individual self) possesses *ātmatva*, for it is responsible for the emergence, sustenance and submergence of the intellect and other sense-organs.[2] But the *jīva* endowed with the property of consciousness is said to possess *ātmatva* in a secondary sense just as the vital force (*prāṇa*) endowed with the quality of being superintendent is regarded as the *ātman* of the sense-organs.[3] The term *puruṣa* connoting pure consciousness applies to both the Absolute and the individual self with the difference, firstly, that the former is eternally invested with the Pure-*Sattva*-Adjunct whereas the latter, being many, come in contact with their *upādhis* in order to reap the fruits of past actions and, secondly, that it is ontologically a part of the former.

---

1. पुरुषस्य प्रकाशरूपत्वे सिद्धे तत्सम्बन्धमात्रेणान्यव्यवहारोपपत्तौ प्रकाशात्मकधर्मकल्पनागौरवमित्यपि बोध्यम् । तेजसश्च प्रकाशाख्यरूपविशेषाग्रहेऽपि स्पर्शपुरस्कारेण ग्रहात् प्रकाशतेजसोर्भेदः सिध्यति । आत्मनस्तु ज्ञानाख्यप्रकाशाग्रहकाले ग्रहणं नास्तीत्यतो लाघवाद् धर्मधर्मिभावशून्यं प्रकाशरूपमेवात्मद्रव्यं कल्प्यते । तस्य च न गुणत्वं संयोगादिमत्त्वात्, अनाश्रितत्वाच्च । तथा च स्मर्यते–
   ज्ञानं नैवात्मनो धर्मो न गुणो वा कथञ्चन ।
   ज्ञानस्वरूप एवात्मा नित्यः पूर्णः सदा शिवः ।। *SPB* (under *sūtra* I-146), p. 85.
   Also compare चैतन्यमेव ह्यस्य स्वरूपमग्नेरौष्ण्यप्रकाशौ नात्र गुणगुणिविभागो विद्यते । *BSS*, III-3-39, pp. 537-38.
2. यो यत आगत्य यदधिष्ठितं यत्र जीवित्वा यत्र लीयते समुद्रतरङ्गादिवत् जीवात् तद्बुद्ध्यादिवच्च स तस्य आत्मा भवति । *VAB*, p. 28.
3. जीवाः चित्शक्तिगुणयोगाद् गौणात्मानः एव, यथाध्यक्षत्वगुणयोगेन प्राणः करणानामात्मा तद्वद् । *Ibid.*, p. 29.
   Also cf. यथा हि देहेन्द्रियाणां बुद्धिपर्यन्तानामुत्पत्तिलयाधारतया तत्साक्षित्वेन अधिष्ठातृत्वादिना च जीवस्तेषामात्मा । *Ibid.*, p. 29.

Vijñānabhikṣu defines the term *jīva* by way of giving its etymology. He says that the root √ *jīv* from which the term *jīva* is derived means 'to possess strength and vitality'. For the *jīva* to possess strength and vitality, it is necessary that it is invested with egoity. To explain it he makes use of the principle of agreement and difference (*anvaya-vyatireka*). He says that the persons who are still under the influence of ego are observed to experience the excellence of strength and possession of vitality and that those who have successfully vanquished the ego experience only the cessation of all mental modifications, since it is the ego which is responsible for generating interest in activity. It is in this sense that Vijñānabhikṣu draws a distinction between two kinds of *puruṣas*. The one is *Kevala Puruṣa*, the Supreme Soul, and the other is invested with the adjunct of internal sense-organ.[1] He literally divides *puruṣas* into two categories: (i) Absolute (*Kevala Puruṣa*) and (ii) other *puruṣas* who are bound to come in contact with the *upādhis* to reap the fruits of their past actions. It is the latter kind of *puruṣa* who in association with ego is called *jīva*, the individual phenomenal self. It is this self, which now is going to be discussed.

Nyāya holds that a quality must inhere in a substance. Desire, knowledge, etc. are qualities and so they must reside in a substance. Consequently Nyāya holds that the substance which is the locus of knowledge is called self.[2] Vijñānabhikṣu suggests that it is more appropriate to assume that consciousness (knowledge) is the very essence (nature) of self. The Naiyāyikas have to postulate four principles in order to explain the event of knowledge. They are: internal sense organ (*manas*), awareness (*vyavasāya*), introspective awareness (*anuvyavasāya*) and the locus of the two kinds of awareness. But on Vijñānabhikṣu's conception of the self, the postulation

---

1. जीव बलप्राणधारणयोरिति व्युत्पत्त्या जीवत्वं प्राणित्वम्, तच्चाहङ्कारविशिष्टपुरुषस्य धर्मो न तु केवलपुरुषस्य । कुतः, अन्वयव्यतिरेकात् । अहङ्कारवतामेव सामर्थ्यातिशयप्राणधारणयोर्दर्शनात् । तच्छून्यानां चित्तवृत्तिनिरोधस्यैव दर्शनात्, प्रवृत्तिहेतुरागोत्पादकस्याहंकारस्याभावादित्यर्थः । तथा चान्तःकरणोपाधिकं जीवस्य परिच्छिन्नत्वं परमात्माख्यात् केवलपुरुषाद् भिन्नत्वं चेति भावः । *SPB* (under *sūtra* VI. 63), p. 242.

   And also आत्मानं द्विविधं प्राहुः परापरविभेदतः ।
   परस्तु निर्गुणः प्रोक्तः अहंकारयुतोऽपरः ।। *Ibid.*, p. 249.

2. ज्ञानाधिकरणमात्मा । *TS*, p. 12. Also cf. *Self and Falsity in Advaita Vedānta*, Ananda Kumar Chaudhuri, p. 18.

of only three principles, namely, internal sense-organ (intellect, *buddhi*), its modes, and the conscious self (in place of introspective awareness) adequately explains the process of knowing. Hence it is less cumbersome.[1] Moreover, subscribing to the view that the self is the receptacle of cognition generated by the epistemological process would result in the modifiability and destructibility of the self. And this contradicts their own point of view that the self (soul) is eternal.[2] To further explain that the self is without any characteristics whatsoever he gives another argument. It is more cumbersome to assume mutability in both *prakṛti* and self while it suffices to conceive *prakṛti* only as a principle that undergoes mutation. And in the event of the self being assumed as undergoing mutation, it (self) might, on account of blind transformation, happen to be lacking knowledge and experiencing doubt even in the case of its own knowledge, desires, etc.[3] It is simpler to assume mind as the locus of knowledge and desire in pursuance of the principle of *anvaya* and *vyatireka* than to assume the individual self as the locus, since in the latter alternative the self's contact with the mind will have to be additionally postulated for the incidence of knowledge.[4] Vijñānabhikṣu refutes another view of the Naiyāyikas who hold that the individual self is the agent saying that on this view the state of liberation would not be satisfactorily explained. Moreover, the psychic state that 'I am the agent' has been mentioned in the scriptures such as the *Bhagavadgītā*, etc. as the cause of *adṛṣṭa*. And since on their view this psychic state is not taken to be false, its termination will not be possible at the rise of the knowledge of reality. It is in this context that Vijñānabhikṣu says that the self, in reality, is not the agent since otherwise it would render untenable the incidence of liberation, as mentioned in the scriptures. As such the self bereft of agency would also cease to be the receptacle of *adṛṣṭa* and its products such as pleasure, pain, etc. But

1. नन्वात्मनो नित्यज्ञानस्वरूपत्वे कीदृशं लाघवमिति चेत्; उच्यते नैयायिकादिभिरन्तःकरणं, व्यवसायानुव्यवसायौ, तदाश्रयश्चेति चत्वारः पदार्थाः कल्प्यन्ते । अस्माभिस्तु अन्तःकरणं, व्यवसायस्थानीया च तद्वृत्तिः अनन्तानुव्यवसायस्थानीयश्च नित्यैकज्ञानरूप आत्मेति त्रयः पदार्थाः कल्प्यन्त इति । *SPB* (under *sūtra* I-147), p. 87.
2. जन्यगुणाङ्गीकारे परिणामित्वापत्तिः । *Ibid.* (under *sūtra* I-146), p. 86.
3. उभयोरेव प्रकृतिपुरुषयोः परिणामहेतुत्वकल्पने गौरवम् । आन्ध्यपरिणामेन कदाचिदज्ञत्वस्यापत्त्या ज्ञानेच्छादिगोचरसंशयापत्तिश्च । *Ibid.*, p. 86.
4. इच्छादिकमन्वयव्यतिरेकाभ्यां मनस्येव लाघवात् सिध्यति मनःसंयोगस्य आत्मनश्चोभयहेतुत्वे गौरवात् । *Ibid.*, p. 86.

to account for the incidence of human effort for liberation, it would be simpler to assume mind as invested with agency and other internally observable phenomena (properties).[1] When the Naiyāyika takes recourse to the empirical evidence 'I know' for the assumption that consciousness is the property of self and consequently it does not incur the defect of cumbersomeness,[2] Vijñānabhikṣu does not accept this view and remarks that it is not only the logical arguments that he has forwarded to establish that the self does not possess any property but the scriptures also endorse his view. The scriptural evidence overrules the so-called empirical evidence that the self has consciousness as its property just as the perception of common people that 'I am fair' is contradicted since fairness obviously is the property of the body and not of the self. In case it were not accepted, the arguments which are used to establish that the self is an entity separate from the body, would be contradicted by the perception: 'I am fair, etc.'[3] So the scriptural evidence should carry more weight vis-a-vis the evidence of reflective awareness 'I know'. And as such the arguments which are used to prove that the self is an entity separate from body, mind, etc. would hold good and the reflective awareness 'I know' would cease to be an evidence to prove that consciousness is the property of self.

Vijñānabhikṣu here refers to a problem concerning the nature of self and offers a solution. The acts of seeing, hearing, etc. culminating in experience may somehow be admitted to be belonging to the immutable self, but how can speakership which is purely an act be said to be related to the immutable self in the above sense.

---

1. अपि च ये तार्किका आत्मनः कर्तृत्वमिच्छन्ति तेषां मोक्षानुपपत्तिः । अहं कर्त्तेति बुद्धेरेव गीतादिष्वदृष्टोत्पत्तिहेतुतयोक्तत्वात्, तस्याश्च तन्मते मिथ्याज्ञानत्वाभावेन तत्त्वज्ञाननिवर्त्यासंभवात् । अतः श्रुत्युक्तमोक्षानुपपत्त्यात्मनोऽकर्तृत्वमस्माभिरिष्यते । अकर्तृत्वाच्चादृष्टसुखाद्यभावः । ततश्च मनसः कृत्यादिहेतुत्वे कल्पनीये लाघवादन्तर्दृश्यगुणत्वावच्छेदेनैतत् कल्प्यते । *SPB*, p. 86.
2. नन्वहं जानामीति धर्मधर्मिभावानुभवात् पुरुषस्य चिद्धर्मकत्वं सिध्यति गौरवस्य प्रामाणिकत्वेनादोषत्वादिति । *Ibid.*, p. 86.
3. भवेदेवं यदि केवलतर्केणास्माभिर्निर्गुणत्वाचिद्धर्मादिकं प्रसाध्यते, किन्तु श्रुत्यापि । अतः श्रुत्या सिद्धस्य निर्गुणत्वादेर्नापलापः सम्भवति, तत्प्रत्यक्षस्य गुणादिप्रत्यक्षस्य श्रुत्यैव बाधात्, अहं गौर इत्यादिप्रत्यक्षवदित्यर्थः । अन्यथा गौरोऽहमिति प्रत्यक्षबलेन देहातिरिक्तात्मसाधिका अपि युक्तयो बाधिताः स्युरिति जितं नास्तिकैः । *Ibid.* (under *sūtra* I-147), pp. 86-87.
   Also see किञ्चाज्ञानामहं जानामीति प्रत्यये प्रमात्वकल्पनायामेव गौरवम् । अनाद्यविद्यादोषस्यानुवर्तमानतया भ्रमत्वस्यैवौत्सर्गिकत्वात् । अतो भ्रमशतान्तःपातित्वेनाप्रामाण्यशङ्कास्कन्दितत्वाच्चैतत्प्रत्यक्षबाधने लाघवतर्काद्यनुगृहीतमनुमानमपि समर्थमिति । *Ibid.*, p. 87.

Vijñānabhikṣu resolves it by explaining that the terms, seership, etc. mean that the act of seeing, etc. belongs to the self in the sense that it causes the functions of seeing, etc. to be performed in the same manner as magnet is said to be causing movement in the needles which lie near it. To illustrate further, he says that the king without himself having to fight is said to be a warrior through the agency of his army, which he has only commanded to wage a war. In a somewhat similar manner, the immutable consciousness (self) assumes the roles of seer, speaker, etc. as it happens to make all the instruments of sense such as eyes, ears, etc. function by virtue of its being in their proximity in the form of conjunction.[1]

Vijñānabhikṣu offers yet another argument to buttress his point of view that the self does not possess properties. It runs like this: Desires, etc. which are said to belong to the self are not eternal since they are perceived to have been brought into existence. And to admit properties in the self, which are produced, definitely entails mutability in it.[2] It goes against the principle already established that self is eternal.

On this view that the self is eternal and conscious, the states of wakefulness, dream and dreamless sleep can be satisfactorily explained by saying that they are witnessed by the self since they occur in the mind. In order to avoid the possibility of the self becoming liable to mutability on account of the states just mentioned, the self has to be assumed to be a witnessing entity different from the mind, which, being an evolute of *prakṛti*, is mutable. Also by not accepting self as different from the mind, the different states of the self would become incongruous since the self being consciousness is bound to remain conscious always.[3]

---

1. ननु द्रष्टृत्वश्रोतृत्वादिकं कदाचिदनुभवे पर्यवसानात् पुरुषाविकारिणोऽपि घटताम् वक्तृत्वादिकं क्रियामात्रं तत् कथं कूटस्थस्य घटताम् इति चेद्, न, अयस्कान्तवत् सान्निध्यमात्रेण दर्शनादिवृत्तिकर्तृत्वस्यैवात्र द्रष्टृत्वादिशब्दार्थत्वात् । यथाहि महाराजः स्वयमव्याप्रियमाणोऽपि सैन्येन करणेन योद्धा भवति आज्ञामात्रेण प्रेरकत्वात्, तथा कूटस्थोऽपि पुरुषश्च चक्षुराद्यखिलकरणैर्द्रष्टा वक्ता संकल्पयिता चेत्येवमादिर्भवति, संयोगाख्यसान्निध्यमात्रेण तेषां प्रेरकत्वादयस्कान्तमणिवदिति । *SPB* (under *sūtra* II-29), p. 113.
2. ननु निर्गुणत्वे का युक्तिरिति चेत्, उच्यते–पुरुषस्येच्छाद्यास्तावन्नित्या न सम्भवन्ति जन्यताप्रत्यक्षात् । जन्यगुणाङ्गीकारे परिणामित्वापत्तिः । *Ibid.* (under *sūtra* I-146), p. 86.
3. ननु यदि प्रकाशरूप एवात्मा तदा सुषुप्त्याद्यवस्थाभेदो नोपपद्यते सदा प्रकाशानपायादिति । तत्राह–सुषुप्त्याद्यस्यावस्थात्रयस्य बुद्धिनिष्ठस्य साक्षित्वमेव पुंसि इत्यर्थः । *Ibid.*, (under *sūtra* I-147), p. 86.
   Also cf. जाग्रत् स्वप्नः सुषुप्तं च गुणतो बुद्धिवृत्तयः ।
   तासां विलक्षणो जीवः साक्षित्वेन व्यवस्थितः ।। *BhāgPu*, XI-13-27.

Vijñānabhikṣu poses a problem in order to bring the conception of self in sharper focus. It concerns the state of deep sleep (*ardhalaya suṣupti*). If the self is not admitted as witness of the state of dreamless sleep, and if all the mental modes instead are assumed to be apprehended by the modes themselves, then this assumption should also extend to the waking and dreaming states. And this would render redundant the separate existence of self.[1] He resolves this problem averring that if the intellectual mode were admitted to invariably cognize itself and its own object, it would incur the fallacy of infinite regress and cumbersomeness[2] since in the former case the cognizing principle would have to be assumed to be as many as there are intellectual modes, which involves more intricacy and hence more cumbersomeness. To elaborate, pleasure, pain, etc. are qualifiers in such modes as 'I am happy', etc. It is necessary in this case that knowledge without qualification be assumed before the qualified knowledge ensues. So an infinite number of qualified modes would necessitate the postulation of an equal number of unqualified modes preceding the former. But as such it will be more intricate and more cumbersome. It is simpler to postulate one eternal principle of knowledge, i.e. self, instead of an infinite number of mental modes. Thus it would suffice to account for the reflective modes such as 'I am happy', etc., by merely admitting that such modes are reflected onto the self. Besides, there will be no need to assume a mutative phenomenon in the self over and above the intellectual ones; since admitting transformation of an independent nature in the self would render it mutable, and it is certainly not acceptable.[3] Witnesshood, too, does not incur any mutation in the self since witnesshood consists only in illuminating the intellectual modes

1. स्यादेतत्–सुषुप्ते यदि सुखदु:खादिगोचरा वृत्तिरिष्यते तर्हि जाग्रदावप्यखिलवृत्तीनां वृत्तिग्राह्यत्वस्वीकार एव युक्त इति व्यर्था तत्साक्षिपुरुषकल्पना स्वगोचरवृत्तित्वेनैव स्वव्यवहारहेतुताया: सामान्यत: सुवचत्वादिति। *SPB* (under *sūtra* I-148), p. 88.
2. मैवम्, नियमेन स्वगोचरवृत्तिकल्पनेऽनवस्थापत्तिर्गौरवं च स्यात् । *Ibid.*, p. 88.
3. कि चाहं सुखीत्यादिवृत्तिषु सुखादीनां विशेषणतया निर्विकल्पकं तज्ज्ञानमादावपेक्ष्यते । तत्र चानन्तनिर्विकल्पवृत्त्यपेक्षया लाघवेन नित्यमेकमेवात्मस्वरूपं ज्ञानं कल्प्यते । अहं सुखीत्यादिविशिष्टज्ञानार्थं बुद्धिवृत्तेरेव तादृशाकारत्वं पुरुषे वृत्तिसारूप्यमात्रस्वीकारेण वृत्त्याकारातिरिक्ताकारानभ्युपगमात्, स्वतन्त्राकारेण परिणामापत्तेरिति । *Ibid.*, p. 88.

reflected in the self.[1]

It would not be out of place to mention here what Vijñānabhikṣu has to say about *suṣupti* (dreamless sleep). He divides it into two kinds: (1) *ardhalaya* (half latency) and (2) *samagralaya* (complete latency). He is of the view that although in the former the mental modification of the form of object does not take place, yet the mind does get modalized into the form of pleasure, pain and confusion inhering in it.[2] The other form of *suṣupti* is constituted by the form of absence of all mental modifications. It is here that Vijñānabhikṣu makes a significant departure from Śaṅkara. He holds that the self ceases to witness the absence of intellectual modes. If this is not accepted, the self will have to be assumed to illuminate even the impregnations (*saṃskāras*) which remain lying in the mind.[3] On the other hand, the Advaitin holds that during deep sleep the internal sense-organ merges into its cause, i.e. *ajñāna* and it is the function of *ajñāna* which constitutes experience and is witnessed by the self. It sheds ample light on Vijñānabhikṣu's scheme of things that in this respect he follows the philosophical principles laid down in the *Yogasūtras*[4] and attempts to interpret the *Brahmasūtras* in that light to establish the theory of Integral Non-dualism.

Vijñānabhikṣu in this context considers the Nyāya view which maintains that pleasure and pain, etc. are the properties of self. Explaining the *Sāṅkhyasūtra* I-141, he criticizes the Nyāya view and propounds that pleasure, pain, etc. belong to the body (in a wider sense which also includes the mind). For if they are admitted to occur in the self, it will result in incurring the subject-object-contradiction. It is the self which experiences pleasure and pain which have been assumed to be its properties. The act of experiencing pleasure and pain occurs only when the experience of the locus of properties, i.e.

---

1. सुषुप्त्यादिसाक्षित्वं तु तादृशबुद्धिवृत्तीनां स्वप्रतिबिम्बितानां प्रकाशनमिति वक्ष्यामः । अतो ज्ञानार्थं पुरुषस्य न परिणामापेक्षेति । *SPB*, p. 88.
2. तत्रार्धलये विषयाकारा वृत्तिर्न भवति, किन्तु स्वगतसुखदुःखमोहाकारैव बुद्धिवृत्तिर्भवति । *Ibid.* (under *sūtra* I-148), p. 87.
3. सा च समग्रसुषुप्तिर्वृत्त्यभावरूपेति पुरुषस्तत्साक्षी न भवति पुरुषस्य वृत्तिमात्रसाक्षित्वात्, अन्यथा संस्कारादेरपि बुद्धिधर्मस्य साक्षिभास्यतापत्तेः । *Ibid.* (under *sūtra* I-148), p. 88.
4. अभावप्रत्ययालम्बना वृत्तिर्निद्रा । *Yogasūtra*, I-10.
   Also compare *VAB*, III-2-10.

intellect has already taken place. Taking the Sāṅkhya line the opponent says that there is no harm if the self is assumed to perceive its own pleasure and pain when these are reflected in the intellectual modes as it does itself. Vijñānabhikṣu retorts by pointing out that even in such an eventuality, it is simpler and less cumbersome to postulate that pleasure, pain, etc. are the properties of the mind than to postulate that they, being the properties of self, are reflected in the modes of the intellect to bring about the phenomenon of experience of pleasure and pain.[1] Moreover, perceptions like 'I am happy', 'I am in pain', etc. do not at all go to establish that they inhere in the self since their belonging to the self may be satisfactorily accounted for by assuming that they belong to the self in the manner a thing belongs to its owner. That it is intellect which actually possesses the properties of pleasure and pain also corroborates the same point of view. The intellect does become an object of the layman's I-cognition which includes both self and the intellect because *ajñāna* has not yet been terminated. But it will not be proper to assume that these cognitions reside only in the self and are reflected in the intellect.[2] For otherwise it would involve cumbersomeness.

Not complying with the view of the Realists (Naiyāyikas) that agency, superintendence, etc., in reality, belong to the self, Vijñānabhikṣu further clarifies that these functions actually relate to the intelligized intellect and that they, because of proximity, are said to be in association with the self in a secondary sense.[3] He explains at this juncture that the mind's process of intelligization by the self does not render the latter liable to mutation since there is no actual contact of the mind with the self as the latter does not actually undergo any transition into the former.[4] In fact, the intelligization

---

1. शरीरादीनां हि यः सुखाद्यात्मकत्वं धर्मः स सुखादिभोक्तरि न सम्भवति स्वयं सुखादिग्रहणे कर्मकर्तृविरोधात्। धर्मिपुरस्कारेणैव सुखाद्यनुभवादिति । ननु बुद्धिवृत्तिप्रतिबिम्बितं स्वसुखादिकं पुरुषेण गृह्यतां स्ववदिति चेन्न । एवं सति बुद्धेरेव सुखादिकल्पनौचित्यात्, पुरुषगतसुखादेः बुद्धौ प्रतिबिम्बकल्पने गौरवात् । *SPB* (under *sūtra* I-141), p. 83.
2. अहं सुखी दुःखी मूढ इत्यादिप्रत्ययास्तु न पुरुषे सुखादिसाधकाः, तत्स्वामित्वेनाप्युपपत्तेः । बुद्धेः सुखादिमत्त्वेनाप्युपपत्तेश्च । लौकिक्यां ह्यहंबुद्धौ अवश्यं बुद्धिरपि विषयो मिथ्याज्ञानवासनादिरूपदोषानुवृत्तेस्तत्प्रतिबिम्बकल्पनायां च गौरवादिति । *Ibid.*, p. 83.
3. ननु पुरुषस्य चेत् सन्निधिमात्रेण गौणमधिष्ठातृत्वं तर्हि मुख्यमधिष्ठातृत्वं कस्येत्याकाङ्क्षायामाह अन्तःकरणस्यानुपचरितमधिष्ठातृत्वम् । *Ibid.* (under *sūtra* I-99), p. 62.
4. न तु चैतन्यमन्तःकरणे संक्रामति येन संगिता स्यात् । *Ibid.* (under *sūtra* I-99), p. 63.

of mind according to Vijñānabhikṣu consists either in a particular relation of the eternally intelligent self or in self's reflection in it brought about by a particular association. And this, Vijñānabhikṣu observes, does not render the self transmutable since generation of properties other than the general ones is to be taken as mutation. It is not the case in the present context.[1]

Vijñānabhikṣu seems to land himself in a much greater problem when he says that it is the self in which experience culminates. At the same time this phenomenon is understood to have caused no mutation in it. He attempts to resolve this enigma by defining experience as the self delimited by the reflection of the mental mode of the form of objects.[2] Thus experiencing objects is construed as presenting the modes in the form of reflection to the self.[3] And this is how he manages to ward off the incurrence of self's mutability even as he accepts the Sāṅkhya view that experience culminates in the self. To put it slightly differently, he ascribes experience causing mutation to the intellect and scrupulously denies its existence in the self in the primary sense.[4] Having shown consciousness as the nature of self, he thus establishes that the self is also beyond the phenomenon of mutation.

The opponent comes up with an alternative suggestion. He says that experience, i.e. *bhoga* is the sole possession of the intellect as implied by the statement that the self seems to experience what is actually experienced by the intellect. Vijñānabhikṣu does not accept this view. To clarify his point of view he takes upon himself the job of explaining what constitutes experience (*bhoga*). According to him the word '*bhoga*' is derived from the root $\sqrt{bhuj}$ meaning both 'protection' and 'eating'. Consequently *bhoga* is of two types. In this context eating means nourishing oneself either by one's own or by external material. That the physical body is nourished by food buttresses the intended sense. Likewise pleasure and pain in the intellect get nourished by the pleasure and pain contained in the

1. नित्योज्ज्वलचैतन्यसंयोगविशेषमात्रस्याथवा संयोगविशेषजन्यचैतन्यप्रतिबिम्बस्यैवान्त:करणोज्ज्वलन-रूपत्वात्. . . . नन्वेवमपि संयोगेन परिणामित्विमिति चेन्न, सामान्यगुणातिरिक्तधर्मोत्पत्तावेव परिणामव्यवहारादिति । *SPB*, p. 63.
2. अर्थोपरक्तवृत्तिप्रतिबिम्बावच्छिन्नं स्वरूपचैतन्यमेव भानं पुरुषस्य भोग: । *Ibid.* (under *sūtra* I-104), p. 66.
3. अपरिणामित्वात् पुरुषस्य विषयभोग: प्रतिबिम्बदानमात्रम् । *Ibid.*, p. 66.
4. अयमेव पारमार्थिको भोग: पुरुषे प्रतिषिध्यते । *Ibid.*, p. 66.

objects since everything is comprised of the nature of pleasure, pain, etc. To further clarify what he means by nourishment in the case of intellect, Vijñānabhikṣu gives another illustration of the sweetness of milk which gets enriched by the sweetness of sugar. This phenomenon occurring in the mind is postulated to be reflected in the self since the latter is assumed to be immutable and the experience or apprehension of pleasure and pain in the form of reflection constitutes the *bhoga* of self. Even in a secondary sense this *bhoga* or experience cannot be said to be belonging to the intellect because of the latter being inanimate and since in that case the very assumption of self would be rendered redundant.[1] What Vijñānabhikṣu wants to emphasize is that, though actual mutation takes place in the mind, the self does not undergo any mutation since according to him the reflection of mental modes which is cast in the self does not cause any mutation in the self in the real sense of the term.

Vijñānabhikṣu further seeks to endorse the immutability of the self by elaborating on the nature of experience. He holds that experience is not an instrument towards any other effect; it should be taken as an end in itself. As such if experience is to be regarded as effect at all, it has to be described as an effect in the manner of the Vaiśeṣikas, who consider ear as nothing but *ākāśa* limited by its external form. So if experience is defined to be of the nature of self, there is no incongruency involved here since the state of being an effect belongs to experience in the same sense as it does to the ear on the Vaiśeṣika view. The nature of experience having been thus defined, the *summum bonum* should be taken to mean as absence of the experience of pain. Alternatively ultimacy belongs to the absence of pleasure and pain by the relation of experienciability and by the same relationship pleasure and pain may be said to be residing in the self as wealth is held to be residing in the owner by the relationship of possessedness. In conclusion, even if experience be

---

1. ननु ''बुद्धेर्भोग इवात्मनि'' इत्यादिवचनात् बुद्धेरेव भोगो नात्मन इति चेन्न, भोगस्य द्वैविध्यात् । भोगो हि 'भुजि पालनाभ्यवहारयो' रित्यनुशासनात् स्वबाह्यवस्तुना पुष्टिः, यथाऽन्नेन स्थूलदेहस्य भोगः । तथा स्वसर्ववस्तूनां सुखदुःखमोहात्मकत्वाद् विषयगतसुखदुःखाभ्यां बुद्धेः सुखदुःखयोः पोषणं बुद्धेर्भोगः दुग्धमाधुर्यस्येव शर्करामाधुर्येण पोषणम् । अयमेव वा भोगश्चेतने प्रतिबिम्बति, तस्याविकारित्वात्, स एव पुरुषस्य भोगः सुखदुःखसाक्षात्काररूपो भवति । न तु सुखदुःखसाक्षात्काररूपो गौणभोगोऽपि बुद्धेः संभवति तस्या अचेतनत्वात् पुरुषकल्पनावैयर्थ्यापत्तेश्चेति । *VAB*, p. 35.

defined as consciousness limited by the intellectual modes, the eternally immutable nature of self remains intact.[1]

Vijñānabhikṣu does not accept the view that bliss constitutes the nature of self. It is a significant departure from the view of Advaitins who hold that consciousness, existence and bliss are absolutely on a par with each other.[2] He seems to be successful in explaining his stand on the scriptural statements about the bliss aspect of self by stating that they may be treated as a case of metaphor, that is, bliss has occurred in such statements in the sense of absence of pain.[3] Before arriving at this conclusion in the true spirit of a Sāṅkhya exponent, he offers arguments to reject the Advaitic point of view and to endorse his own viewpoint.

Taking consciousness and knowledge (experience) as identical, Vijñānabhikṣu avers that when pleasure is different from its experience, it logically follows that bliss does not constitute the nature of self. To further strengthen his view about the difference of pleasure and its experience, he gives an example. In the event of pain being cognized, pleasure remains unexperienced. It is only possible when pleasure and its experience are distinct. Should bliss constitute the nature of self which is not different from experience, it would occasion the simultaneity of the cognition of pain and that of the absence of pleasure. It never happens at the level of experience. Even then to save the situation, if the Advaitin advances the argument that a specific act of knowing is considered to be pleasure, it would only cause embarrassment to him since the view that knowledge as the nature of self is one undivided whole gets compromised in the process. That is why it cannot be justified that pleasure is covered when the experience of consciousness occurs. Moreover, the covering of bliss would bring about the absence of experience of consciousness since both are held to be undivided and on a par

---

1. भोगस्तु नान्यस्य साधनम्, अत स एव फलमिति मुख्यः सिद्धान्तः । भोगस्य पुरुषस्वरूपत्वेऽपि वैशेषिकाणां मते श्रोत्रवत् कार्यता बोध्या सुखाद्यवच्छिन्नचितेरेव भोगत्वात् ।अस्मिंश्च भोगस्य फलत्वपक्षे दुःखभोगाभाव एवापवर्गो बोध्यः । अथवा भोग्यतारूपस्वत्वसम्बन्धेन सुखदुःखाभावयोरेव फलत्वमस्तु तेन सम्बन्धेन धनादेरिव सुखादेरपि पुरुषनिष्ठत्वादिति । *SPB* (under *sūtra* I-106), p. 67.
2. Kalidas Bhattacharyya, *A Modern Understanding of Advaita Vedānta*, p. 41 fns. 2 and 3. Also see *Pañcadaśī, Ānanda-Pañcakam*, for a detailed account of the bliss aspect of the self.
3. दुःखनिवृत्त्याऽऽत्मनि श्रौत आनन्दशब्दो गौण इत्यर्थः । *SPB* (under *sūtra* V-67), p. 193. Also *YV* on *Yogasūtra*, II-42 and III-18.

with each other, that is, identical. As a consequence the experience of pain continues to remain unsubstantiated. And to accommodate the Advaitic viewpoint it does not seem reasonable to hold that the self has divisions so that the phenomenon of pain-experience may become possible even when the bliss aspect of self remains covered. The reason is that it would entail the impermanence of self and it does not either help resolve the dilemma just mentioned.[1]

When the Advaitin says that the arguments put forward by Vijñānabhikṣu to prove that bliss does not constitute the nature of self are fallacious, the latter refuses to accept it. To further endorse his view, Vijñānabhikṣu refers to the scriptural statements which propound that bliss does not exist in the self; rather it is the absence of bliss which inheres in it. So in deference to the scriptural position, the arguments put forward by Vijñānabhikṣu to prove his view should be given weightage since they are endorsing the view expressed in the scriptures.[2] Keeping this aspect of the arguments in view the scriptural statements to this effect can satisfactorily be explained by interpreting the bliss aspect of self as absolute absence of pain.[3]

Should the Advaitin persist in proving the bliss aspect of self by means of the phenomenon of natural love for the self, he should be told forthwith that such concern for the self can be explained equally convincingly by viewing 'absence of sorrow' as probans (*hetu*) in the syllogism used to prove the opposite. Like the state of pleasure, selfhood is also responsible for giving rise to the phenomenon of love for self. Otherwise if pleasure alone is understood to be the cause of the incidence of love for self, it would lead to the phenomenon of love invariably occurring even in the case of others'

---

1. एकधर्मिण आनन्दचैतन्योभयरूपत्वं न भवति दुःखज्ञानकाले सुखाननुभवेन सुखज्ञानयोर्भेदादित्यर्थः । न च ज्ञानविशेषः सुखमिति वक्तुं शक्यते, आत्मस्वरूपज्ञानस्याखण्डत्वात् । अत एव चैतन्यानुभवकाले सुखस्यावरणमपि वक्तुं न शक्यते । अखण्डत्वेनान्दावरणे दुःखं जानामीत्यनुभवानुपपत्तेः । न ह्यात्मनोऽंशभेदोऽस्ति येनानन्दांशावरणेऽपि चैतन्यांशो भायादिति । *SPB* (under *sūtra* V-66), p. 193.
2. न च श्रुतिबलेनैतेऽसत्तर्का इति वाच्यम् नानन्दं न निरानन्दमित्यादिश्रुत्या 'अदुःखमसुखं ब्रह्म भूतभव्यभवात्मकमि' त्यादिस्मृत्या चानन्दाभावस्यापि प्रतिपादितत्वेन तर्कस्यैवादर्तव्यादिति । *Ibid.*, p. 193.
3. दुःखनिवृत्त्याऽऽत्मनि श्रौत आनन्दशब्दो गौणः । *Ibid.*, p. 193. Also cf. *YV* on *Yogasūtra*, III-18 in *SYD*, p. 334, fn. 3 and *YV* on *Yogasūtra* II-16, *op. cit.*, p. 188.

pleasure, which is not always the case.[1] Thus he dismisses the inferential argument used by the Advaitin to prove the bliss aspect of self. Equally cogently Vijñānabhikṣu substitutes the Advaitic probans 'the state of pleasure' by 'the state of soulhood' to prove the occurrence of the phenomenon of love for the self.

Vijñānabhikṣu now addresses himself to the task of delineating the existence-aspect of self. Though he does not accept the view that self exists as an independent entity at the ontological plane, yet to put his viewpoint in the right perspective, it seems to be necessary to know what he means by 'existence'. He defines existence in terms of a state having a property conducive to the emergence of a meaningful activity.[2] The incidence of meaningful activity depends primarily on the adjuncts. That is why he postulates the adjunct (*upādhi*) being associated with which the self becomes able to perform a meaningful activity and hence fit to be defined in terms of existence. But the adjuncts, Vijñānabhikṣu points out, become totally inoperative at the time of dissolution. As a consequence selves are said to be existing during creation only. Such is not the case with the Absolute, since It remains eternally invested with the Pure-*Sattva*-Adjunct and perceives the whole world even at the time of dissolution. In other words, the meaningful activity of perception exists in the case of the Absolute even at the time of dissolution just as it exists in It during creation with the only difference that *prakṛti* and *puruṣas* having ceased to perform such functions as are performed by them during creation, lie in It as if fast asleep.[3] It would be of advantage to point out here that Vijñānabhikṣu accords ontological reality only to the Absolute. The self is not ontologically real since, according to him, reality consists in having a state of practical efficiency or a state producing an effective action, which in the case of selves is possible only during creation during which they remain invested with their operative adjuncts. The point which Vijñānabhikṣu wants to make

---

1. यत्तु निरुपाधिप्रियत्वेनात्मनः सुखरूपत्वानुमानं कश्चिदाह; तन्न, दुःखाभावरूपतयापि प्रेमोपपत्तेः । सुखत्वादिवदात्मत्वस्यापि प्रेमप्रयोजकत्वाच्च, अन्यथा परसुखेऽपि प्रेमोपपत्तेरिति । *SPB* (under *sūtra* V-67), p. 194.
Also cf. *Pañcadaśī, Ānandapañcakam.*
2. पुरुषार्थक्रियाकारित्वमेव लोके सत्त्वमिति व्यवह्रियते । *VAB,* p. 58.
3. प्रलयेऽपि इदानीमिव कुर्वदास्ते प्रकृतिपुरुषादयस्तु सृष्ट्यादिलक्षणस्वकार्येभ्य उपरता एव सुषुप्तास्तिष्ठन्तीति । *Ibid.,* pp. 57-58.

here is that the status of self is both real and unreal or it is real on the empirical plane only.[1]

It may be noted with caution at this juncture that in respect of self's conception Vijñānabhikṣu seems to be overwhelmingly influenced by the Nyāya-Vaiśeṣika view. He holds that the self endowed with the capacity of consciousness is *ātman* only in a secondary sense.[2] The expression 'endowed with the capacity of consciousness' implies that consciousness as a characteristic of self is contingent, and not essential. He makes his position absolutely clear when he says that selves cease to have the property of consciousness at the time of dissolution. He compares them with *prakṛti* in this respect and further avers that it is Īśvara (Absolute) who confers consciousness upon selves during creation. So the consciousness of selves being contingent in nature remains restricted to speech.[3] In other words, self's possessing consciousness should be viewed as an effect. But, if Vijñānabhikṣu's arguments are followed, self is virtually reduced to the status of the inanimate. Nonetheless he endeavours to bring out a clear distinction between the nature of self and that of *prakṛti*. The latter does not have the capacity to assume consciousness whereas the former has it. It is another matter that they are said to be completely submerged in, and become one with, the Absolute at the time of dissolution. The selves, then, give up their characteristic of consciousness consisting in the manifestation of objects.[4]

Vijñānabhikṣu further tells us that the self is not an ultimate agent of the acts of seeing, hearing, speaking, etc. He rather confers the ultimate agency of these acts on the Absolute in the following way. He says that just as self is held to be the agent of the act of speech through the speech-instrument, the Absolute (Īśvara) can likewise be said to be the referent of the pronoun 'I' through the instrumen-

---

1. सदसद्रूपत्वमेव व्यावहारिकसत्त्वम् । *VAB*, p. 55.
2. जीवाश्चिच्छक्तिगुणयोगाद् गौणात्मान एव । *Ibid.*, p. 29.
3. उच्यते, एतादृशं तदक्षरमन्तर्यामि यतोऽतिरिक्तजीवादयः सर्वे अन्धा एव प्रलये, जीवानामपि प्रकृत्यादिवच्च चैतन्यफलोपधानाभावात् । ईश्वरदत्तस्य सृष्टिकालीनस्य चैतन्यफलोपधानस्य कादाचित्कत्वेन वाचारम्भणमात्रत्वात् । *Ibid.*, p. 273.
   Also cf.—सर्गकाले च तदिच्छया तत एव लब्धचैतन्यफलोपधाना आविर्भवन्ति पितुरिव पुत्रा अतो जीवा ब्रह्मांशा भवन्ति । *Ibid.*, p. 27 and किन्तु जीवेषु चैतन्यफलोपधानं कादाचित्कतया वाचारम्भणमात्रमीश्वरपरतन्त्रं सदल्पं चेति । *Ibid.*, p. 29.
4. चिन्मात्रे ब्रह्मणि नित्यसर्वावभासके विषयभासनरूपं स्वलक्षणं विहाय लक्षणानन्यत्वं गच्छति । *Ibid.*, p. 27.

tality of the self which is usually understood to be the referent of 'I'. In other words, though the act of speech apparently belongs to the organ of speech, yet it is said to be belonging to the self. In a similar manner for the sake of general usage it may safely be stated that whatever belongs to the self, may also be attributed to the Absolute.[1] At another place, Vijñānabhikṣu minces no words about it and affirms that the self is only an instrument of the Absolute. In this way, self's ownership and doership (agency) of every epistemological process of seeing, hearing, intellection and intimately knowing belong to the Inner Controller, since these processes take effect under His superintendence.[2]

After having discussed in brief how Vijñānabhikṣu differs from the Advaitins on the one hand and the Naiyāyikas on the other about the nature of self, we should now address ourselves to the aspect of self-luminosity of the self. In order to discuss this view he refers to and quotes the definition of self-luminosity as given by Citsukhācārya in his *Tattvapradīpikā*. He analyzes it threadbare and refutes it altogether. Citsukha defines self-luminosity as 'the capability of being called immediately known without being an object of cognition'.[3] This view of the Advaitins has already been discussed elaborately in the context of self-luminosity of the Absolute. In the present context it would suffice to mention that the self does become an object of its own perception in the form of its own reflection in the intellect. But in this way, the Advaitin retorts, the subject-object-contradiction will result. Vijñānabhikṣu dispels this undesirable contingency replying that there would be no such contradiction involved if the reflection of self in the intellect be accorded the status of an object and self as the archetype of reflection (*bimba*) be understood to be the subject of that particular cognition. He drives this point home with the help of an illustration. The sun, as the original (archetype), assumes subjectivity but as reflection, it becomes an object of its manifesta-

1. Cf. न चेश्वरस्य सम्बोध्यत्वप्रयोक्तृत्वाभावात् कथं त्वहंशब्दार्थता स्यादिति वाच्यम्, वागिन्द्रियद्वारा जीवस्य प्रयोक्तृत्ववज्जीवाख्यकरणद्वारा ब्रह्मण एव सम्बोध्यत्वादिसकलव्यवहारप्रतिपादनायैव तत्त्वमसीत्युपदेशादिति । तथा च श्रुत्यन्तरम्–'नान्योऽतोऽस्ति द्रष्टा श्रोता मन्ता बोद्धे' त्यादिना परमात्मन एव दर्शनश्रवणादिसर्वव्यवहारकर्तृत्वमाह । *VAB*, p. 31.
2. किं च जीवदर्शनश्रवणमननविज्ञानानामप्यन्तर्याम्यात्ततया अन्तर्यामिण एव तानि भवन्ति तत्स्वामिकत्वात् तत्कर्तृकत्वाद् येन तु करणस्थानीयस्य जीवस्येति महिमोत्कीर्तनादिति । *Ibid.*, p. 273.
3. V.A. Sharma, *Citsukha's Contribution to Advaita*, Mysore, 1974, p. 44.

tion.[1] When both the original and its reflection differ in some respect, he views that there is no incurrence of the subject-object-contradiction. Vijñānabhikṣu further adds that even the etymological meaning of '*svaprakāśa*' does not justify what has been made out to mean by the definition put forward in *Tattvapradīpikā* since the compound '*svaprakāśa*' even from the grammar point of view yields only one sense, that is, 'knowable by itself'.[2] To put it differently, he does not accept such self-luminosity as does not admit of knowability.[3] To further clarify this point of view, he adds that the illuminating aspect of light becomes manifest when the relation between the illuminator and the illuminated comes into force. For, to avoid the subject-object-contradiction no direct relation of the illuminator with itself is admitted. He points out that since he takes the mental mode to be a means of cognition, it enables him to satisfactorily account for the incidence of subject-object-relationship with regard to the same entity. The self in the form of reflection in the mode may be understood to be related to itself as the original just as it has been explained in the case of the relationship of the sun with its reflection in water.[4] Interpreting the *Sāṅkhyasūtra* VI-50 Vijñānabhikṣu says that the aphorism does not at all convey the sense that the self (consciousness) only illuminates the unconscious objects, and not itself, since in that case the self is rendered unknowable and as such the very existence of self is jeopardized for want of logical evidence which is an essential prerequisite to prove the existence of an entity.[5]

Insofar as the scriptural statements pertaining to the self-luminosity of the self are concerned, they should be construed as referring to the illumination aspect which does not depend upon any other adjunct of any other self.[6]

---

1. सूर्यो बिम्बरूपेण प्रकाशक: प्रतिबिम्बरूपेण च प्रकाश्य इति न कर्मकर्तृविरोध: । *VAB*, p. 42.
2. स्वप्रकाशशब्दस्यास्मिन्नर्थे यौगिकत्वमपि न सम्भवति, स्वज्ञेयत्वस्यैव योगतो लाभात् । *Ibid.*, p. 38.
3. अज्ञेयत्वरूपं तावत्स्वप्रकाशत्वमस्माभिर्नाभ्युपगम्यते । *Ibid.*, p. 39.
4. प्रकाश्यप्रकाशकसम्बन्धे हि प्रकाशनमालोकादिषु दृष्टं स्वस्य साक्षात् स्वस्मिन् सम्बन्धश्च विरुद्ध इति । अस्मन्मते तु बुद्धिवृत्त्याख्यप्रमाणाङ्गीकारात् तद्द्वारा प्रतिबिम्बरूपस्य स्वस्य बिम्बरूपे स्वस्मिन् सम्बन्धो घटते । यथा सूर्ये जलद्वारा प्रतिबिम्बरूपसम्बन्ध इति भाव: । *SPB* (under *sūtra* VI-41), pp. 235-36.
5. अस्मिंश्च सूत्रे जडमेव प्रकाशयति चिद्रूपो न त्वात्मानमिति नार्थ: । *Ibid.* (under *sūtra* VI-50), p. 236. Also cf. प्रमेयसिद्धि: प्रमाणाद्धि । *Sāṅkhyakārikā*, 4c.
6. आत्मन: स्वप्रकाशत्वश्रुतिस्त्वनन्योपाधिप्रकाशादिपरा बोध्या । *SPB* (under *sūtra* VI-49), p. 236.

Vijñānabhikṣu holds the view that the reflection of the individual self is cast in the intellect. This is known as *cicchāyāpatti.* This reflection of consciousness is a modalized form of the intellect in the same way as the intellect assumes the form of a pitcher, etc. He clarifies it stating that the reflection of self in the intellect is postulated to account for the cognition of the self in order to avoid the subject-object-contradiction just mentioned.[1] And this modalized form of the intellect is capable of being reflected on to the self so that the act of cognition may come into existence.[2]

From the foregoing account, it becomes clear that Vijñānabhikṣu does not subscribe to the Advaitic view of self-luminosity of the self and offers the theory of double reflection to resolve the problem of self-awareness to prove which the Advaitins have postulated the self-luminosity of the self.

1. यच्च बुद्धौ चेतनस्य प्रतिबिम्बनं तद् बुद्धेश्चिच्छायापत्तिरित्युच्यते । तच्च बुद्धेः घटाद्याकारवच्चैतन्याकार-परिणामः। स च चैतन्यभानार्थं कल्प्यते, साक्षात्स्वदर्शने कर्मकर्तृविरोधात् । *VAB*, p. 40.
2. बुद्धिवृत्तेरेव चेतने साक्षात्प्रतिबिम्बनसामर्थ्यं नेतरस्येति ।तस्मादर्थोपरक्तवृत्तिस्फुरणार्थं चेतने तत्प्रतिबिम्बः सिध्यति । *Ibid.*, p. 40.

4

CONCEPT OF *PRAKṚTI*

Prakṛti is the opposite polarity of consciousness (*puruṣa*). As power of the Absolute, it inheres in It along with the *puruṣas.* On the empirical plane, *prakṛti* represents the object aspect of experience, though at the unreflective stage consciousness remains an undistinguished associate of the mental body which appears as subject. It has been said so since it is only consciousness that appears to transcend even the mind at the reflective stage and consequently fulfils the criterion of being the subject even though its being the subject gets crystallized only when it is juxtaposed with the object. The primordial materiality which represents the object aspect of experience but which may also be said to represent the subject aspect at the unreflective stage is variously called *prakṛti*, power, unborn, *pradhāna,* unmanifest, *tamas, māyā, avidyā,* etc.[1] Vijñānabhikṣu spells out the nature of *prakṛti* by way of etymologically explaining the term *pradhāna.* He says that *prakṛti* is called *pradhāna* since all its effects from *mahat* to gross elements reside in it.[2] He means thereby that all the effects manifest themselves and also get submerged in it. To put it differently, he considers *prakṛti* to be the material cause of the manifest universe—both physical and psychological. He also remarks tha. it is possible only when the effects are, in some sense, different from the cause (*prakṛti*), since in the case of identity between cause and effect the former cannot become the repository of the latter.[3] In pursuance of the principle that it is the valid means

---

1. प्रकृतिः शक्तिरजा प्रधानमव्यक्तं तमो मायाऽविद्येत्यादयः प्रकृतेः पर्यायाः । *SS,* p. 9.
2. प्रधीयन्तेऽस्मिन् हि कार्यजातानीति प्रधानमुच्यते । *SPB* (under *sūtra* I-125), p. 76.
3. तच्च कार्यकारणयोर्भेदाभेदौ विना न घटते, अत्यन्ताभेदे स्वस्याधारत्वासम्भवादित्यर्थः । *Ibid.,* p. 76.

of knowledge that establishes the existence and reality of an independent category, he offers an argument to prove the ontological status of *prakṛti*. In the process he makes use of the theory that effect pre-exists in the cause.

The various objects that we perceive must have emerged from something positive, which ought to be different from them. Vijñānabhikṣu says that everybody accepts the threefold classification of effects from the temporal point of view, viz., past, present and future. In case the effect were not accepted to be existing at all times, the threefold classification would be rendered untenable. Had the pitcher, cloth, etc. been non-existent in the past, how could they have been assumed to be possessing the attribute of being existent in the past since there is no relationship between what is present and what is not present.[1] It is therefore proper that the effect be admitted to possess eternality and the different states of past, future and present are attributed to it.[2] For, it is not cogent to hold that only the present effect possesses the characteristic of being existent, while the past and future ones do not.[3] He does not subscribe to the Nyāya view that non-existence is a separate category.[4] What logically follows from it is that the effect already exists in the cause. This is what is known as *satkāryavāda*, the theory of pre-existent effect, which is contrary to *ārambhavāda* held by those who accept non-existence as a separate category. The other arguments supporting the theory of pre-existent effect set forth in his comments on the *Sāṅkhyasūtras* I-114-118 appear to be merely a restatement of what the *Sāṅkhyakārikā* 9 says.

Reiterating the theory of pre-existent effect, Vijñānabhikṣu views that the cause of manifold effects must be admitted as uncaused to avoid the incurrence of infinite regress. And it is this uncaused ultimate cause which is known as *prakṛti*.[5] K.C. Bhattacharyya also gives an ontological argument to this effect. He says "Viveka is

---

1. अथ सर्वं कार्यं त्रिविधं सर्ववादिसिद्धमतीतमनागतं वर्तमानमिति । तत्र यदि कार्यं सन्नेष्यते तदा त्रिविधत्वानुपपत्तिः ।अतीतादिकाले घटाद्यभावेन घटादेरतीतादिधर्मकत्वानुपपत्तेः, सदसतोः सम्बन्धानुपपत्तेः । *SPB* (under *sūtra* I-113), p. 70.
2. तस्मान्नित्यस्यैव कार्यस्यातीतानागतवर्त्तमानावस्थाभेदा एव वक्तव्याः । *Ibid.* (under *sūtra* I-113), p. 70.
3. नत्वेकस्य भावविषयत्वमन्ययोश्चाभावविषयत्वमिति । *Ibid.* (under *sūtra* I-113), p. 70.
4. नास्मत्सिद्धान्तेऽभावोऽतिरिक्तः। *Ibid.* (under *sūtra* I-113), p. 70.
5. अतो यत्र पर्यवसानं सैव नित्या प्रकृतिः । प्रकृतिरिह मूलकारणस्य संज्ञामात्रमित्यर्थः । *SPB* (under *sūtra* I-68), p. 46.

primarily the distinguishing of buddhi from puruṣa through which the conception of prakṛti and of its unmanifest distinction of buddhi from puruṣa emerges. In the order of being, the distinction of buddhi from puruṣa is derived from that of prakṛti from puruṣa".[1] In this way the fact of experience, in'·rential evidence and the ontological argument establish the independent status *of prakṛti.*

Let's now take up the definition and nature of *prakṛti* for discussion. Vijñānabhikṣu defines *prakṛti* as constituted by the three substances, namely, *sattva, rajas* and *tamas* when they are in a state of equilibrium,[2] that is, when they have not become a collocation of the different constituents in a greater or smaller degree.[3] To put it differently, *sattva, rajas* and *tamas* are called *prakṛti* when they undergo similar modification and are yet to start undergoing dissimilar modification. To ensure that *prakṛti* does not cease to be called so even when the state of equilibrium no longer remains, Vijñānabhikṣu has inserted the term *upalakṣita* in the definition. Although the term conveys the sense of a characteristic that is not an integral part of the characterized as is clear from the illustration *kākavanto devadattasya gṛhāḥ,* yet what Vijñānabhikṣu intends to convey by it is that *prakṛti* continues to be called so since it does, at least, remain in a state of equilibrium before creation and after dissolution, which is not the case with the effects.[4] And the causal *sattva, rajas* and *tamas,* therefore, continue to be called *prakṛti* since they do not cease to exist during the process of dissimilar modification. This, according to Vijñānabhikṣu, is implied by the word *upalakṣita.*[5] Moreover, it also ensures that the definition does not overpervade to the product-*sattva,* product-*rajas* and product-*tamas,* since they are never in a state of equilibrium, i.e. causal state.[6]

Keeping in view that Vijñānabhikṣu subscribes to the Sāṅkhya view of *satkāryavāda,* we may say that though the effects of *prakṛti* may

---

1. *SP,* p. 198.
2. सा च साम्यावस्थयोपलक्षितं सत्त्वादिद्रव्यत्रयम् । *SS,* p. 9.
3. साम्यावस्था च न्यूनाधिकभावेनासंहननावस्था, अकार्यावस्थेति यावत् । *SS,* p. 9.
4. In this context what K.C. Bhattacharyya observes is also important to note: "Sāmyāvasthā of prakṛti is retained even along with the visadṛśa pariṇāma emerging as distinct in prakṛti." *SP,* p. 200.
5. महदादिकन्तु कार्यसत्त्वादिकं न कदाप्यकार्यावस्थं भवतीति तद्व्यावृत्तिः । वैषम्यावस्थायामपि प्रकृतित्वसिद्धये उपलक्षितमित्युक्तम् । अकार्यमिति तूपलक्षितान्तस्य निष्कृष्टार्थः । *SS,* p. 9. Also compare *SPB,* p. 38.
6. कार्यसत्त्वादिवारणायोपलक्षितान्तम् । *SS,* p. 9.

have distinctive features at a certain stage of evolution, they are not essentially different from the cause. Since the effects are assumed to be inhering in the cause and since it is the nature of cause to permeate the effects, which have no reality over and above the cause, it follows that a relation of identity and difference exists between *prakṛti* and its evolutes. For fear that *prakṛti* might cease to be called so during the state of creation, that is, during dissimilar modification, Vijñānabhikṣu has defined *prakṛti* in a manner different from that in which it has been defined traditionally[1]—the three substances, namely, *sattva, rajas* and *tamas* constitute *prakṛti* when they are in a state of equilibrium.

The definition of *prakṛti* in terms of *sattva, rajas* and *tamas* gives rise to the problem about the status of these substances vis-a-vis *prakṛti*. Do they belong to *prakṛti* as parts do to the whole? The genesis of the problem may be attributed to the fact that *sattva, rajas* and *tamas* are called *guṇas*. According to the Nyāya-Vaiśeṣika system of philosophy, the *guṇas* are postulated to inhere in the substances (*dravyas*) and hence they cannot be understood in the sense in which they are used in the Sāṅkhya Philosophy. Vijñānabhikṣu clarifies it. He maintains that these *guṇas* can't be qualities in the sense in which the Naiyāyikas and the Vaiśeṣikas take them to be since conjunction and disjunction which are themselves postulated as qualities in the Nyāya-Vaiśeṣika system of philosophy are admitted to inhere in them. But on their view the qualities are not assumed to inhere in other qualities. Since *sattva, rajas* and *tamas* themselves have the characteristics of lightness, motion and inertia, and since they do not fulfil the Nyāya-Vaiśeṣika criterion of being a quality they should be substances only.[2] Even being substances, they are not assumed to be belonging to *prakṛti* as its parts because the effects are stated to emerge from these very substances and because, as such, to postulate *prakṛti* over and above these substances would be redundant.[3] Then why have they been designated as *guṇas*? Vijñānabhikṣu adduces the following two grounds[4] to answer this question:

---

1. प्रकरोतीति प्रकृति: प्रधानं सत्त्वरजस्तमसां साम्यावस्था । *STK* on *SK*, 3.
2. सत्त्वादीनि द्रव्याणि न वैशेषिका गुणा: संयोगविभागवत्त्वात् लघुत्वचलत्वगुरुत्वादिधर्मवत्त्वाच्च । *SPB* (under *sūtra* I-61), p. 38.
3. गुणेभ्य एव कार्योत्पत्तौ तदन्यप्रकृतिकल्पनावैयर्थ्याच्च । *SS*, p. 10.
4. तेषु अत्र शास्त्रे श्रुत्यादौ च गुणशब्द: पुरुषोपकरणत्वात् पुरुषबन्धकत्रिगुणात्मकमहदादिरज्जुनिर्मातृत्वाच्च प्रयुज्यते । *SPB* (under *sūtra* I-61), p. 38.

1. They serve as instruments of the self to experience pleasure, pain, etc.
2. They make the rope in the form of *mahat*, etc. which binds the self.

The use of the term *guṇa* with respect to *sattva, rajas* and *tamas* being thus consistent, the expression *prakṛterguṇāḥ* could be interpreted in the manner in which the usage *vanasya vṛkṣāḥ* is construed. The three substances are the very being of *prakṛti* just as the trees constitute the very being of the forest which cannot be conceived as a category separate from them.[1] *Sāṅkhyasāra* further endorses the same point of view. It says that they are not the qualities of *prakṛti* since they in reality constitute its nature. And the denial that *sattva, rajas* and *tamas* are qualities also implies that they are the very essence of *prakṛti*.[2] Patañjali and Vyāsa also support this view.[3]

The postulation of the three *guṇas* depends on the three modes of feeling—*sukha* (pleasure), *duḥkha* (pain) and *moha* (indolence). Pleasure is a mode of *bhoga* which is a feeling of conscious detachment or freedom from the object. It implies a beginning of reflection.[4] Whenever we come into contact with an object which gives rise to the feeling of pleasure, we tend to continue with the feeling of pleasure transcending its cause, i.e. object. It may be interpreted as freedom from the object. The attendant feeling of lightness in the body or mind may be compared with the lightness which is felt in the noble qualities of sincerity, truthfulness, purity, forgiveness.[5] In the Freudian sense it is the release of tension. It is due to *sattva guṇa*. In other words, the experience of pleasure points towards the existence of *sattva guṇa*. Pain implies the active wish to be free from pain, which remains however unfulfilled so long as it is pain. The feeling of pain is thus a freeing activity.[6] This is the mode of *bhoga* which is reflected in the qualities of hatred, anxiety, etc. and points towards the existence of *rajas*. The third mode of feeling is *moha* or indolence. It seems to be a conscious feeling of not being

---

1. प्रकृतेर्गुणा इत्यादिवाक्यन्तु वनस्य वृक्षा इतिवद् बोध्यम् । *SS*, p. 10.
2. "सत्त्वादीनामतद्धर्मत्वं तद्रूपत्वात्" इति सांख्यसूत्रेण सत्त्वादीनां प्रकृतिस्वरूपत्वहेतुना प्रकृतिधर्मत्वप्रतिषेधात् । *Ibid.*, pp. 9-10.
3. योगसूत्रतद्भाष्याभ्यामपि गुणानामेव प्रकृतित्ववचनाच्च । *Ibid.*, p. 10.
4. *SP*, p. 207, section 141.
5. *Ibid.*, p. 207, section 142.
6. *Ibid.*, p. 207, section 141.

able to feel. There is a want of freedom in *moha* and also there is no wish or will to be free. It is still a positive feeling, feeling of indolence in mind and body, feeling of being stupefied before the object or being fascinated by the object. It is reflected in the qualities of ignorance, pride, fear, etc. These three feelings are all positive and they are different from one another. But they are capable of being combined into a unitary feeling and hence the justification why the three substances are called the 'unitary' *prakṛti.*[1] *Sukha, duḥkha* and *moha* are primarily the felt mental qualities of lightness (freedom, *laghutva*), restlessness (*calatva*) and heaviness (*gurutva*), and their analogues in the object are expression (*prakāśa*), action (*kriyā*) and standing being or persistence (*sthiti*). The necessity and sufficiency of the triple characterization of the object are justified by the introspective testimony about the necessity and sufficiency of the elementary feelings.[2] This is the psychological justification for the postulation of these three elementary substances constituting *prakṛti.*

The diversity of the visible universe can be explained by varying permutations and combinations of these basic elements. The manifest objects do not essentially differ from the *guṇas* from which they have emerged since the cause is admitted to be immanent in the effects. These effects point towards the unmanifest *guṇas,* the ultimate nature of which does not come within the range of ordinary perception[3] for various reasons like distance, minuteness,[4] etc., but it does not mean that the ultimate principle does not exist. If non-perception were admitted to be a cause of the non-existence of such reals as are not perceived, then many other reals which have been scientifically established would be rendered liable to become non-existent because of their being beyond ordinary perception. This is not desirable. To avoid such an eventuality, the ultimate positive principle must be assumed to exist, even though it may be beyond perception since the universe which is obviously an effect must come out of something positive and since it is only something positive which brings forth a positive product. And it is pursuant to the theory of effect pre-existing in the cause (*satkāryavāda*) that the universe, the visible positive product, should have as its cause *prakṛti* constituted by the three *guṇas.*

1. *SP*, p. 207, section 141, *loc. cit.*
2. *Ibid.*, pp. 207-08, section 142.
3. गुणानां परमं रूपं न दृष्टिपथमृच्छति । Quoted in *Vyāsabhāṣya* on *Yogasūtra,* IV.13.
4. *SPB* (under *sūtras* I-108-9), pp. 68-69 and also *Sāṅkhyakārikā,* 7.

Vijñānabhikṣu approvingly says that these three *guṇas* are all-pervading and adds that each of the three *guṇas* has innumerable individuals. His arguments in support of the innumerability of *guṇas* are as follows:

If the three ultimate reals, i.e. *guṇas* were admitted to be only three in number, then growth, decay, etc., would remain unaccounted for since one *guṇa* undergoing decay at one place cannot simultaneously be responsible for growth in another object at another place. This anomaly can be removed by assuming that each *guṇa* has innumerable individuals. Besides, if the three *guṇas* are assumed to be determined by means of limiting conditions, then their collective form, *pradhāna,* would be similarly determined. As such the infinite number of emerging universes as propounded in the scriptures are rendered unjustifiable. It is therefore necessary that to also justify the scriptural statements the *guṇas* should be assumed to be infinite in number. So far as their description as being three is concerned, Vijñānabhikṣu observes that it is so from the points of view of similarity and dissimilarity. Besides, it facilitates the *sādhaka* to discriminate between *prakṛti* and consciousness.[1]

The visible variety of effects also warrants that the three all-pervasive *guṇas* be admitted to possess infinite number of similar individuals since intermingling (or union) of the three *guṇas* only cannot bring about an extra peculiarity in the effects to explain their infinitely diverse nature.[2]

The *Sāṅkhyasūtra* I-128 which mentions similar and dissimilar features of the three *guṇas* also corroborates what Vijñānabhikṣu says about the numerical aspect of the *guṇas*.[3] Explaining this *sūtra,* he says that there is a similarity of *sattva*-individuals by virtue of the features of lightness, etc. residing in them. *Rajas* and *tamas* are different from *sattva* because they possess the characteristics of movement, etc. and heaviness, etc. respectively and not lightness, etc. It is on account of this similarity that *sattva* individuals are said

---

1. गुणानां सत्त्वादीनामेकैकव्यक्तिमात्रत्वे वृद्धिह्रासादिकं नोपपद्यते तथा परिच्छिन्नत्त्वे च तत्समूहरूपस्य प्रधानस्य परिच्छिन्नत्वापत्त्या श्रुतिस्मृतिसिद्धमेकदाऽसङ्ख्यब्रह्माण्डादिकं नोपपद्यते । अतोऽसङ्ख्यत्वेऽपि गुणानां त्रित्वसङ्ख्योपपादनाय विवेकाद्यर्थं च तेषां साधर्म्यवैधर्म्ये प्रतिपादयति ।
SPB (under *sūtra* I-127), p. 78. Also compare *SS*, pp. 10-11.
2. सत्त्वादित्रयमपि व्यक्तिभेदादनन्तम् । अन्यथा हि विभुमात्रत्वे गुणविमर्दवैचित्र्यात् कार्यवैचित्र्यमिति सिद्धान्तो नोपपद्यते विमर्देऽवान्तरभेदासम्भवात् । *Ibid.*, p. 78.
3. लघ्वादिधर्मैः साधर्म्यं वैधर्म्यं च गुणानाम् । *Sāṅkhyasūtra*, I-128.

to constitute one basic element just as manifold products of earth are said to be one because of one genus residing in them. The assumption of infinite number of *sattva, rajas* and *tamas* individuals also accounts for the simultaneous increase and decrease occurring in the individual products at different places since there are now many individuals of one kind acting on those of another kind.[1]

Vijñānabhikṣu further adds that it is all the more established that each of the causal *guṇas* has infinite individuals, since otherwise it would not be proper to say that lightness, etc. are similarities. It is only the property of similars which constitutes similarity. And it cannot be said that lightness, etc. constitute similarity because of the diversity of effect-*sattva* (*kārya-sattva*), etc. because in that case the similarity of effect-*sattva*, etc. with respect to lightness, etc. cannot be proved. It is clear from the examples of a pitcher, etc. which are essentially made of three *guṇas* and which are of the form of effect-*sattva*, etc. but which are not light. It would, therefore, be proper to hold that it is with respect to the causal *guṇas* that similarity and dissimilarity have been expounded and, therefore, it is the causal *guṇas* (*kāraṇa sattva, kāraṇa rajas* and *kāraṇa tamas*) which are said to have the innumerable individual manifestations.[2] Moreover, the use of the term *gaṇa* in this context corroborates this standpoint.[3]

Vijñānabhikṣu appears to be ambivalent while commenting on the behaviour of the *guṇas*. In the *Vijñānāmṛtabhāṣya* he does not admit that there is any activity in the *guṇas* during the state of dissolution or prior to creation. He says that *puruṣa* and *prakṛti* bereft of activity lie submerged in the Absolute at the time of dissolution. Vijñānabhikṣu likens them to the dead snakes lying in a pit.[4] Apparently here he does not subscribe to the Sāṅkhya view that

---

1. लघुत्वादिधर्मेण सर्वासां सत्त्वव्यक्तीनां पृथिवीत्वेनेव सत्त्वव्यक्तीनामेकजातीयतयैकता सजातीयोपष्टम्भादिना वृद्धिह्रासादिकं च युक्तमित्याशय: । एवं च चलत्वादिधर्मेण सर्वासां रजोव्यक्तीनां साधर्म्यं सत्त्वतमोभ्यां च वैधर्म्यं शेषं पूर्ववत् । एवं गुरुत्वादिधर्मेण सर्वासां तमोव्यक्तीनां साधर्म्यं सत्त्वरजोभ्यां वैधर्म्यं शेषं पूर्ववदिति । *SPB* (under *sūtra* I-128), p. 78.
2. अत्र सूत्रे सत्त्वादीनां कारणद्रव्याणां प्रत्येकमनेकव्यक्तिकत्वं सिद्धम् । अन्यथा लघुत्वादीनां साधर्म्यत्वानुपपत्ते: समानां धर्मस्यैव साधर्म्यत्वात् । न च कार्यसत्त्वादीनामनेकतया लघुत्वादिकं साधर्म्यं स्यादिति वाच्यं त्रिगुणात्मकत्वेन घटादीनामपि कार्यसत्त्वादिरूपतया लघुत्वादीनां सत्त्वादिसाधर्म्यत्वानुपपत्ते: । तस्मात्कारणगुणानामेवात्र साधर्म्यादिकमुच्यत इति । *Ibid.* (under *sūtra* I-128), p. 78.
3. सत्त्वादीनां प्रत्येकव्यक्त्यानन्त्यं गणशब्दो वक्ति । *Ibid.* (under *sūtra* I-61), p. 38.
4. नासीदिति विरतव्यापारतया कारणरूपेण गर्तस्थमृतसर्पवद् विलीनमासीदित्यर्थ: । *VAB*, p. 19. Also प्रकृतिपुरुषादयस्तु सृष्ट्यादिलक्षणस्वकार्येभ्य उपरता एव सुषुप्तास्तिष्ठन्तीति । *Ibid.*, p. 58.

the *guṇas (prakṛti)* are eternally in flux. But on the other hand when we scrutinize *Sāṅkhyapravacanabhāṣya, Yogavārttika* and *Sāṅkhyasāra,* Vijñānabhikṣu's adherence to the view that the *guṇas* are always in flux seems to become more pronounced. This ambivalence can be understood in the right perspective, if we keep in view his role as a commentator. He performs it faithfully, while commenting on the *Sāṅkhya* and *Yogasūtras,* he says that the *guṇas* never cease to function[1] whereas he evinces his predilection for the Vedāntic view that Brahman is the Absolute Reality when he comments on the *Brahmasūtras.* It is in this perspective that Vijñānabhikṣu considers it logically necessary to deny any meaningful activity—conducive to dissimilar modification—to *prakṛti* and *puruṣa* at the time of dissolution so that the ultimate nature of the Absolute may be preserved intact.

Before taking up for discussion the process of evolution, it would be proper to determine the status of *prakṛti* more pointedly. It has been explained earlier that Vijñānabhikṣu admits that the Absolute is the only Reality. It is, therefore, implied that *prakṛti* is not independently real as has been accepted in the traditional Sāṅkhya. He has his own view about the concept of reality. Reality, according to Vijñānabhikṣu, consists in having a meaningful activity and so far as the principles of *puruṣa* and *prakṛti* are concerned they are meaningfully active only during creation. They cease to perform any meaningful function after the dissolution has set in. At that time they remain in the Absolute without performing any meaningful activity whereas the Absolute does remain meaningfully active even during the state of dissolution since It continues to perceive with the aid of Its Pure-*Sattva*-Adjunct the mode reflecting the universe, otherwise the creation of the universe by It would be rendered untenable.[2]

Vijñānabhikṣu himself refers to this view saying that a section of thinkers who follow Sāṅkhya and Yoga hold that *prakṛti* and *puruṣas* are real in their own right and that *prakṛti* itself starts functioning to fulfil the needs of selves after coming into contact with the latter. The

1. प्रदीपावयवानामिव बुद्ध्यवयवानां गुणानां वृत्तं क्रिया चञ्चला प्रतिक्षणमन्याऽन्या च भवति न तु निर्व्यापारा गुणास्तिष्ठन्ति । *YV* on *Yogasūtra* II-15. Also cf. *SPB* on VI-42 and *YB* on *Yogasūtra* III-13.
2. ब्रह्मचेतनस्य तु लयो नास्ति "आत्मा वा इदमेक एवाग्र आसीन्नान्यत् किंचन मिषद्" इत्यादिश्रुतिभिर्ब्रह्मणो विश्वावभासनरूपव्यापारस्य प्रलयेऽपि सत्त्वात् । ईश्वरोपाधौ विश्वाकारवृत्तेर्नित्यत्वात् इच्छाकृतिवत्, अन्यथा विश्वनिर्माणानुपपत्तेः । *VAB,* p. 51.

stock example offered in this context is that of iron and the magnet. Iron does not require anything else for its movement to come in contact with the latter except that it is near the magnet. Similarly *prakṛti* in the vicinity of selves is propelled to come in contact with the latter to fulfil their objectives and does not stand in need of any Higher Conscious Being for its propulsion. Vijñānabhikṣu does not accept this view. He has his own point of view in this regard. He says that it is Īśvara Who brings the selves into contact with *prakṛti*[1] and enters into them only by meditation.[2] It is consistent with his philosophy of Integral Non-duality that *prakṛti* assumes activity under the superintendence of the Absolute.

It will become evident from the following that the evolutionary process of creation in the Sāṅkhya system is not substantially different from the one propounded by Vijñānabhikṣu. But his account of the process of creation bears the stamp of Purāṇic literature.

Mahat which is also called *buddhi* evolves out of *prakṛti.* This first evolute is called *mahat* since it is endowed with the superb qualities like virtue, etc.[3] Vijñānabhikṣu says that *mahat* assumes three functions for the three deities, viz., Brahmā, Viṣṇu and Maheśa. It is predominantly *sāttvika* when it becomes the adjunct of Viṣṇu; it is *rājasa,* when it becomes the *upādhi* of Brahmā and when it is with Maheśvara, it is *tāmasa.* It means that like *ahaṅkāra, mahat* is also of three kinds because of the preponderance of one quality or the other.[4] And there is no harm if these are understood in terms of three functions of the power of the Absolute Lord,[5] which continue to be performed every moment during creation both at the micro and macro levels in respect of creation, sustenance and dissolution. The deities relating to these functions in the respective order are popu-

---

1. प्रकृतिस्वातन्त्र्यवादिभ्यां सांख्ययोगिभ्यां पुरुषार्थप्रयुक्ता प्रकृतिः स्वयमेव पुरुषेण आद्यजीवेन संयुज्यत इत्यभ्युपगम्यते अयस्कान्तेन लोहवत् । अस्माभिस्तु प्रकृतिपुरुषसंयोग ईश्वरेण क्रियत इत्यभ्युपगम्यते । *VAB*, p. 18. See also *ibid.*, pp. 19, 68 and 69.
2. प्रकृतिपुरुषयोश्चेश्वरस्य प्रवेशः शास्त्रवदवधानमात्रम् । *Ibid.*, p. 17.
3. प्रकृतेः सकाशाद् बुद्ध्याख्यं महत्तत्त्वं जायते; तस्य धर्मादिरूपप्रकृष्टगुणयोगात् महत्संज्ञा, तदेव च लक्षणम्। *SS*, p. 12.

   See also सविकारात् प्रधानात्तु महत्तत्त्वमजायत । महानिति यतः ख्यातिलोकानां जायते सदा । *SS*, p. 13.
4. सात्त्विको राजसश्चैव तामसश्च त्रिधा मताः । *VP* quoted in *SS*, p. 12.
5. गुणेभ्यः क्षोभमाणेभ्यस्त्रयो देवा विजज्ञिरे ।

   एका मूर्तिस्त्रयो देवा ब्रह्मविष्णुमहेश्वराः ।। *MP* quoted in *SS*, p. 13.

larly known as Brahmā, Viṣṇu and Maheśvara.

After having been partially agitated by *rajas* and *tamas*, when *mahat* undergoes transformation it also becomes the limiting adjuncts of selves.[1] It is just opposite in nature to the *mahat* at the cosmic level as is clear from the *Sāṅkhyasūtra* '*mahaduparāgādviparītam*'. To elaborate, *mahat* at the micro-level is afflicted with *rajas* and *tamas* and it is because of this affliction that vice, ignorance, attachment and absence of lordly power result. It is *sattva* which predominates in it at the macro-level and as a consequence it acquires the qualities of virtue, wisdom, non-attachment, lordship, etc.[2]

The chief and unique characteristic of *mahat* (intellect) is the intellectual mode of ascertainment.[3] It is the last limit in an ascending order, upto which the subjective and objective continue to be differentiated. Or in other words, at this stage of evolution, the subject and object aspects of experience had not yet emerged.[4]

Vijñānabhikṣu in conformity with Sāṅkhya holds that the intellectual mode (*vṛtti*) is substantial (*dravyarūpā*) like a flame[5] and that it also performs the function of maintaining itself. K.C. Bhattacharyya here observes that these two functions of *mahat* have to be distinguished: The self-maintaining[6] function of the intellect is not substantial. To explain, the intellect maintains itself with the help of desire, etc., just as it sustains itself with the aid of substantial modes of its own.[7] It seems that Vijñānabhikṣu denies the status of substance to desires, etc. while he confers the same on the intellectual modes. But taking into consideration what K.C. Bhattacharyya says in this context, we may say that Vijñānabhikṣu's statement suffers from

---

1. इदमेव महत्तत्त्वमंशतो रजस्तमःसम्भेदेन परिणतं सद् व्यष्टिजीवानामुपाधिधर्मादियुक्तं क्षुद्रमपि भवति । *SS*, p. 13.
2. धर्मज्ञानैश्वर्याण्यपि बुद्ध्युपादानकानि नाहङ्काराद्युपादानकानि बुद्धेरेव निरतिशयसत्त्वकार्यत्वादिति । *SPB* (under *sūtra* II-14), p. 106.
   and तदेव महत्तत्त्वं रजस्तभोभ्यामुपरागाद्विपरीतं क्षुद्रधर्माज्ञानावैराग्यानैश्वर्यधर्मकमपि भवतीत्यर्थः । *Ibid.*, p. 106.
3. महत्तत्त्वस्य प्राधान्येनासाधारण्येन चाध्यक्सायो वृत्तिः । *SS*, p. 13.
   Also see महदाख्यमाद्यं कार्यं तन्मनो मननवृत्तिकम् । मननमत्र निश्चयस्तद्वृत्तिका बुद्धिरित्यर्थः । *SPB* (under *sūtra* I-71), p. 48.
4. Sarasvati Chennakesavan, *Concept of Mind in Indian Philosophy*, Motilal Banarsidass, 1980, p. 24.
5. बुद्धिवृत्तिरपि प्रदीपशिखावद् द्रव्यरूप एव परिणामः । *SPB* (under *sūtra* V-107), p. 208.
6. स्वस्थितिहेतुर्व्यापारः । *Ibid.* (under *sūtra* V-108), p. 208.
7. तत्र यथा द्रव्यरूपया वृत्त्या बुद्धिर्जीवति, तथेच्छादिभिरपीति तेऽपि वृत्तयः । *Ibid.*, p. 209.

ambiguity since according to him even in the self-maintaining sense, the function of the intellect is substantial because of its being a self-maintaining *tattva.*[1] It may be mentioned here that K.C. Bhattacharyya calls this function *bhāva.* According to him it is merely a function of referring to, or being conscious of, the objects. It is, therefore, not substantial like the mental mode in which the intellect actually assumes the form of object. *Bhāva* and *vṛtti* obviously depend on each other for their existence. *Bhāva* does not take place without *vṛtti* and there is no *vṛtti* without *bhāva,* that is, without conscious reference to the object. *Bhāva* is a subjective function by which an object is manifested non-causally.[2]

Thus *mahat* (*buddhi*) performs two functions, viz., subjective and objective. It is on account of *aviveka* that both subjective and objective aspects (consciousness and matter) remain indistinct. It is in this condition of indistinctness that *buddhi* continues to exist. And no sooner is the intellectual mode reflecting distinction between *mahat* (*buddhi*) and the self brought about than *mahat* lapses into its cause, *prakṛti* spelling an end to creation for the self. It means that the self has attained liberation from the cycle of creation at the rise of discriminatory knowledge (*vivekakhyāti*).

The *mahat-tattva* is the seed-stage of the internal sense-organ, i.e. mental or intellectual apparatus constituted by *mahat* (*buddhi*), *ahaṃkāra* and *manas.*[3] It helps establish its relation with the self and hence, in a sense, is responsible for its bondage. Vijñānabhikṣu mentions here that there is only scriptural testimony so far as order in the evolutionary process is concerned. He admits that inference helps only in arriving at the conclusion in general that effects have their causes. He clarifies further that it is not possible for the inferential proposition to infer a specific order of elemental substances or the internal apparatus in the process of creation, since there is no manifest indicator which becomes the basis of such a conclusion.[4] Vijñānabhikṣu here intends to make the point that an intellectual mode comes into existence when through senses the

1. *SP,* p. 186. Vijñānabhikṣu's view as improved upon by K.C. Bhattacharyya.
2. *Ibid.,* pp. 186-87.
3. महदहङ्कारमनस्त्रितयात्मकस्यान्तःकरणस्य महत्तत्त्वं बीजावस्थेति । *SS,* p. 13.
4. अत्र प्रकृतेर्महान् महतोऽहङ्कार इत्यादिसृष्टिक्रमे शास्त्रमेव प्रमाणम्, अनुमानेन सामान्यतः कार्याणां सकारणत्वमात्रसिद्धेः, न तु सृष्टौ भूतादिक्रमो वान्तःकरणादिक्रमो वेत्येकतरावधारकमनुमानं सम्भवति, स्पष्टलिङ्गाभावात् । *SS,* p. 13.

intellect is modalized into the form of objects. The precedence of the mode of intellect (*antaḥkaraṇavṛtti*) over the whole creation except that of the internal apparatus, therefore, means that *mahat, ahaṃkāra* and *manas* are created before everything else. He illustrates this point with the help of an example of the creation of a water-pot which is produced only after it has been conceived in the mind of the potter.[1]

Mahat issues forth from the selves and *prakṛti* when brought into union by Īśvara. Vijñānabhikṣu calls this particular evolute both *prāṇa* and *buddhi* from the points of view of activity and ascertainment respectively. Out of the two it is the creation of *prāṇa* which precedes that of *buddhi.*[2] In *Sāṅkhyapravacanabhāṣya*[3] Vijñānabhikṣu points out that *prāṇa* is nothing but *mahat.* Another reason why the first evolute is called *mahat* is that it teems with potentialities and pervades all the effects that evolve out of it.[4]

Vijñānabhikṣu raises a query about the status of *mahat:* Why should it not be admitted to be eternal even when it houses virtue, lordship, etc.? Why is it instead assumed to be an effect of *prakṛti*? He answers: The residue of *karma, vāsanās,* etc. resides in the germinal form in *mahat,* which still forming a part of *prakṛti* is merely a particular form of *sattva.* This seed of *mahat* may be understood to be a sprout during the causal state of knowledge[5] and may also be taken both as eternal and non-eternal like *ākāśa.*[6] Just as *ākāśa* in its causal state, in which it does not possess sound which is its distinctive mark is spoken of as *prakṛti,* similarly *mahat* in the causal state is spoken of only as *prakṛti* and not treated as *buddhi* on account of the

---

1. घटसृष्टिवदन्तःकरणातिरिक्ताखिलसृष्टेरन्तःकरणवृत्तिपूर्वकत्वानुमानम् । *SPB* (under *sūtra* II-10), p. 104.
2. प्रथमं तावदीश्वराधिष्ठानेन संयुक्ताभ्यां जीवप्रधानाभ्यां महानुत्पद्यते । स च क्रियाशक्त्या प्राणः निश्चयशक्त्या च बुद्धिः, तयोर्मध्ये प्रथमं प्राणवृत्तिरुत्पद्यते । *VAB*, p. 218.
3. अतोऽस्यां श्रुतौ प्राण एव महत्तत्त्वम् । *SPB*, p. 104.
4. अस्याश्च बुद्धेर्महत्त्वं स्वेतरसकलकार्यव्यापकत्वान्महैश्वर्याच्च मन्तव्यम् । *Ibid.* (under *sūtra* II-13), p. 106.
5. नन्वेवं धर्माद्यवस्थानार्थं बुद्धेरेव नित्यत्वात् कथं कार्यतेति चेन्न । प्रकृत्यंशरूपे बीजावस्थमहत्तत्त्वे सत्त्वविशेषे कर्मवासनादीनामवस्थानात्, तस्यैव ज्ञानकारणावस्थायामङ्कुरवदुपपत्त्यङ्गीकारात् । *Ibid.* (under *sūtra* II-15), pp. 106-7.
   Cf. also अन्तःकरणावस्थे प्रकृत्यंशविशेषेऽन्तःकरणे धर्माधर्मसंस्कारादिकं तिष्ठतीति । *Ibid.* (under *sūtra* V-25), p. 177.
6. तथा चाकाशवदेव नित्यानित्योभयरूपा बुद्धिः । *Ibid.* (under *sūtra* II-15), p. 107.

non-availability of the function of ascertainment which is the distinctive mark of *buddhi*.

Ākāśa as causal is the manifesting process of the unmanifest and it is distinct from *ākāśa* as an evolute or effect.[1] K.C. Bhattacharyya refers to this *ākāśa* as the causal prototype of *ākāśa* as *bhūta* and that this is interpreted "as the form of changes implied in every metaphysical object and, therefore, in prakṛti itself, change is through combination and combination is for change. What changes is a complex and elements combine for the production of a new unity. Change is real time and combination is real space. Each implies the other, their unity being called ākāśa, ākāśa as the general form of change that is inherent in the real object. Such ākāśa is implied in prakṛti as the potentiality of change."[2]

Time is understood as a moment of this *kāraṇa ākāśa* and is, therefore, inherent in *prakṛti* itself. In a sense, it is real becoming of a manifest effect. Within *prakṛti* it is becoming as mere self-reproduction of a *guṇa* (*sadṛśapariṇāma*). *Sadṛśapariṇāma*, i.e. process of self-reproduction, is construed as active persisting by K.C. Bhattacharyya. During this state of self-reproduction, it is becoming in the sense of changing when it is not yet changing, which accords reality to everything that persists in such a manner.[3] K.C. Bhattacharyya further adds that change or persistence is a time function whereas unrelated plurality as during self-reproduction is the space-function. Both these functions inhere in *prakṛti* itself.[4] Vijñānabhikṣu's view is that the eternal time and space which are the cause of *ākāśa* are the special qualities of *prakṛti* and nothing more.[5]

The concepts of time and space having incidentally been discussed, what falls in proper sequence is *ahaṃkāra*. The internal organ is called *ahaṃkāra* when it performs the special function of *abhimāna* which in essence is the conscious identification of the self with a finite being; it may be expressed either as 'I am this being' or as 'I am going to become this being'. This finitizing function is a

1. *SP*, p. 165.
2. *Ibid.*, pp. 169-70.
3. Vijñānabhikṣu appears to have a different view on this since according to him reality consists in giving rise to meaningful activity which is only possible during *visadṛśapariṇāma*.
4. *SP*, p. 170.
5. नित्यौ यौ दिक्कालौ तावाकाशप्रकृतिभूतौ प्रकृतेर्गुणविशेषावेव । *SPB* (under *sūtra* II-12), p. 105.

bhāva of *buddhi,*[1] which may also be called *vṛtti* as has been just pointed out in the foregoing that *vṛtti* is not always substantial. As such the definition of *ahaṃkāra* as offered by Vijñānabhikṣu corresponds to the one just given.[2] He likens it to *kumbhakāra* and explains that the mind (or agent) which brings 'I' into existence is *ahaṃkāra* just as a potter is one who brings the pot into existence.

When the mind (or agent) performs the function of knowing itself as 'I am I', it is called *buddhi.*[3] The knowing self may be finite but this finitude is not manifest in the knowing.[4] But when the agent makes itself know that it has become this or that, it is called *ahaṃkāra.* It evolves out of *mahat* (*buddhi*) as a tree grows out of the sprout.[5]

Vijñānabhikṣu rightly points out that the mental function known as willing, i.e. 'I am this' or 'this is mine', is possible only with respect to the object or condition which has already been determined by *buddhi,* the principle of certitude. Since the willing function becomes manifest only after *buddhi* has determined something, it may rightly be assumed that the organ having the function of knowing is the cause of the one possessing the function of willing.[6] *Abhimāna,* according to K.C. Bhattacharyya, corresponds to self-willing since *buddhi* as self-knowing becomes *ahaṃkāra* as self-willing. Interpreting the *Sāṅkhyasūtra* VI-54 which says that the agent is *ahaṃkāra,* he adds that the finite egohood of the self (which is in essence an infinite individual) is manifested in willing. The knowing self may be finite but the finiteness is not manifest in the knowing. "Ahaṃkāra is the finite egohood of the mind as willing and willing in the (gross) body and directed towards the external object presupposes willing in the mind towards itself, the mind as active 'I' becoming the standing me. This is the self-willing of the mind which answers to ahaṃkāra."[7] It is a modification of the universal *buddhi* in which *rajas* predominates.[8]

---

1. *SP,* p. 182.
2. तस्य चाभिमानवृत्तिकत्वादहङ्कारसंज्ञा । *SS,* p. 13.
3. *SP,* p. 183.
4. *Ibid.,* p. 181.
5. महत्तत्त्वादहङ्कार उत्पद्यते, अङ्कुरात् शाखिवत् । *SS,* p. 13.
6. बुद्ध्या निश्चित एवार्थे अहङ्कारममकारौ जायेते । अतो वृत्त्योः कार्यकारणभावानुसारेण वृत्तिमतोरपि कार्यकारणभाव उन्नीयत इति । *SPB* (under *sūtra* II-16), p. 107.
7. *SP,* pp. 181-82 (quoted with slight alteration).
8. S. Chennakesavan, *Concept of Mind in Indian Philosophy,* p. 25.

Ahaṃkāra has been described as *vaikārika, taijasa* and *tāmasa* depending on the preponderance of *sattva, rajas* and *tamas* respectively. Senses including the mind on the one hand and the *tanmātras* on the other evolve out of *ahaṃkāra*. These may be taken as co-ordinates, i.e. two equally significant evolutes, though having different characteristics. Such is not the case with the rest of the evolution which is linear. The division of *ahaṃkāra* into three types has significance in the sense that *manas, jñānendriyas* along with *karmendriyas* and *tanmātras* are said to have emerged out of *vaikṛta, rājasa* and *tāmasa ahaṃkāra* respectively. In other words, as Vijñānabhikṣu says, all the senses possess less *sattva* than *manas* and as such are said to have been produced from *rājasa ahaṃkāra, manas* being *sāttvika,* from *vaikṛta ahaṃkāra* and *tanmātras,* from *tāmasa ahaṃkāra.*[1] This order of creation of *manas*, sense-organs along with motor organs and *tanmātras* as given by Vijñānabhikṣu is in consonance with the *Bhāgavata Purāṇa* which has also been quoted by him in this context.[2]

Vijñānabhikṣu's view is different from that of other interpreters of the Sāṅkhya system. The view held by Vācaspati Miśra and Aniruddha is that *manas* along with sensory and motor organs emerges from *sāttvika ahaṃkāra* and *tanmātras,* from *tāmasa ahaṃkāra.* By implication, *rājasa ahaṃkāra* could be taken to be aiding in the process of evolution in general. As Vijñānabhikṣu has a predilection for the Purāṇas, he construes the word *ekādaśakaḥ* occurring in *Sāṅkhyakārikā* 25 in the same manner as he interprets the word *ekādaśakam* in *Sāṅkhyasūtra* II-18. According to him the latter (word) stands for *manas.* In this sense it means 'eleventh' or 'what completes a group of eleven' so the word *ekādaśakaḥ* of the *Sāṅkhyakārikā* should also mean 'eleventh' or 'what completes a group of eleven, he avers. But this interpretation appears to be a little stretched since it (*ekādaśakaḥ*) obviously connotes 'a group of eleven.'[3] Bālarāma Udāsīna refers to this anomalous interpretation

---

1. एकादशानां पूरणमेकादशकं मनः षोडशात्मगणमध्ये सात्त्विकम् । अतस्तद् वैकृतात् सात्त्विकादहङ्काराज्जायत इत्यर्थः । अतश्च राजसाहङ्काराद् दशेन्द्रियाणि तामसाहङ्काराच्च तन्मात्राणीत्यवगन्तव्यम् । *SPB* (under *sūtra* II-18), p. 108.
2. *Ibid.*, p. 108.
3. सात्त्विक एकादशकः प्रवर्तते वैकृतादहङ्काराद् ।
भूतादेस्तन्मात्रः, स तामसस्तैजसादुभयम् ।। *Sāṅkhyakārikā*, 25.

by Vijñānabhikṣu and rejects it.[1] Nevertheless as shown by R.S. Bhattacharyya in the footnotes, these two views seem to be fairly prevalent in the relevant literature.[2]

According to Vijñānabhikṣu, a sense-organ is a product of *ahaṃkāra* which becomes instrumental in the emergence of cognition.[3] He does not accept the Nyāya-Vaiśeṣika view that the sense-organs are the products of different elemental substances. In other words, nose, tongue, eyes, skin and ears are respectively the products of earth, water, fire, air and *ākāśa.* In case the latter view were accepted, the order in the process of evolution as described in Sāṅkhya, Yoga, etc. would stand reversed. On Vijñānabhikṣu's view which is consistent with the Purāṇic account, it is *ahaṃkāra* which is the cause of the eleven sense-organs on the one hand and five *tanmātras* on the other hand. The five *tanmātras* are, in turn, responsible for the emergence of the five *bhūtas.* Vijñānabhikṣu is particular in this respect and assumes the existence of scriptural enunciation (*śruti*) to this effect since such statements do exist in the Smṛti-literature.[4] Another argument that looks to be convincing on the epistemological ground is that, since both *ahaṃkāra* and the senses share the common characteristic of being illuminator, it is quite in order to hold the view that the senses are the effects of the internal sense-organ, i.e. *ahaṃkāra.*[5]

Being both a sense and motor organ, *manas* occupies an important place. In this regard the Advaitins have divergent viewpoints. The Bhāmatī school holds the view that it is a sense-organ whereas the Vivaraṇa school does not accept this point of view. It is of advantage to take note of what K.C. Bhattacharyya has to say in this context. He says that *manas* is both an *indriya* and *antaḥkaraṇa.*[6] In

---

1. विज्ञानभिक्षुस्तु पुराणेषु, सात्त्विकाहङ्कारात् इन्द्रियाधिष्ठातारो देवा मनश्चजातं, राजसात् दशेन्द्रियाणि जातानि, तामसाच्च तन्मात्राणि इति प्रक्रियाप्रदर्शनेनात्रापि "सात्त्विक एकादशक इत्यनेन मनो ग्राह्यं, तैजसादुभयम् इत्युभयपदेन च द्विविधमिन्द्रियं ग्राह्यम्" इत्याह, नैतत्सुन्दरम्, एकादशकशब्दस्य एकादशसङ्ख्यापरिमिते गणे शक्तत्वेन मनोमात्रप्रत्यायनेऽशक्तत्वं, न च पूरणप्रत्ययान्तात्स्वार्थे केऽभिमतलाभः इत्यभिमन्तव्यम्, तथा सति एकादशकमित्यस्यैवौचित्येन पुल्लिङ्गनिर्देशायोगात् ।
Bālarāma Udāsīna, *Vidvattoṣiṇī* on *Sāṅkhyakārikā* and *Tattvakaumudī*, pp.177-78.
2. R.S. Bhattacharya, *SPB*, p. 108, footnotes 1 and 2.
3. अहङ्कारकार्यत्वे सति करणत्वमिन्द्रियत्वम् । *SPB* (under *sūtra* II-19), p. 109.
4. आहङ्कारिकत्वे च प्रमाणभूता श्रुतिः काललुप्ताचार्यवाक्यान्मन्वाद्यखिलस्मृतिभ्यश्चानुमीयते । *Ibid.* (under *sūtra* II-20), p. 110.
5. प्रकाशकत्वसाम्येनान्तःकरणोपादानत्वस्यैवोचिततयाहङ्कारिकत्वश्रुतेरेव मुख्यत्वात् । *Ibid.*, p. 110.
6. *SP*, p. 188.

case the *indriya* is understood to be a motor organ in this context, Vijñānabhikṣu's view on the status of *manas* is vindicated. Its specific function is *saṅkalpa,* which consists in distinguishing the *viśeṣaṇa* or determinant in the *viśeṣya* or determinate object of the external senses. As it only makes manifest what was already known implicitly in the determinate sense cognition, *manas* is itself a sense, the internal sense. It shares with *ahaṃkāra* and *buddhi* the character of being concerned with all time, unlike the external senses which are concerned with the present alone.[1] Since it shares the characteristic of both external and internal sense-organ, it must, at least, be called both external and internal sense-organ irrespective of what the Vivaraṇa school says in this regard.

According to Vijñānabhikṣu, *manas* performs the functions of willing and doubting.[2] It not only co-ordinates the *vṛttis* or functions of the external cognitive senses but also those of the external active senses and these two sets of functions with one another. Vijñānabhikṣu further adds that in the hierarchy of cognitive senses *manas* holds the principal position when it is considered with respect to the operations of the external senses but it is relegated to the second place when compared with the functions of *ahaṃkāra* and *buddhi.*[3]

Before the evolutionary description of the internal sense-organs is wound up, it would not be out of place to add a few words on the divergent views on the question of the causal order of the evolution of *manas,* sense and motor organs on the one hand and *tanmātras* on the other. Though the view that *manas* emerges from *sāttvika* or *vaikṛta ahaṃkāra,* the ten sense and motor organs, from *rājasa ahaṃkāra* and *tanmātras,* from *tāmasa ahaṃkāra* has been supported with ample Purāṇic quotations by Vijñānabhikṣu and though Vācaspati and Aniruddha support the other view that *manas* along with ten sense and motor organs evolves out of *sāttvika ahaṃkāra* and *tanmātras,* from *tāmasa ahaṃkāra,* while *rājasa ahaṃkāra* may be taken to play the role of a catalyst in the process of evolution, yet it may be submitted in the form of an amendment that *manas* may be assumed to emerge out of *sāttvika ahaṃkāra,* sense-organs out of

---

1. *SP,* p. 188. Cf. also साम्प्रतकालं बाह्यं त्रिकालमाभ्यन्तरं करणम् । *SK,* 33 cd.
2. संकल्पविकल्पौ मनस इत्यायातम् । संकल्पश्चिकीर्षा . . . . विकल्पश्च संशयः । *SPB* (under *sūtra* II-30), pp. 113-14.
3. चक्षुरादिव्यापारेषु मनः प्रधानम्, मनोव्यापारे चाहङ्कारोऽहङ्कारव्यापारे च बुद्धिः प्रधानम् । *Ibid.* (under *sūtra* II-45), p. 120.

sāttvika ahaṃkāra with a tinge of *rājasa* and motor organs from *rājasa ahaṃkāra* while *tanmātras* may be admitted to evolve out of *tāmasa ahaṃkāra*, since there is a difference in the functions of the sense-organs from those of the motor organs which commence functioning only after the sense-organs have done their job. It would also conform to the view that both of them do not share the characteristic of being the illuminator (*prakāśakatva*) as has been said by Vijñānabhikṣu.

The sense-organs of hearing, smell, touch, taste and seeing originate from *ahaṃkāra*. The organs of action: larynx, hands, feet, and organs of generation and excretion also emerge out of the same *ahaṃkāra*. The sense-organs receive the stimuli and reflect them. It is their *vṛtti* or function. When co-ordinated by *manas* they get reflected in the intellectual mode which is finally reflected in the self resulting in the incidence of experience. The nature of the organs of action is different from that of the sense-organs. They may be taken to be in the form of motor nerves which impart motion to different muscles. The motor nerves responsible for the generation of motion or activity in the external organs of action may be construed as real organs of action. To illustrate, the motor nerves which actually issue from centres in the motor area of the brain and which give impetus to the organs of action, that is, feet, hands, etc. may be named as the motor organs: *pāda, hasta*, etc., since the particular capacity lies in the specific motor nerves. It is the capacity which should be understood as the actual motor organ though feet, hands, etc. are their most obvious manifestations. In case a particular capacity is paralyzed, the corresponding motor organ ceases to perform its function, as, e.g. in the case of hemiplegia.

It is only the achievement of the purpose of the self that causes these organs to function.[1] They perform their functions in a planned manner as if they knew each other very well.[2] The triad of internal organs in union with one of the organs of the outer sense functions either simultaneously or in succession[3] so that although a higher function implies a lower one, the latter does not imply and may, in fact, psychologically precede the higher one. All the lower *karaṇas* yield their contents ultimately to *buddhi*. The object is reflected in

1. पुरुषार्थ एव हेतुर्न केनचित् कार्यते करणम् । *SK*, 31 cd.
2. स्वां स्वां प्रतिपद्यन्ते परस्पराकूतहेतुकां वृत्तिम् । *Ibid.*, 31 ab.
3. युगपच्चतुष्टयस्य तु वृत्तिः क्रमशश्च तस्य निर्दिष्टा । *Ibid.*, 30 ab.

a *vṛtti* of the external sense, that again in a *vṛtti* of *manas* and so on; *buddhi-vṛtti* further is said to be reflected in the self.[1]

Tanmātras which are said to have emerged out of *tāmasika ahaṃkāra* act as cause in the emergence of five *bhūtas*, viz., *ākāśa, vāyu, agni, ap* and *pṛthivī*. Vijñānabhikṣu points out that since there is a mention of the word *sthūla* in *Sāṅkhyasūtra* I-61, these *tanmātras* have been assumed as subtle-elements. And unlike Nyāya-Vaiśeṣika and like Vedānta, he, in consonance with the theory of *satkāryavāda*, says that the five *tanmātras*—*śabda-tanmātra, sparśa-tanmātra, rūpa-tanmātra, rasa-tanmātra* and *gandha-tanmātra*—have come into existence in this order. From *śabda-tanmātra* emerges *sparśa-tanmātra* with the characteristics of both sound and touch. The three *tanmātras* that follow arise out of the preceding *tanmātras* with the increase of one quality in the succeeding one.[2] Later on the five gross elements evolve *mutatis mutandis* out of these five subtle elements.[3]

Manas along with ten *indriyas* on the one hand and *tanmātras* on the other which have evolved out of *ahaṃkāra* have different features. The former are non-causal since there is no evidence for their being causal whereas there is a Purāṇic evidence[4] so far as the causal nature of the *tanmātras* is considered. Moreover, since there is no causal relationship between *indriyas* and *tanmātras*, there is no order of precedence or succession between them.[5]

The preceding account of the evolutes of *prakṛti* points towards the existence of two bodies: mental and physical. It gets confirmed in two kinds of reflection as has been explained by K.C. Bhattacharyya: 'The two bodies are known in two grades of reflection, one in which the material body is distinguished from the mental body which here appears as the self, and the other in which the mental body is distinguished from the pure self. The first reflection is identical with the reflection that has been taken to be implied in the wish to be free from pain which is explicitly felt in the body. The second reflection

1. *SP*, p. 189.
2. शब्दतन्मात्राद् वक्ष्यमाणक्रमेण स्पर्शतन्मात्रं शब्दस्पर्शोभयगुणकम्, एवं क्रमेणैकैकगुणवृद्ध्या परतन्मात्रत्रयं पूर्वपूर्वतन्मात्रेभ्य उत्पद्यते । *SS*, pp. 14-15.
3. ततश्च पञ्चतन्मात्रेभ्यः पञ्चभूतानि जायन्ते । *Ibid.*, p. 15.
4. *Ibid.*, p. 15.
5. इन्द्रियतन्मात्रयोश्च कार्यकारणभावस्याभावात् क्रमनियमो नास्ति । तत्रेन्द्रियेषु नास्त्यवान्तरकार्यकारणभावः, प्रमाणाभावात्, तन्मात्रेषु त्वस्ति । *Ibid.*, p. 14.

is what was called spiritual reflection, reflection on the first reflection.'[1]

The theories of *karma* and eternal nature of the self also necessitate the postulation of two bodies. The physical body obviously perishes with death and so it has to be the subtle body which serves as vehicle for the self to migrate to another body to reap the fruits of what it has done in the previous incarnations. Vijñānabhikṣu, unlike Patañjali,[2] admits that there is only one subtle body for each *puruṣa* (self) from the time it has assumed embodied existence till it attains liberation. But it raises a problem. The subtle body of an unemancipated self is said not to exist at the time of dissolution. How does the unliberated self take on another body during the following creation in order to exhaust its *karmas* so that there is no loss of what it has already done (*kṛtahāni*). Explaining Vijñānabhikṣu's view on this, K.C. Bhattacharyya observes, "It is conceived at the time of dissolution either to be no body at all, being aviveka itself or karma by itself or to be the mental body of a previous cycle surviving it."[3]

Vijñānabhikṣu's observations on the status of subtle body are worth mentioning. He says that the subtle body is an aggregate of seventeen components and as such does not constitute a whole over and above these seventeen constituents. To substantiate his view he takes recourse to the word *saptadaśaka* occurring in the quotation from the *Mahābhārata*.[4] Moreover, the assumption of a whole over and above the seventeen elements, according to him, suffers from the defect of being cumbersome, whereas a whole in the form of physical body should be postulated in pursuance to the fact that it is perceived.[5]

Mahādeva Vedāntin[6] and Aniruddha[7] interpret *Sāṅkhyasūtra* III-

1. *SP*, p. 156.
2. Pulinbihari Chakravarti, *Origin and Development of the Sāṁkhya System of Thought*, Delhi, 1975, p. 290.
3. *SP*, pp. 156-57. Also see *SPB*, p. 244 :
"यद्यपि प्रलये लिङ्गशरीरं नास्ति तथापि तत्कारणमविवेककर्मादिकं पूर्वसर्गीयलिङ्गशरीरजन्यमस्ति ।"
4. कर्मात्मा पुरुषो योऽसौ बन्धमोक्षैः प्रयुज्यते ।
ससप्तदशकेनापि राशिना युज्यते च सः ।। Quoted in *SPB*, p. 126.
5. राशिशब्देन स्थूलदेहवल्लिंगदेहस्यावयवित्वं निराकृतं अवयविरूपेण द्रव्यान्तरकल्पनायां गौरवात्, स्थूलदेहस्यावयवित्वमेकतादिप्रत्यक्षानुरोधेन कल्प्यत इति । *SPB*, p. 126.
6. *Sāṃkhya Sūtrāṇi with Sāṅkhyavṛttisāra*, ed. Swami Dwarika Das Shastri, Varanasi, 1987, p. 48.
7. *Sāṅkhya Sūtras with the Vṛtti of Aniruddha*, ed. Ram Shankar Bhattacharya, Varanasi, 1964, p. 64.

9 to mean that the subtle body consists of seventeen and one element, i.e. eighteen elements. Vijñānabhikṣu rejects this interpretation in *Sāṅkhyapravacanabhāṣya.*[1]

The subtle body is of two kinds: (1) macrocosmic and microcosmic. The macrocosmic subtle body comes into existence at the beginning of creation.[2] It is an aggregate of the microcosmic subtle bodies. It is the manifestor of self as fuel is considered to be that of fire.[3] It becomes many by giving birth to microcosmic (individual) *sūkṣmaśarīras* or *liṅga-śarīras* in the same way as father's subtle body brings forth those of sons and daughters.[4] The reason why different individual subtle bodies issue forth from the one macrocosmic *liṅga-śarīra* is that the individual selves have to undergo different experiences determined by the actions performed by them individually.[5] It means that the *liṅga-śarīra* is the actual locus where good and bad deeds are fruitioned.

The macrocosmic subtle and gross bodies are known as Hiraṇyagarbha and Virāj respectively. It is the macrocosmic gross body, i.e. Virāj, which created the four-headed self-born Brahmā and through him all other individual gross bodies.[6]

What is worth mentioning in this context is that Vijñānabhikṣu admits the existence of three bodies: (1) *Liṅga-śarīra,* (2) *Adhiṣṭhāna-śarīra,* and (3) *Sthūla-śarīra.* It is the *adhiṣṭhāna-śarīra* which requires some explanation. He explains it saying that just as a shadow or a picture does not exist without the support, the *liṅga-śarīra* similarly cannot exist without its vehicle which is the *adhiṣṭhāna-śarīra* with the

---

1. वक्ष्यमाणप्रमाणादेतान्येव सप्तदशलिङ्गं मन्तव्यं न तु सप्तदशमेकं चेत्यष्टादशतया व्याख्येयम् । *Op. cit.,* p. 126.
2. सूक्ष्मशरीरमप्याधाराधेयभावेन द्विविधं भवति । तत्र सप्तदश मिलित्वा लिङ्गशरीरं, तच्च सर्गादौ समष्टिरूपमेकमेव भवतीत्यर्थः । *SPB* (under *sūtra* III-9), p. 125 and also *SS,* p. 15.
3. वह्नेरिन्धनवदात्मनोऽभिव्यक्तिस्थानत्वात् । *SS,* p. 15.
4. यद्यपि सर्गादौ हिरण्यगर्भोपाधिरूपमेकमेव लिङ्गं तथापि तस्य पश्चात् व्यक्तिभेदो व्यक्तिरूपेणांशतो नानात्वम् भवति पुत्रकन्यादिलिङ्गदेहरूपेण । *SPB* (under *sūtra* III-10), p. 127. And also *SS,* p. 15.
5. व्यक्तिभेदः कर्मविशेषात् । *Sāṅkhyasūtra,* III-10. And also जीवान्तराणां भोगहेतुकर्मादेरित्यर्थः । *SPB* on this *sūtra.*
6. Compare—स नारायणो विराट् शरीरी स्वनाभिकमलकर्णिकास्थानीयस्य सुमेरोरुपरि चतुर्मुखाख्यस्वयंभुवं सृष्ट्वा तद्द्वारा अन्यानपि व्यष्टिशरीरिणः ससर्ज । *SS,* pp. 16-17.

help of which it migrates to other regions.[1] The third body is the manifest physical body.

Contrary to the Advaitic philosophy and in consonance with Sāṅkhya and Nyāya, Vijñānabhikṣu subscribes to the view that the gross body does not have all the five elemental substances as its material cause since substances which are different in genus cannot become the material cause of a single product. So far as products such as pots and cloth, etc. are concerned, they have clay and thread, etc. as their material causes respectively and these material causes individually do not have different genera. How, then, can the different substances having different universals be the material cause of a single product such as this physical body? So far as the convention of regarding it as made up of elements is concerned, it may be said that though the body is mainly composed of earth yet all other four substances have been helpful in its emergence and that as such it may be said to have been composed of five elemental substances.[2]

The description of the evolutionary and cosmological process of creation bears significance in that it helps cultivate the capacity to reflect so that the self may be discriminated from what is not self. In preliminary reflection one clearly distinguishes oneself as one's body from other bodies, things, etc., that, e.g., one is not Mohan, book, etc. At the second stage of reflection one succeeds in distinguishing oneself as the inner self, as the mental body (*sūkṣma-śarīra* or subtle body) from one's own physical body. At this level the physical body appears to be other than the internal self. But at this stage also the self still remains identified (confused) with the complex of seventeen *tattvas.*

The gross physical body may be said to lapse when it stands distinguished from the subtle body. "In the regressive process of dissolution (pratisañcara) manas indeed lapses into ahaṃkāra and this into buddhi."[3] K.C. Bhattacharyya further adds that so long as *buddhi* does not tend to lapse, the mental body stands represented

---

1. तल्लिङ्गशरीरं तदृतेऽधिष्ठानं विना स्वातन्त्र्यान्न तिष्ठति । यथा छाया निराधारा न तिष्ठति यथा वा चित्रमित्यर्थः। तथा च स्थूलदेहं त्यक्त्वा लोकान्तरगमनाय लिङ्गदेहस्याधारभूतं शरीरान्तरं सिध्यतीति भावः । *SPB* (under *sūtra* III-12), p. 128. Cf. also *SK*, 41.
2. बहूनां भिन्नजातीयानां चोपादानत्वं घटपटादिस्थले न दृष्टमिति सजातीयमेवोपादानम् । इतरच्च भूतचतुष्टयमुपष्टम्भकमित्याशयेन पाञ्चभौतिकव्यवहारः । *SPB* (under *sūtra* V-102), pp. 205-06.
3. *SP*, p. 157.

in *buddhi.* It means that all the three *karaṇas—buddhi, ahaṃkāra* and *manas* stand or lapse together. In other words, the mental body stands or lapses as a whole.[1]

It is quite obvious that the gross body (*sthūla-śarīra*) is only mediately identified with the self. Even the lower factors of the mental body cannot be said to be identified with the self mediately through the identification of the higher factors[2] with the self, since in reflection the physical body does not appear conscious. The mental body on the other hand appears conscious even though consciousness is not one of its characteristics. It only appears so on account of *aviveka.* In other words, it may be said that consciousness is an undistinguished associate of the mental body. The discontinuity of the mental body with the gross is a felt phenomenon. Such discontinuity, however, does not exist among the constituents of the mental body. Each factor appears conscious and none appears as unconscious to any other in the way the material body appears to the mental body, "The knowing mind is aware of the willing mind (ahaṃkāra) not as an object but as subjective or conscious like itself, and so, too, is the willing mind aware of the sentient mind. Mind as a whole to viveka, but below the stage of viveka, every factor of the mind appears endowed with the I-form and never as mere object relatively to any other factor."[3]

Discrimination or *viveka* is a mental function which appears conscious and does not imply an immediate lapse of the mental body into the unmanifest *prakṛti.* When the knowledge of the lapse of *buddhi* into *prakṛti* dawns, it brings *aviveka* to end and ushers in the state of liberation which is nothing but detachment of both the mental and material bodies from the self in knowledge. It means that the self that has attained *viveka* no longer subjectively confuses itself with the body which still mysteriously remains undistinguished from the self.[4]

The state of *vivekakhyāti,* that is, recognition by the self that it is other than *prakṛti* and more so than its evolutes, frees the self from bondage which was brought about by *aviveka.* But Vijñānabhikṣu says that this liberation is of the lesser kind. The nature of this liberation and that of the higher one will be discussed in greater detail in the sixth chapter: Doctrine of Bondage and Liberation.

1. *Loc. cit.*
2. *Loc. cit.*
3. *Loc. cit.*
4. *Loc. cit.*

5

THEORY OF DOUBLE REFLECTION

I

The act of knowing presupposes the existence of a self and its being related to the act in a manner that its agency may be attributed to the self. The systems of Sāṅkhya, Yoga and Vedānta hold this relationship between the self and the act to be unreal (whether the former is unified with the reflection of modes of the mind (*buddhivṛttis*) in the self or the real modes are unified with the reflection of the self in the mind). The self appears to be in bondage on account of the image of the modes in the former case while it is the modes which seem to enter into relationship with the image of the self in the latter case. To talk of bondage or freedom of the image of the self does not carry conviction though it looks reasonable when the states of freedom and bondage are referred to the real self, notwithstanding the nature of this relationship. It is the emphasis on the falsehood of this relationship between *buddhivṛttis* and the self which is responsible for the emergence of both the views mentioned above. Vijñānabhikṣu advocates the first view known as the double reflection theory. This theory has been referred to approvingly by J.N. Sinha[1] and supported by K.C. Bhattacharyya[2]—though with amendments to be discussed at the end of this chapter. It would be preferable first to discuss Vācaspati Miśra who holds the second view so that Vijñānabhikṣu's theory may be presented and understood better in contrast.

Vācaspati, in his commentary on *Sāṅkhyakārikā*, *Tattvakaumudī*,

1. *IPP*, p. 125.
2. *SP*, pp. 190-91.

says, "The self on the other hand is conscious and admits of no contact with knowledge, pleasure, etc. That self, having been reflected in the mind (*buddhi*) and identified with it, appears to possess knowledge, pleasure, etc. which actually subsist in the mind."[1] He means thereby that it is the reflection of self in the mind which appears to experience pleasure, pain, etc. while in fact they are modes of the mind only. This can be illustrated through an example. The image of the moon in water appears to take on the characteristics of water. If there is a movement in the water on account of a draft of air, the image of the moon also appears to be moving and if there is red colour in the water, red appears the moon. In the same manner, the self appears to take on the characteristics of the mind in which it has been reflected. It is only due to the real modes of the mind that the self seems to feel serene, sad and indolent.[2] In other words, Vācaspati holds that the agency of experience belongs to the reflected self—which implies that admitting the real modes being reflected in the self would become cumbersome. This is what is traditionally known as the theory of single reflection.

Bālarāma Udāsīna, supporting Vācaspati, clarifies that, though the reflection in a medium does seem to take on its characteristics, the original is not affected thereby. Similarly the self is reflected in the mind which is created out of the *sattva* portion of *prakṛti* and the reflection of the self takes on the modes of the mind while the original self remains unaffected. It is, therefore, unwarranted to hold that the modes are reflected back in the self. Knowership, in the single reflection theory, is held to be belonging to the reflected self because its imputation on the real self would incur its transmutation and the presence of contact in it; these are denied by the scriptures.[3]

The law of parsimony also favours the view of single reflection as the acts of perception, knowledge, etc. can be explained adequately

---

1. पुरुषस्तु सुखाद्यननुषङ्गी चेतनः, सोऽयं बुद्धितत्त्ववर्तिना ज्ञानसुखादिना तत्प्रतिबिम्बतस्तच्छायापत्त्या ज्ञानसुखादिमानिव भवतीति । *STK* on *Kārikā* 5.
2. शान्तघोरमूढरूपाया बुद्धेश्चैतन्यबिम्बोद्ग्राहेण चैतन्यस्य शान्ताद्याकाराध्यारोपः चन्द्रमस इव स्वच्छसलिलप्रतिबिम्बितस्य तत्कम्पनात्कम्पनारोपः । *TV* in *SYD*, p. 351. See also *ibid.*, pp. 432-35.
3. पूर्वोक्तयुक्त्युपेतवाक्यजातेभ्यो बुद्धितत्त्वप्रतिबिम्बितस्य पुंसः कथञ्चित् प्रमातृत्वेऽपि शुद्धस्य प्रमातृत्वायोगाद् 'ध्यायतीव लेलायतीव' इत्यादिश्रुतिष्वौपाधिकप्रमातृत्वादिश्रवणाच्च, 'असङ्गो ह्ययं पुरुष' इत्यत्रासङ्गत्वाम्नानाच्च । *VT*, p. 53.

with the help of this theory. In the Sāṅkhya Philosophy the effect in a sense is identical with the cause. In this case the reflecting of the self is the effect of the original self. Therefore, the acts of perception, knowledge, etc. which appear to belong to the reflection can also be taken to belong to the original self. This being the case, it may fairly be assumed that the view that experience belongs to the reflection of the self is not an altogether new and unjustified formulation within the scope of the philosophies of Sāṅkhya, Yoga and Vedānta, while the view of the modes of the mind being reflected in the real self is without any precedent.[1]

In Sāṅkhya and Yoga, the self is held to be devoid of any contact or qualifications. It means that it does not possess perceptibility which is an essential condition of a medium. The self, being devoid of perceptibility, cannot become the medium for the reverse reflection of the mental modes—which is the view held by Vijñānabhikṣu. In case, the self is taken to be a medium, it would cease to be devoid of contact and decay. And this, says the opponent, would contradict the Smṛtis.[2] The objection of the supporters of the theory of double reflection, viz., that the existence of self cannot be proved unless it is admitted that it perceives and experiences, is countered by Bālarāma Udāsīna on the ground that this role can be conferred on the reflected self. The existence of self may further be proved by taking recourse to *arthāpatti* : The reflection of the self can't take place in the mind unless there is the original self.[3] Moreover, the act of witnessing whatever happens in the mind also proves that the self exists.

Bālarāma Udāsīna has also refuted Vijñānabhikṣu's view that, if experience, perception, etc. do not belong to the self but to the reflection thereof, as Vācaspati holds, it would entail abandoning the proper meaning of the word *'pauruṣeya'* in *pauruṣeyabodha.* He asserts that its meaning should be either 'ownership of the self' or 'simply subsisting in the self' instead of 'really subsisting in the

---

1. *VK*, p. 183.
2. ज्ञानं नैवात्मनो धर्मो न गुणो वा कथञ्चन ।
ज्ञानस्वरूप एवात्मा नित्यः सर्वगतः शिवः ।। *SPr*, XI.25.
3. यच्चोक्तं – बुद्धेरेव प्रमातृत्वे पुरुषो न सिद्ध्येद् इति, तदति फल्गु, न वयं केवलं बुद्धितत्त्वं प्रमातृ इत्याचक्ष्महे येनैवमुपालभ्येमहि किन्तु 'उपरागात् कर्तृत्वं चित्सान्निध्याद्' इति साङ्ख्यसूत्राद् उपसङ्क्रान्तचिति प्रतिबिम्बमेव तत्प्रमातृ इति ब्रूमहे तथा च प्रतिबिम्बत्वान्यथानुपपत्त्या साक्षितया च पुरुषसिद्धेः कथंकारमुपालभ्येमहि इत्यलं बहुना । *VT*, p. 53.

self' which Vijñānabhikṣu has suggested. Both the meanings, ownership and subsistence, can be either real or superimposed. It does not lie within the denotative power of the word *'pauruṣeya'* to distinguish between one meaning and the other. Consequently adherence to the view that experience belongs to the reflected self does not incur relinquishing the accepted lexical and grammatical connotation of the word '*pauruṣeya*' in *pauruṣeyabodha.*[1] Though it is not proper to attribute real activity to the reflection of something inanimate, yet there is no incongruity if a reflection of the conscious self is said to be performing a real activity.[2] The original and its reflection are clearly different. The experiencership superimposed on the reflected self stands justified by virtue of this distinction.

Bālarāma Udāsīna also disputes the claim of Vijñānabhikṣu that his view of mutual reflection is based on a statement to this effect from *Yogavāsiṣṭha.*[3] He says that the latter interprets the above-statement to suit his theory of double reflection. This interpretation seems based on sheer speculation. Why can't '*cid-darpaṇa*' mean 'the mirror of the reflection of self in the mind' as against 'the mirror of the self' as contended by Vijñānabhikṣu. The self which is reflected in the mind appears to be identical with it and the modes of the mind, therefore, get reflected in it.[4] Due to ignorance, the self seems to undergo the experience of pleasure, pain, indolence, etc. The possibility of such an interpretation being there, the theory of double reflection is doomed to remain without foundation.

Bālarāma Udāsīna also points out a contradiction in Vijñānabhikṣu's *Yogavārttika* on *Yogasūtra* II-20. The latter, according to Bālarāma, says that the agency of seeing is unreal because of the superimposed activity on the reflection whereas the self has a real status as witness. Thus Vijñānabhikṣu is in conflict with himself

---

1. न हि पारमार्थिकत्वघटितमेव पुरुषनिष्ठत्वं यथाश्रुत: पौरुषेयशब्दार्थ: किं तर्हि पुरुषस्वत्वं पुरुषनिष्ठत्वं वा, तच्च पारमार्थिकं वौपचारिकं वेति नाग्रह:, प्रकृते च मुख्यस्यासम्भवादौपचारिकं तन्निष्ठत्वमाश्रीयतेऽतो न यथाश्रुतार्थत्यागापत्ति: । *VT*, p. 62.
2. जडप्रतिबिम्बस्यार्थक्रियाकारित्वाभावेऽपि चेतनप्रतिबिम्बस्यार्थक्रियाकारित्वसम्भवात् । *Ibid.*, p. 62.
3. तस्मिंश्चिद्दर्पणे स्फारे समस्ता वस्तुदृष्टय: ।
   इमास्ता: प्रतिबिम्बन्ति सरसीव तटद्रुमा: ।। *YVS, Upaśama,* XCI-113.
4. यास्तु 'तस्मिंश्चिद्दर्पणे. . . .' इत्यादिस्मृतयस्ता अपि सूत्राद्यानुगुण्येन बुद्धिदर्पणप्रतिबिम्बितत्वेन तत्तादात्म्यापन्ने दर्पणवत् स्वच्छे चेतने इमा वस्तुदृष्टय: बुद्धेर्धर्मभूतानि ज्ञानानि अविवेकात् प्रतिभासन्ते इत्येवमर्थपरतया नेया: । *VT*, p. 62.

when at one place he conjures up the superimposed agency of seeing and at another he holds that self's being witness is real. His point of view, therefore, merits rejection.[1]

It is generally seen that the fruition to be brought about by some action manifests itself at the site of the causal action. This co-existence of the result and the action can only be accounted for satisfactorily with the help of the view of single reflection of the self in the mind, according to which the resultant cognition and the corresponding mode of the mind co-exist as the action and its fruition take place in the same locus, i.e. mind; the mind is modalized into the form of an object and the resultant cognition also gets effected in the mind where the self is present in the form of its own reflection.[2]

Vijñānabhikṣu himself points out one more objection to his theory of double reflection saying that the mistaken identity between the self and the mind which obtains in experiences such as 'I know, I am happy' can be explained in the same manner as the illusory oneness between the two trees at a distance because of some defect in the eyes. Moreover, the objects can be cognized through self's contact with the modes of the mind just as the pitcher full of water, etc. becomes manifest on account of its contact with the rays of the sun. It is, therefore, no use admitting the reflection of the modes of the mind in the self and vice versa to explain the phenomenon of experience and knowing, and the illusory identity between the self and the mind.[3]

II

The problem of the agency of experience, which has been discussed

---

1. अपि च 'आरोपितक्रियया कल्पितं दर्शनकर्तृत्वं वस्तुतस्तु बुद्धेः साक्ष्येव पुरुष' इति स्वोक्त्या सह विरोधादश्रद्धेयं पुरुषस्य मुख्यप्रमाश्रयत्वेन प्रमातृत्वाभिधानम् । *VT*, p. 62.
2. *VK*, p. 185. See also— कश्चित्तु बुद्धिगतया चिच्छायया बुद्धेरेव सर्वार्थज्ञातृत्वमिच्छादिभिर्ज्ञानस्य सामानाधिकरण्यानुभवादन्यस्य ज्ञानेनान्यस्य प्रवृत्त्यनौचित्याच्चेत्याह । तदात्माज्ञानमूलकत्वादुपेक्षणीयम् । एवं हि बुद्धेरेव ज्ञातृत्वे चिदवसानो भोग इत्यागामिसूत्रद्वयविरोधः । पुरुषे प्रमाणाभावश्च पुरुषलिङ्गस्य भोगस्य बुद्धावेव स्वीकारात् । *SPB* (under *sūtra* I-99), pp. 63-64.
3. ननु सविषयवृत्तेः स्फुरणं चेतनसंयोगादेव भवतु यथा सजलघटादिप्रकाशः सूर्यसम्बन्धात् । अतः किमर्थं चैतन्ये वृत्तिप्रतिबिम्बं वृत्तौ वा वक्ष्यमाणचैतन्यप्रतिबिम्बं कल्प्यते । सुख्यहं जानामीति बुद्धिपुरुषयोरेकताभ्रमस्तु परस्परं प्रतिबिम्बं विनाऽपि दूरस्थवनस्पत्योरिव दोषवशादेव सम्भवति । *YV* in *SYD*, p. 21.

above in the light of *STK* and *VT*, provides the pivot around which Vijñānabhikṣu weaves his theory of double reflection. He holds that not only is the self reflected in the mind but the modes of the mind, which take shape when the inner senses through outer senses come in contact with the objects of experience, also are reflected in the self. The latter reflection phenomenalizes the self and seems to confer experiencership on it. However, if we accept, as Vācaspati Miśra holds, only the reflection of the self in the mind, which takes on the characteristics of the modes of the mind and hence also the agency of experience the following problems would crop up:

The phenomenon of bondage and liberation becomes redundant as it belongs to the reflection of self and not to the real self. There is no meaning in bondage and liberation of the reflection; it also points out the worthlessness of efforts which man is exhorted to put in in order to attain liberation. The reflection neither is nor can conceivably be substantial. It, therefore, cannot assume the agency of any real activity. In case it is given such status, the assumption of the original self would be rendered meaningless.[1]

Bālarāma Udāsīna has criticized Vijñānabhikṣu's view that the agency of experience cannot be attributed to the reflection of self as it lacks substantiality.[2] In other words, he says that the reflection of self can be assumed to be doing a real activity,[3] though the reflection of an inanimate object does not possess such a capacity. This criticism by Bālarāma Udāsīna seems to be untenable, as there is no basic difference between the reflection of an object and that of the conscious self. This can be elucidated by taking an instance from daily life. When I stand before a mirror with a white ball in my hand, both I and the ball would appear red if the surface of the mirror is smeared with red colour. If the mirror is moved, both I and the ball would seem to be moving. In taking on the characteristics of the medium of reflection, there does not lie any difference whether the original is conscious or not. It is not in the reflection that we have to

1. यत् तु कश्चिदविवेकी वदति, बुद्धिप्रतिबिम्बितपुरुषस्य कर्मेति, तन्न, योगभाष्येऽस्मदुक्तप्रकारस्यैवोक्तत्वेनान्यप्रकारस्याप्रामाणिकत्वात्, प्रतिबिम्बस्यावस्तुत्वेन कर्माद्यसंभवाच्च । अन्यथा प्रतिबिम्बस्य कर्मतद्भोगाङ्गीकारे बिम्बत्वाभिमतपुरुषकल्पनावैयर्थ्यस्य पूर्वं प्रतिपादितत्वात् । *SPB* (under *sūtra* II-46), p. 120.

2. प्रतिबिम्बस्य तुच्छतया अर्थभानरूपत्वानुपपत्तेश्च, प्रतिबिम्बस्य प्रकाशाद्यर्थक्रियाकारिताया क्वाप्यदर्शनाच्च । *YV* in *SYD*, p. 30.

3. जडप्रतिबिम्बस्यार्थक्रियाकारित्वाभावेऽपि चेतनप्रतिबिम्बस्यार्थक्रियाकारित्वसंभवात् । *VT*, p. 62.

grope for substantiality but in the original, as it is the latter which matters and not the reflection. A reflection qua reflection, is unsubstantial of whatever it may be. That is why Bālarāma Udāsīna's refutation of Vijñānabhikṣu's view of the worthlessness of human endeavour for liberation, if the agency belongs to the reflection, does not hold good.

The self is considered to be motionless, neutral, etc. Such nature of the self can be consistently maintained only by attributing agency to the reflected self. This is the view held by Vācaspati Miśra and his supporters. Vijñānabhikṣu on the other hand maintains that the motionless and neutral nature of the self does not present any contingency of change if the reflection of the modes of the mind in the self is accepted. We know that if a China rose is lying near a crystal, the crystal would look red without undergoing any substantial change. In the same manner the reflection of the modes in the self does not and can't bring about any substantial change in it. Likewise, the self may appear to be perceiving, experiencing, etc. without undergoing any basic change in its nature.

The invocation of the law of parsimony in support of the theory of single reflection is equally unconvincing. Admitting the relation of cause and effect, which is one of identity, between the reflection and its original and consequently superimposing agency on the original do not sound rational, as the original remains absolutely unaffected by whatever happens to the reflection on account of its medium. The phenomenon of some action accruing to the reflection has its origin either in the medium or in the original. It is the original conscious self which may appear affected by the characteristics of the medium when the reflection, in any form, is carried to it. If it stops at the reflection level, it is of no significance. I may mistake myself or the ball to be red only when the apparent redness is reflected back on to the retina of my eyes. The law of parsimony does not stand refuted if the fact demands that the reflection of the modes in the self is essential to satisfactorily account for the epistemological phenomena. Moreover, the theory of double reflection does absolve itself of the charge of being without a precedent, when it finds itself based on a scriptural evidence from *Yogavāsiṣṭha.*[1] If

1. तस्मिंश्चिद्दर्पणे स्फारे समस्ता वस्तुदृष्टयः ।
इमास्ताः प्रतिबिम्बन्ति सरसीव तटद्रुमाः ।। *YVS*, Upaśama, XCI-113.

'*ciddarpaṇa*' is taken to mean 'the mirror of consciousness' instead of 'the mirror of the reflection of consciousness in the mind', Vijñānabhikṣu's interpretation, supported by Ānandabodhendra Sarasvatī,[1] seems to be quite in order. On the other hand, the interpretation offered by Bālarāma Udāsīna looks not only laboured but is also insignificant. When translated, according to Vijñānabhikṣu, the couplet would read: 'Just as the trees on the bank are reflected in the lake so also are reflected in the clear mirror of the conscious self all the mental modes of the form of objects.' Since this reflection in the self does not affect its basic nature, neither would the scriptural statements concerning the nature of self be contradicted, nor would the purity and neutrality of self be in jeopardy, as Bālarāma Udāsīna fears.[2]

Another possible objection implicit in Bālarāma Udāsīna's criticism of Vijñānabhikṣu's double reflection theory can be formulated and put forward like this. Both the single and double reflection theories admit that the self is reflected in the mind (*buddhi*) and that the latter, being a medium of reflection, is perceptible to the former. In case mental modes are also assumed to be reflected in the self, Bālarāma Udāsīna would point out, then the property of perceptibility will have to be accepted as residing in the self since for that matter both, mind and self, are the mediums of reflection. As a consequence the self will have to lose its nature of being propertyless. Vijñānabhikṣu would meet the objection in the following manner. It is indeed necessary to admit that the self becomes an object of experience to account for the prevailing usage in scriptures. It is his considered opinion that nothing becomes an object of usage until and unless it has been experienced at some stage or the other.[3] The self, too, is perceived at a stage of very deep reflection but it is perceived in the form of its own reflection. And it is everybody's experience that reflection as such does not bring about any substantial change in the medium, i.e. self. As a consequence the self would not have to relinquish its nature of propertylessness.

Vijñānabhikṣu maintains that the process of the emergence of the knowledge of Brahman or self does not differ from that concerning

---

1. *VMTP* on the above.
2. *VT*, p. 53.
3. अपि च वेदनस्य सर्वव्यवहारकारणतया वेद्यत्वाभावे व्यवहारासंभवात् । *VAB*, p. 43.

external objects.[1] Consequently he differs substantially with the Advaitins on the emergence of the mode 'I am Brahman' which he describes thus. After the *tamas* of the mind has been purged either by the study of scriptures or by the capacity acquired through the practice of Yoga, the mind is modalized in the form of Brahman which is of the form 'I am Brahman'. This is what he calls a valid means of knowledge which is reflected in the self. The resultant knowledge resting in the self in the form of reflection is known as the knowledge of Brahman or soul. He, however, points out that this mode differs from that of the external objects, only in one respect. The former does away with egoity (*abhimāna*) while the latter does not invariably annihilate it. What he wants to emphasize here is that knowability which belongs to both external and internal objects consists in being pervaded by the mental mode reflected in the self.[2]

This view is said to be suffering from the subject-object-contradiction. To meet this charge, he says that the sun is an illuminator and becomes an object of illumination in the form of its own reflection.[3] So far as the illumination of reflection is concerned, it should be attributed to the rays of the sun and not to the reflection itself.[4] The eye does not see itself as such but it does see itself when reflected in a mirror. So by admitting a distinction in the mode of perception of the self from that of the object, Vijñānabhikṣu has brought about resolution of the problem of subject-object-contradiction. The non-acceptance of such a view would entail the meaninglessness of scriptural utterances.[5] It is in this context that the criticism of the

---

1. या चेयं ज्ञानोत्पत्तिप्रक्रिया बहिर्विषयेष्ववधारिता एषैवात्मन्यपि प्रत्येतव्या । *VAB*, p. 41.
2. तथाहि, शास्त्रादिना, योगधर्मेण वा बुद्धेस्तमोऽभिभवे सति निर्मलायां बुद्धौ आत्माकारा वृत्तिर्जायते 'अहं ब्रह्मास्मि' इत्यादिरूपा । सा प्रमाणम् । सा वृत्तिर्जायमानेव चेतने प्रतिबिम्बिता सती भासते । तदेतत्पुरुषनिष्ठं फलमात्मज्ञानमुच्यते । घटादिज्ञानाच्चात्मज्ञानस्यायं विशेषो यदात्मतत्त्वाकारवृत्त्या अभिमानो निवर्त्यते, घटाद्याकारबुद्धिवृत्तिभिस्तु मिथ्याज्ञानं न नियमेन निवर्त्यत इति । चेतनप्रतिबिम्बितबुद्धिवृत्तिव्याप्यत्वमेव बाह्याभ्यन्तरसाधारणं ज्ञेयत्वं बोध्यम् । *Ibid.*, p. 41.
3. सूर्यो बिम्बरूपेण प्रकाशकः प्रतिबिम्बरूपेण च प्रकाश्यः इति न कर्मकर्तृविरोधः । *Ibid.*, p. 42.
4. यश्चसर्यादिप्रतिबिम्बेऽपि प्रकाशो दृश्यते स किरणोपाधिकः । *Ibid.*, p. 40.
5. मनसैवानुद्रष्टव्यम् । *BṛhadUp*, 4-4-19.
   आत्मा वा अरे द्रष्टव्यः श्रोतव्यो मन्तव्यो निदिध्यासितव्यो मैत्रेयि आत्मनि खल्वरे दृष्टे श्रुते मते विज्ञात इदं सर्वं विज्ञातं भवति । *Ibid.*, 4-5-6.
   दृश्यते त्वग्र्यया बुद्ध्या सूक्ष्मया सूक्ष्मदर्शिभिः । *KUp*, 3-12.

Advaitins' view of self-luminosity by Vijñānabhikṣu comes in. According to him, the meaning of self-luminosity cannot be derived, as indeed the Advaitins seek to do, from the word *sva-prakāśa*, even when it is understood from the point of view of grammar. The grammatically proper connotation would be 'that which is capable of being known by itself'.[1] As a consequence, Citsukha's definition of *svaprakāśa* that that, being unknowable, can become an object of immediate intuition as found in the scriptures, cannot be accepted.[2] Notwithstanding the rejection of the concept of *svaprakāśa* of the Advaitins, he subscribes to the view that the self being self-luminous —not knowable with the aid of any other light except its own—does admit of knowability.[3]

The scriptural utterances showing inaccessibility of Brahman[4] can be interpreted thus: Brahman is not accessible to persons of ordinary perception, but It can surely be experienced by those who have attained absolute purity of mind through sustained yogic meditation. The resolution of subject-object-contradiction also sets Vijñānabhikṣu against the Advaitins holding the view of partless and non-dual[5] Reality. On the contrary, he holds that Brahman is constituted by selves and *prakṛti* which being real cannot be sublated at the time of the final removal of ignorance.

The direct connotation of a term, if possible, is to be preferred to an indirect one. It shows that Bālarāma Udāsīna is not right in not agreeing with Vijñānabhikṣu on the import of *pauruṣeya*. So far as Pāṇini is concerned,[6] two direct meanings of *pauruṣeya* emerge: (1) existing in (the self), (2) belonging to (the self). These are acceptable only when the reflection of mental modes in the self is accepted. Accepting the direct connotation will lend plausibility to the relationship of 'ownership and owned' by providing acceptable meanings to the relata. The self is owner of the reflection of the mental

1. स्वप्रकाशशब्दस्यास्मिन्नर्थे यौगिकत्वमपि न संभवति, स्वज्ञेयत्वस्यैव योगतो लाभात् । *VAB*, p. 43.
2. अवेद्यत्वे सति अपरोक्षव्यवहारयोग्यतायास्तल्लक्षणत्वात् । *TP*, p. 16.
3. अज्ञेयत्वरूपं तावत्स्वप्रकाशत्वमस्माभिर्नाभ्युपगम्यते । *VAB*, p. 39.
4. यतो वाचो निवर्तन्ते अप्राप्य मनसा सह । *TaittUp*, 2-4.
   and ज्ञानप्रसादेन विशुद्धसत्त्वस्ततस्तु तं पश्यति निष्कलं ध्यायमान: । *MuUp*, 3-1-8.
5. नापि जीवब्रह्मणोरखण्डत्वं येन जीवस्य ब्रह्मज्ञाने कर्मकर्तृविरोध: स्यात् । *VAB*, p. 39.
6. तत्रभव: । Pāṇini, 4-3-53.
   तस्येदम् । Pāṇini, 4-3-120.

mode, which constitutes its *bhoga,* without compromising its basic nature, while its possession consists in possessing the subliminal impressions of the modes of the mind which, in the form of reflection, have been enjoyed by the self.[1] The phenomenon of emancipation in which total cessation of mental transformations results in ending the reflection in the self and thereby annihilating relationship, buttresses Vijñānabhikṣu's interpretation of the word *'pauruṣeya'*.[2]

The contradiction pointed out by Bālarāma Udāsīna in the statement of Vijñānabhikṣu is also not tenable if the instance given by the former is not torn away from the context,[3] as the latter has not indicated anywhere that seership is superimposed and witnesshood is real. Seen in the context, it becomes crystal clear that both seership and witnesshood are superimposed. The self appears to cognize the mind with its modes when they are reflected in it. The modalized mind is reflected in the self like an echo. The resultant sense is that the self directly witnesses the mind along with its transformations. Keeping this in view, we arrive at the conclusion that seership consists in the state of being the subject of seeing which is effected by the superimposed activity in the form of reflection. Vijñānabhikṣu has maintained uniformly that the mind undergoes real changes and projects them on to the self to confer on it illusory agency and thus keep it in bondage.

Vijñānabhikṣu[4] does not consider the principle of the result coexisting with the causal action in the same locus worth invoking to endorse the theory of single reflection, for the principle, when invoked, would give rise to several problems: (1) Giving up of the meaning of belonging to the self indicated by the word *'pauruṣeya'*, as the reflection of the self is insignificant. (2) Subject-object-contradiction remaining unresolved because it is the reflection of the self in the mind which can experience itself in the final stage of

---

1. स्वत्वं च स्वभुक्तवृत्तिवासनावत्त्वं । *SPB* (under *sūtra* I-19), p. 18.
2. बिम्बनिरोधे प्रतिबिम्बस्यापि निरोधादिति । *Ibid.* (under *sūtra* V-30), p. 229.
   See also—तथापि बिम्बरूपाणां विषयाणामेव प्रतिबिम्बरूपेणैव भानात् प्रतिबिम्बरूपतया चैतन्ये बाधेऽपि स्वतो बाधाभावादिति । *VAB*, p. 41.
3. संवेदिन्या बुद्धेः प्रतिसंवेदी पुरुषः संवेदनमर्थाकारवृत्तिः तस्याः प्रतिसंवेदनं प्रतिध्वनिवत् प्रतिबिम्बं यत्र स पुरुष इत्यर्थः, बुद्धेः साक्षीति तु पर्यवसितोऽर्थः, एतेन प्रतिबिम्बरूपयारोपितक्रियया कल्पितं दर्शनकर्तृत्वं द्रष्टृत्वमित्यपि सूचितम् । *YV* in *SYD*, p. 214.
4. *Ibid.*, p. 30.

samprajñāta samādhi. (3) Rendering untenable the concept of self, for the reflection of self in the mind, being a characteristic of the latter, can very well account for the phenomenon of experiencership. (4) Incurrence of the contradiction of scriptural and traditional texts, which, establishing mutual reflection, also associate the fruit of knowledge with the self conditioned by the reflection of the mental modes. In view of these consequences, the principle of co-existence need not be invoked and adhered to.

The genesis of the concept of dual reflection does not lie only in the refutation of the arguments advanced by the adherents of the opposite view of single reflection, but it also owes its formulation to the epistemological necessity which Vijñānabhikṣu has justified by adducing cogent arguments. The occurrence of dual reflection is caused by a particular conjunction between the self and the mind,[1] which takes place through the transformation in the form of predominance of *sattva* in the mind as it is not possible to admit instrumental causality in the self; it otherwise would be liable to transmutation.[2] Before going into the arguments which Vijñānabhikṣu buttresses to support his theory of double reflection, it seems necessary to become familiar with what he says about the process of knowledge.

After the *tamas* of the mind is removed by the senses coming in contact with objects like the dirt of clothes, the pure *sattva* of the mind takes on the form of objects through sense-contact just as a clean cloth takes on the form of *kusumbha* flower, i.e. takes on its colour, coming in contact with it. This state of the mind which has taken the form of objects is called *buddhivṛtti* (mode of the mind).[3] This mode of the mind is immediately followed by an experience of the self because the mode is the direct means of experience of the self as chariot becomes a means for the charioteer to reach the village.[4] The mode of the mind thus being generated is reflected in

---

1. अयमेव च संयोगविशेषो बुद्ध्यात्मनोरन्योऽन्यप्रतिबिम्बने हेतुः। *SPB* (under *sūtra* I-99), p. 63.
2. अयं च संयोगविशेषोऽन्तःकरणस्यैव सत्त्वोद्रेकरूपात् परिणामाद् भवतीति फलबलात्कल्प्यते, पुरुषस्यापरिणामित्वेन संयोगे तन्निमित्तकविशेषासम्भवादिति । *Ibid.*, p. 63.
3. विषयेन्द्रियसंयोगादिना वस्त्रमालिन्यस्येव बौद्धतमोद्रव्यस्यापसारणे सति यथा निर्मलवस्त्रे कुसुम्भसंयोगात्तु कुसुम्भाकारता भवति, तथैव निर्मले बुद्धिसत्त्वे विषयसंयोगाद् विषयाकारता भवति । सा बुद्ध्यवस्था विषयाकारा बुद्धिवृत्तिरित्युच्यते । *VAB*, p. 39.
4. वृत्तेश्च प्रमाणत्वमनुभवाख्यफलायोगव्यवच्छिन्नत्वात्, रथारूढस्य ग्रामसम्बन्धे रथस्येव चेतनस्य विषयसम्बन्धे द्वारत्वाच्च । *Ibid.*, p. 39.

the self. This reflected mode of the mind which is coloured by the object is manifested by the self, the seat of reflection, just as the cloth dyed in the *kusumbha*, which is reflected in the crystal wall, gets illuminated by the latter.[1] In this manner the modes of the mind along with their contents when reflected in the consciousness (self) are cognized by the self in exactly the same manner as the water superimposed on the rays of the sun in a desert is made illusorily manifest by them (rays).[2]

A serious anomaly of self's omniscience would arise if we do not accept this process of knowledge. The self, being omnipresent consciousness, would know all as it is in contact with everything just as the pitcher is not invisible when it is in the light of the sun.[3] But obviously it is not the case. If, to avoid this eventuality, ignorance is admitted in the self, a more undesirable situation would crop up, namely, that of accepting ignorance in the self which is of the nature of eternal knowledge. How can ignorance and eternal knowledge coexist? If on the other hand, double reflection is accepted, the anomaly would be easily removed, for the mental modes which are of intermittently delimiting nature can give rise to intermittent and delimited knowledge[4] when they are reflected in the self. Knowledge, according to Vijñānabhikṣu, consists in self's receiving the reflection of the modes of the mind which owe their emergence to the senses coming into contact with the objects. Thus the problem of self's omniscience which is removed so easily[5] otherwise becomes impervious to solution on the single reflection theory.

Though contact with the objects is common yet the eye can comprehend only their form to the exclusion of taste, etc. Similarly the self being in contact with each and everything receives only the reflection of the modes of its own mind, for the reception of objects

---

1. सा च वृत्तिर्जायमानैव चेतने प्रतिबिम्बिता भवति. . . .ततश्च स्वप्रतिबिम्बितां विषयोपरक्तां तां बुद्धिवृत्तिं स एव प्रतिबिम्बाधिष्ठानचेतनोऽवभासयति, यथा स्वप्रतिबिम्बितकुसुम्भरक्तवस्त्रं स्फटिकभित्तिः । *VAB*, p. 39.
2. तथा च चेतने प्रतिबिम्बनादेव बुद्धिवृत्तितद्विषययोर्भानं मरुमरीचिकाध्यस्तजलस्येव मरीचिना प्रकाशनमिति । *Ibid.*, p. 39.
3. अन्यथाकूटस्थनित्यविभुचैतन्यस्य सर्वसम्बन्धात् सदैव सर्वं वस्तु सर्वैर्ज्ञायेत, न हि सूर्यसम्बन्धे सति घटाद्यप्रकाशो दृष्ट इति । *YV* in *SYD*, p. 22. See also *VAB*, p. 40.
4. *YV* in *SYD*, p. 22.
5. अस्मदुक्तप्रकारे तु बुद्धिवृत्तेः कादाचित्कत्वेनाप्रतिबन्धात् विषयप्रतिबिम्बस्य कादाचिकत्वं परिच्छिन्नत्वं चोपपद्यते । *VAB*, p. 40.

in the self is possible only in the form of the form of objects; and this cannot be other than the reflection. The empirical modes, therefore, to the exclusion of everything else, are capable of being immediately reflected in the self. So, for the sake of the cognition of the modes in the form of objects, it is essential to accept their reflection in the self.[1]

Vijñānabhikṣu offers an additional textual evidence from *Sāṅkhyasūtra* and *Yogasūtra* in support of his theory as he holds that the logical arguments bereft of authentic textual proofs do not carry weight. When the self appears as experiencer, it must be the real self and not the self as reflected in the mind. *Sāṅkhyasūtras* I-104, I-143, I-161, II-35 and *Yogasūtra* 1-4[2] prove beyond doubt that agency is an apparent feature of the self, though this agency consists in the self's receiving the reflection of the mode of its mind, which also incidentally clarifies why one self does not know what happens in other minds. In case Vācaspati's view is accepted, the above-mentioned five aphorisms would have to be subjected to forced interpretation. In addition, we will have to resort to the indirect meanings of the terms which are otherwise amenable to smooth and rational interpretation in accordance with Vijñānabhikṣu's view. These five *sūtras* when interpreted in keeping with the theory of double reflection would read as follows:

1. Experience belongs to the self in the form of reflection and not to the reflection of self in the intellect. (In the latter case the phenomena of bondage and liberation would remain without significance.)
2. Since self is the experiencer of the mental modes when they are reflected in it, it is different from them (the mental modes).
3. The self is witness, which means that it directly perceives the mind along with its modes of the form of objects. It is possible only when it is held that the self receives their reflection

1. यथा च सन्निकर्षसाम्येऽपि चक्षू रूपमेव गृह्णाति न रसं तथैव सर्वसंयुक्तोऽप्यात्मा स्वबुद्धिवृत्तिमेव साक्षाद् गृह्णाति नेतरद् इति फलबलात् क्लृप्तम् । अर्थाकारतयैव चार्थग्रहणं, सा च कूटस्थे प्रतिबिम्बान्नान्यद्युक्ता । अतो बुद्धिवृत्तेरेव चेतने साक्षात्प्रतिबिम्बनसामर्थ्यं नेतरस्येति । तस्मादर्थोपरक्तवृत्तिस्फुरणार्थं चेतने तत्प्रतिबिम्बः सिध्यति । *VAB*, p. 40.
2. चिदवसानो भोगः, भोक्तृभावात्, साक्षात्सम्बन्धात् साक्षित्वम्, कुसुमवच्च मणिः, वृत्तिसारूप्यमितरत्र in the respective order.

without the interference of other instruments in the form of senses.

4. The self behaves in the manner of the crystal which becomes red in the proximity of a China flower. (Here the mental mode may be compared with China flower while the redness of the crystal with the reflection of modes in the self.)
5. The self has similarity with the mental modes. This similarity also consists in the self's receiving the reflection of the mind which has been modalized in the form of objects.

III

Besides, Vijñānabhikṣu has been accepted by K.C. Bhattacharyya so far as the reflection-aspect in the self is concerned. Vijñānabhikṣu says that the reflection of the mind with its modes occurs in the self, but K.C. Bhattacharyya seems to offer an amendment when he says that the dual function of the mind is reflected in the self in the following way. The dual function comprises both the reflecting and the manifesting aspects of the mind itself. While reflecting the object, the mind functions causally, for, during the process of reflection, it is modalized into a substantial *vṛtti* similar to the object. On the other hand while manifesting the object, the mind functions non-causally,[1] as it does not undergo any transformation as in the case of the substantial mode. The mental function of the latter kind is known as subjective function of *bhāva*, without which no object can become an object of knowledge.

The primordial non-discrimination caused a peculiar kind of relationship between the self and the mind, which relationship in turn was responsible for mutual reflection.[2] As a consequence of the reflection of self in the mind, the latter seems to appropriate the consciousness of the former.[3] This apparently conscious mode of the mind, as K.C. Bhattacharyya explains, has two functions—(1) *bhāva*, the non-causal and non-substantial function and (2) *vṛtti*, the substantially modalized form of the object. Accordingly, the mode of

1. *SP*, p. 191.
2. अयमेव च संयोगविशेषो बुद्ध्यात्मनोरन्योऽन्यप्रतिबिम्बने हेतुः । *SPB*, p. 63.
3. तस्मात्तत्संयोगादचेतनं चेतनावदिव लिङ्गम् । *SK*, 20, first half.

the mind (*vṛtti*), K.C. Bhattacharyya continues to assert, appears as self reflecting the object and *bhāva* as the self apprehending the object. These two functions are illusorily referred to the self. The self appears to take the reflection of the substantial mode of the mind which has taken the form of the object. The self also appears to be itself reflected in the subjective function of the mind which apprehends the objects, which means that the object, after shedding its unmanifestness assumes knownness.

Bhāva (subjective function) and *vṛtti* (substantial mode) remain undistinguished at the unreflective stage just as does the apparent unification of the self and the mind caused by the primordial non-discrimination, a function of *prakṛti*.[1] This non-distinction between the subject and object (mind) percolates to the physical level. An example may be given to elucidate it. Though the self appears to be unified with the mind and the body, yet during preliminary reflection the body stands distinguished from the mind still confused with the self. The mind appropriates subjectivity (a conscious function) on account of the reflection of the self in it just as the body does at the unreflective stage. A higher reflection, a deeper meditation, is essential to put an end to the confusion between the self and the mind. The emergence of *viveka* — a pure *bhāva* of *buddhi* — during *samprajñāta samādhi* makes short work of this confusion between the self and the mind, and the self is known as having been distinguished from the mind.

According to Vijñānabhikṣu in the highest stage of *samprajñāta samādhi* the reflection of self in the mind is taken to mean the substantial mode for self-knowledge, which has taken on the form of the self. This substantial mode is on a par with the real mode of the mind of the form of the object for object-knowledge. This presented *me* according to K.C. Bhattacharyya, explains self-knowledge in the scheme of Vijñānabhikṣu. It means that, if the self is known, it is known in the mental mode of the form of self. To clarify it, the substantial mode reflecting the self confers knownness (manifestness) on the self, when this mental mode is reflected in the self, just as the mental mode reflecting the object is reflected in the self in order that the reflected object may be known. That the reflection of self in *vṛtti* is a real mode of the mind has been singled out by K.C. Bhattacharyya to point out in Vijñānabhikṣu's theory of double reflection an

1. *SP*, p. 158.

inadequacy that the self will be known merely as *me* not as *I.*

It is this inadequacy of Vijñānabhikṣu's theory, which possibly has prompted K.C. Bhattacharyya to offer an amendment in the form of distinguishing a substantial function of the mind from its non-substantial, non-causal function known as *bhāva* or apprehension. He seems to hold that the object of knowledge is an evolute of *prakṛti* and the mind, therefore, is substantially modalized in the form of the object, but the self is not an evolute of *prakṛti* or of mind for that matter. The mind, therefore, does not undergo substantial transformation for the emergence of the knowledge of the self. K.C. Bhattacharyya here differs with Vijñānabhikṣu who holds that the reflection of self in *vṛtti* is a real mental mode while the former asserts that this reflection is an illusory embodiment of the self in the subjective state of mind, that is, in *buddhi-bhāva.* The necessity of assigning illusory character to the reflection of self in *buddhi-bhāva* arises because of the fact that the real Sāṅkhya view seems to be that the self is known as what mind is not[1] and that it is known in *viveka* (*bhāva*—the subjective knowing function of the mind), which implies a mental mode of the form 'I am I'. It seems that *bhāva* is a state of the mind superior to *vṛtti,* which appears to give rise to the former, the subjective function of the mind in which the self is known as what mind is not in the final stage of meditation. The emergence of the states—(1) *vṛtti* in which the self knows itself as illusorily embodied in the *buddhi-bhāva* and (2) *bhāva* in which the self knows itself as distinct from *buddhi,* what *buddhi* is not—takes place in the mind speeding on the path leading to its own dissolution. The state of *viveka* which severs the primordial confusion between the self and the mind constitutes both the referring function and the real mode being referred to. It seems to be the innate disposition of the mind to attain dissolution into the primordial *prakṛti* (*aliṅga*) after the *vṛtti* 'I am I' and its resultant *bhāva* 'I am distinct from *buddhi*' have been reflected in the self. This illusory reference of the dual function of the mind to the self looks like an improvement on the view of Vijñānabhikṣu that only the real mode of the mind of the form of the self is reflected back on to the self.

1. *SP,* p. 191.

6

DOCTRINE OF BONDAGE AND LIBERATION

I

The quest for absolute freedom from pain is as universal as the longing to live for infinity. Almost every Indian philosophical system, therefore, legitimately attempts to define the nature of the *summum bonum* along with its metaphysical principles, which when thoroughly comprehended and imbibed facilitate the seeker to pursue the highest good. The inculcation of conviction and faith which are consequent upon insight into the nature of the Ultimate Reality, is essential for him to overcome hindrances that are likely to be encountered in his pursuits to attain liberation. For this insight to take effect, it is necessary that the status of an individual self during the state of liberation, the nature of liberation and the means to it are discussed and understood at some length.

Vijñānabhikṣu presents a fairly elaborate account of ontology in his commentaries. To put his metaphysical views in a nutshell, he describes the Ultimate Reality as one integral whole in which the individual selves and *prakṛti* inhere inseparably as Its powers distinguishably during creation and indistinguishably, like sugar dissolved in milk, at the time of dissolution.[1] To put it differently, the nature of Brahman, according to him, is Integral Non-dualism (*avibhāgādvaita*). It differs from that of the Absolute as propounded by Śaṅkara in the following two respects:

(1) Vijñānabhikṣu does not include bliss (*ānanda*) into the

1. *VAB,* pp. 21, 51, 57, 58 and 59. And also compare his definition of the Locative Cause (*adhiṣṭhāna kāraṇa*). *Ibid.*, p. 50.

defining characteristics of the Absolute, and also of the individual self for that matter, and holds that only *sat* and *cit* constitute Its nature. Śaṅkara, on the other hand, adds *ānanda* also to the defining characteristics of the Absolute.

(2) Like Śaṅkara, he does not postulate that the Ultimate Reality is one undivided whole. This means that there is total identity between the Absolute and the individual self according to Śaṅkara, whereas Vijñānabhikṣu holds the view that the Absolute and the individual self are ontologically different despite their being inseparable all through.

This difference in their viewpoints regarding the ontological status of Brahman and that of *jīva* leads to the following conclusions which have bearing upon the subject-matter to be discussed in the following:

1. Given Vijñānabhikṣu's metaphysical position, it becomes quite clear that the individual self does not experience bliss, or, to be a little more correct, does not discover itself as bliss,[1] as Śaṅkara holds, after the cause of bondage, i.e. ignorance, has been annihilated.
2. The individual self attains permanent release from bondage as a consequence of discriminatory knowledge (*vivekakhyāti*) whereas according to Śaṅkara it is the knowledge of identity between the Absolute and the individual self which liberates the latter.
3. The individual selves and the Absolute being ontologically different and real, Vijñānabhikṣu does not have to postulate *māyā*, a logical pedant of the theory of the Absolute as non-dual, as it renders unreal the status of individual selves and the world.

II

Before we take up for discussion the nature of the cause of bondage, it would be of advantage to first mention those views which Vijñānabhikṣu summarily rejects for one reason or the other.

Vijñānabhikṣu says that time, space, conjunction, body, enjoined and prohibited actions, etc. cannot be the cause of bondage. If time

1. *VAB*, p. 34.

were taken to be the cause of bondage, the contingency of all the individual selves remaining in bondage eternally would be incurred as time, being eternal, all-pervasive and all-encompassing, would always continue to be in contact with all *puruṣas*, bound or released.[1] The views visualizing space and conjunction as the cause of bondage should be dismissed in the same manner.[2] The insentient body also cannot share the characteristic of being the cause of bondage. The body is a particular combination of the elements of *prakṛti* and if it is assumed to be the direct cause of bondage of someone other than itself, it will bring upon itself the inevitable consequence that the liberated selves still continue to be in bondage, since there is nothing which can remove this fault.[3] So far as the prescribed and prohibited actions are concerned, they too, being the property of the not-self, cannot be admitted to possess causality to avoid the incurrence of the same fault as has just been mentioned. If, for the avoidance of the fault, it is assumed that bondage be accepted as caused by the actions of respective adjuncts (*upādhis*), it would nonetheless incur bondage in the form of conjunction with pain even during dissolution,[4] as no such incidence of experience of pain, etc. at that time is mentioned in the scriptures though the adjuncts, then, do remain in existence without being active. Moreover, he says that it is not the actions which bind the individual self. If this were so, the plausibility of bondage and liberation would not be explained as the individual self is not supposed to witness the reflections of actions. In that case actions are not related to the self in any immediate manner, much less causing bondage of the latter.[5]

---

1. नापि कालसम्बन्धनिमित्तकः पुरुषस्य बन्धः कुतः, व्यापिनो नित्यस्य कालस्य सर्वावच्छेदेन सर्वदा मुक्तामुक्तसकलपुरुषसम्बन्धात् सर्वावच्छेदेन सदा सकलपुरुषाणां बन्धापत्तेः । *SPB* (under *sūtra* I-12), p. 14.
2. *Ibid.*, pp. 15 and 18.
3. संघातविशेषरूपताख्या देहरूपा याऽवस्था न तन्निमित्तोऽपि पुरुषस्य बन्धः, कुतः, तस्या अवस्थाया देहधर्मत्वात्, अचेतनधर्मत्वादित्यर्थः । अन्यधर्मस्य साक्षादन्यबन्धकत्वेऽतिप्रसङ्गात् मुक्तस्यापि बन्धापत्तेरित्यर्थः । *Ibid.* (under *sūtra* I-14), p. 15.
4. न हि विहितनिषिद्धकर्मणापि पुरुषस्य बन्धः, कर्मणामनात्मधर्मत्वात् । अन्यधर्मेण साक्षादन्यस्य बन्धे च मुक्तस्यापि बन्धापत्तेः । ननु स्वस्वोपाधिकर्मणा बन्धाङ्गीकारे नायं दोष इत्याशयेन हेत्वन्तरमाह अतिप्रसक्तेश्चेति । प्रलयादावपि दुःखयोगरूपबन्धापत्तेश्चेत्यर्थः । *Ibid.* (under *sūtra* I-16), p. 15.
5. कर्मादिभिर्बन्धाभ्युपगमे त्वेवं व्याख्या न घटते कर्मादीनां साक्षिभास्यत्वाभावेन साक्षात्पुरुषेष्वप्रतिबिम्बनात् । *Ibid.* (under *sūtra* I-58), p. 36.

Vijñānabhikṣu's own view about the cause of bondage is that it is non-discrimination which causes bondage by means of producing a conjunction between the individual self and the body, intellect, senses, etc.[1] It (non-discrimination) inheres in the intellect as a latent impression (*vāsanā*) before it brings forth the aforesaid conjunction,[2] which, in turn, leads to the incidence of individual self's experience of pain, pleasure, etc. He clarifies that non-discrimination is not of the nature of absence, as is indicated by the compound-form of the word *'a-viveka'* (*nañ-tatpuruṣa*). He proceeds to show that it is not appropriate to hold that ignorance is non-entity.[3] In that case, it, being unsubstantial, cannot bring about bondage, as the unsubstantial dream-rope is not seen to bind anybody. The Advaitic view that, in pursuance of the unsubstantial nature of ignorance, bondage may also be taken to be unreal does not seem acceptable to Vijñānabhikṣu. He explains that such an eventuality does not arise when *avidyā* is understood to be as real as the empirical objects. In any case, it lacks transcendental reality in the form of immutability and eternality. Thus ignorance or non-discrimination being empirically real can safely be assumed to be the cause of bondage, whereas on the Advaitic view the incidence of bondage cannot be satisfactorily accounted for.[4]

Unlike Advaita, Vijñānabhikṣu holds the view that non-discrimination is not the direct cause of bondage. There are two reasons for this. One, should non-discrimination be assumed to be causing bondage directly, it would incur the existence of bondage along with non-discrimination even at the time of dissolution, which lacks congruity. Two, even though non-discrimination in the case of the

---

1. तदेवं संयोगाख्यजन्मद्वारा बन्धाख्यहेयस्य मूलकारणमविवेक इति । *SPB* (under *sūtra* I-55), p. 33.
2. अस्मन्मते वासनारूपस्यैवाविवेकस्य संयोगजन्महेतुतया. . . .। *Ibid.* (under *sūtra* I-55), p. 32.
3. अत एव चाविद्या नाभावोऽपितु विद्याविरोधिज्ञानान्तरमिति । *Ibid.* (under *sūtra* I-55), p. 32. It may be mentioned here that Vijñānabhikṣu seldom distinguishes between *avidyā* and *aviveka*.
4. (i) अद्वैतवादिनां तेषामविद्याया अप्यवस्तुत्वेन तया बन्धानौचित्यात् । न हि स्वाप्नरज्ज्वा बन्धनं दृष्टमित्यर्थः । *Ibid.* (under *sūtra* I-20), p. 20.
   (ii) अनयैव रीत्या नवीनानामपि प्रच्छन्नबौद्धानां मायावादिनामविद्यामात्रस्य तुच्छस्य बन्धहेतुत्वं निराकृतं वेदितव्यम् । अस्मन्मते तु अविद्याया कूटस्थनित्यतारूपपरमार्थत्वाभावेऽपि घटादिवद् वास्तवत्वेन वक्ष्यमाणसंयोगद्वारा बन्धहेतुत्वे यथोक्तबाधानवकाशः । *Ibid.* (under *sūtra* I-22), p. 21.

emancipated person has been annihilated, he is seen to continue experiencing pain which, according to him, is nothing but bondage. There is inconstancy of co-presence (*anvaya-vyabhicāra*)* in the former case, as non-discrimination continues to exist, although its effect, experience of pain, does not exist at the time of dissolution. In the latter case, inconstancy of co-absence (*vyatireka-vyabhicāra*)* is entailed, as even after the destruction of non-discrimination, conjunction in the form of birth and consequent experience of the fruits of past actions still continue to remain in existence even during the liberated state of life. Vijñānabhikṣu says that this incurrence of inconstancy does not arise if non-discrimination is not assumed as the direct cause of bondage.[1] On the assumption that *aviveka* is not the direct cause of bondage, it may be maintained that though the cause of bondage through birth-conjunction has been removed, still the latter (the intermediary conjunction in the form of present life) does not come to an end as its immediate cause, the remaining *prārabdha*, has not yet been exhausted.

After establishing non-discrimination as the cause of bondage, Vijñānabhikṣu proceeds to define it as the cognition which embraces both *prakṛti* and *puruṣa* as its objects but which fails to comprehend the absence of contact between them.[2] He further adds that by non-discrimination is not meant the knowledge of identity between *puruṣa* and *prakṛti* since it does not exist earlier than their particular contact, but it may mean either antecedent non-existence of non-discrimination or its latent impression.[3] Vijñānabhikṣu prefers the latter connotation to the former as it will be made clear in the following that absence is not the nature of non-discrimination

---

* What Vijñānabhikṣu means is that both *anvaya-vyabhicāra* and *vyatireka-vyabhicāra* relate to necessary concomitance of direct cause and its effect. Either inconstancy is involved when either of the two (cause and effect) being present, the other remains absent or when either being absent, the other continues to be present.

1. अपि चाविद्याया: साक्षादेव दु:खाख्यबन्धहेतुत्वे ज्ञानेनाविद्याक्षयानन्तरं प्रारब्धभोगानुपपत्ति:, बन्धपर्यायदु:खभोगस्य कारणनाशादिति । अस्मदादिमते तु नायं दोष:, संयोगद्वारैवाविद्याकर्मादीनां बन्धहेतुत्वात् । जन्माख्यसंयोग: प्रारब्धसमाप्तिं विना न नश्यतीति । *SPB* (under *sūtra* I-24), p. 22. And also see अविवेकश्च संयोगद्वारैव बन्धकारणं प्रलये बन्धादर्शनात् । अविवेकनाशेऽपि जीवन्मुक्तस्य दु:खभोगदर्शनाच्च । अत: साक्षादविवेको बन्धकारणं प्राङ् नोक्त: । *Ibid.* (under *sūtra* I-55), p. 31.
2. अगृहीतासंसर्गकमुभयविषयज्ञानमविवेक: । *Ibid.* (under *sūtra* VI-12), p. 224.
3. नन्वविवेकोऽत्र न प्रकृतिपुरुषाभेदसाक्षात्कार: संयोगात्प्रागसत्त्वात् किन्तु विवेकप्रागभावोऽविवेकाख्यवासना वा । *Ibid.* (under *sūtra* I-55), p. 31.

and that it can very well exist in the form of a tendency even before the conjunction takes place. According to him it is a beginningless property of the intellect which continues to exist as a latent impression even at the time of dissolution. Were it not accepted as beginningless, two faults would result. One, even the liberated selves would become subject to bondage, if it were assumed as *cause sui.* Two, should this non-discrimination be understood to be generated by actions, etc., it would become necessary to look for another non-discrimination as it has been itself accepted as the cause of actions. Thus it would lead to the consequence of infinite regress.[1]

Elsewhere Vijñānabhikṣu has told explicitly that non-discrimination does not constitute conjunction. It cannot mean conjunction simply because the latter is accepted as produced by the former. Should the absence of discrimination in any case come to mean conjunction, it would entail the incidence of experience of pain, pleasure, etc. even during dissolution since there does exist the conjunction between *prakṛti* and *puruṣa* at that particular time also. And if one accepts the other view visualizing that conjunction consists in non-discrimination in the form of false knowledge, it would become liable to suffer from the fallacy of arguing in a circle (*ātmāśraya*) inasmuch as conjunction is the cause of this very false knowledge. This is why the word 'yoga' occurring in the scriptural statement '*ātmendriyamanoyuktam*'[2] should be taken to mean something more than merely non-discrimination, and that should be conjunction, since there is no reason for any other supposition.[3] And non-discrimination also cannot be taken to connote either bondage or liberation as it has already been established that the phenomenon of bondage and liberation owes its incidence to *aviveka.*[4]

---

1. स च प्रवाहरूपेणानादिश्चित्तधर्मः प्रलये वासनारूपेण तिष्ठति । अन्यथा तस्य सादित्वे दोषद्वयप्रसङ्गात् । सादित्वे हि स्वत एवोत्पादे मुक्तस्यापि बन्धापत्तिः । कर्मादिजन्यत्वे च कर्मादिकं प्रत्यपि कारणत्वेन अविवेकान्तरान्वेषणेऽनवस्थेत्यर्थः । *SPB* (under *sūtra* VI-12), p. 224.
2. *Kaṭhopaniṣad,* I-3-4, Vijñānabhikṣu has used the word 'yoga' in the sense of '*yuktam*' occurring in the citation.
3. किं च विवेकाभावरूपस्याविवेकस्य संयोगत्वे प्रलयादावपि प्रकृतिपुरुषसंयोगसत्त्वेन भोगाद्यापत्तिः, मिथ्याज्ञानरूपस्याविवेकस्य संयोगत्वे आत्माश्रयः, पुम्प्रकृतिसंयोगस्याज्ञानहेतुत्वादिति । तस्मादविवेकातिरिक्तो योगो वक्तव्यः । स च संयोग एवान्यस्याप्रामाणिकत्वात् । *SPB* (under *sūtra* I-19), p. 18.
4. अविवेकस्य पुरुषेषु बन्धमोक्षनिमित्तत्वमेव पुरोक्तं न तु अविवेक एव ताविति. . . अविवेकनिमित्तात् प्रकृतिपुरुषसंयोगः । *Ibid.* (under *sūtra* III-74), p. 151.

Rejecting other views on the cause of bondage and establishing the view that it is non-discrimination alone that causes bondage through the birth-conjunction, Vijñānabhikṣu addresses himself to another aspect of the problem of bondage. This relates to the springing up of the first activity in *prakṛti*. Why does it commence functioning for the sake of the individual selves, even though the latter do not solicit[1] the former to do so? He answers that it is its nature to act for the sake of the selves, but not in a general[2] way. Since if it were to function in general and in an unbridled manner, the incidence of bondage and liberation would be rendered meaningless. That is why he assumes that it is due to its teleological role for the sake of the individual selves that it is motivated to act. To clarify, *prakṛti* proceeds to act in respect of that particular self to which it has the tendency to show itself without discriminating[3] and ceases to act for that very self upon which it has conferred the knowledge of discrimination (*vivekakhyāti*).[4] Thus *prakṛti* is regulated and guided in performing its teleological function by a proper cause.[5]

So in this way the first activity that springs forth in *prakṛti* to bind the individual self is also due to non-discrimination. And the conjunction which is brought about by non-discrimination should not be the same as the eternal and general contact which always obtains between *prakṛti* and *puruṣa* as both of them are thought to be eternal and all-pervading. As such the nature of the conjunction causing birth is terminable. Vijñānabhikṣu calls our attention to the fact that though the individual self and the intellect in its causal state (*prakṛti*) are eternal, a terminable conjunction through the limitation of the constituents or qualities of *prakṛti* does take place. Were it not so, the evolution of *mahat, ahaṃkāra,* etc. would be rendered incongruous since in the absence of any contact, there would be no relationship of *puruṣa* with the three constituents of *prakṛti*. But this relationship of the individual self with the three elements, *sattva,*

1. पुरुषाणां नैरपेक्ष्येऽपि . . . . *SPB* (under *sūtra* III-68), p. 149.
2. पुरुषार्थमेव प्रधानस्य प्रवृत्तिस्वभावो न तु सामान्येन । *Ibid.* (under *sūtra* III-6), p. 149.
3. तथा च यस्मै पुरुषायात्मानमविविच्य दर्शयितुं वासना वर्तते तं प्रत्येव प्रधानं प्रवर्तते इत्येव नियामकमिति भाव: । *Ibid.* (under *sūtra* III-68), p. 149. Also *ibid.*, p. 36.
4. Cf. तथा यस्मै विवेकेनात्मानं दर्शितवती तमेव स्ववियोगद्वारा मोचयति वासनोच्छेदादिति । *Ibid.* (under *sūtra* I-58), p. 36.
5. यथा प्रवृत्तिस्तथा निवृत्तिश्च प्रधानस्य स्वभाव एव, योग्येन हेतुना निवृत्तिराविर्भवति प्रवृत्तिर्वेति । *Ibid.*, p. 149, fn. 3.

rajas and *tamas,* takes effect owing to the conjunction occurring between the individual self and *prakṛti* (intellect) because of non-discrimination. This relationship in a sense is a concatenation of one conjunction to another (*saṃyogaja saṃyoga*). Vijñānabhikṣu further elucidates the 'conjunction through limitation' by remarking that such a contact between the two all-pervading substances takes place solely because of a contact with a constituent which has become limited to fulfil a teleological purpose like a conjunction which takes place in relation to space limited by a pot by means of the conjunction of earth with the pot.[1] It would not be out of place to remark at this point that Vijñānabhikṣu discounts the possibility of the figurative usage of conjunction in the sense of capacity of the experiencer and the experienced, which being beginningless as the relationship between the possessor and the possessed defies being explained as the effect. Moreover, should this capacity be taken to be interminable, it would contradict the scriptural statement to the effect that the discrimination-knowledge brings about its termination. And if it were assumed to be terminable, the contingency of mutation in the otherwise immutable individual self would follow.[2]

Vijñānabhikṣu does not consider this conjunction to be of the nature of mutation as according to him it is the production of an additional characteristic in a thing other than the general attributes, which merits to be called mutation, else, the universality as omnipresence of the individual self would be rendered untenable.[3] He observes in this context that the immutable self does not undergo any modification because of the conjunction. According to Vijñānabhikṣu it can be explained in terms of the absence of

---

1. यद्यपि कारणावस्थबुद्धिः पुरुषश्च विभुः, तथा तयोः संयोगः परिच्छिन्नगुणान्तरावच्छेदेन सम्भवत्येव महदाद्यखिलपरिणामानां त्रिगुणसंयोगं विना अनुत्पत्तेः, स च संयोगजः संयोगः न तु कर्मजः । अवयव-संयोगाद् अवयविसंयोगवद् अवच्छेदकीभूतगुणसंयोगादेव विभुनोः संयोगोत्पत्तेः, भूतलस्य घटसंयोगेन घटावच्छिन्नाकाशसंयोगोत्पत्तिवद् । *YV* in *SYD*, p. 191.

   Also cf.—ननु तथापि कथं नित्ययोः प्रकृतिपुरुषयोर्महदादिहेतुरनित्यः संयोगो घटत इति चेन्न । प्रकृतेः परिच्छिन्नापरिच्छिन्नत्रिविधगुणसमुदायरूपतया परिच्छिन्नगुणावच्छेदेन पुरुषसंयोगोत्पत्तेः संभवात् । *SPB* (under *sūtra* I-19), p. 18.
2. न भोक्तृभोग्यतैवौपचारिकोऽत्र संयोगो वक्तव्यः, तस्याः स्वस्वामिभावरूपत्वेनानादितया कार्यत्वस्याञ्जसानुपपत्तेः । किं च तस्या अविनाशित्वे ज्ञाननाश्यत्ववचनविरोधः, नाशित्वे च परिणामः पुरुषस्य स्यादिति । *YV* in *SYD*, pp. 191-92.
3. संयोगश्च न परिणामः सामान्यगुणातिरिक्तधर्मोत्पत्त्यैव परिणामित्वव्यवहारात् । अन्यथा कूटस्थस्य सर्वगतत्वरूपविभुत्वानुपपत्तेः । *SPB* (under *sūtra* I-19), p. 18.

mutation in space due to its contact with a pot, the absence of mutation in the individual self due to its being qualified by twoness, etc. and the absence of any change in the lotus leaf due to water existing on it. Calling our attention to the third illustration, he clarifies that it is because of the absence of any change in the lotus leaf that it is believed and widely mentioned in the scriptures that there exists no contact between the lotus leaf and water.[1]

Vijñānabhikṣu explains that the conjunction in this context connotes birth and that it consists in a particular contact with *prakṛti* reduced into the forms of different intellects to discharge the teleological function.[2] And it is on account of the adjunctival functions of the intellect that the individual self comes in contact with pain, which is nothing but intellectual mode as reflected in the individual self.[3] To recapitulate, non-discrimination aided by conjunction binds the individual self. This bondage consists in the reflection of the intellectual modes in the self.[4] But this should not be taken as effect of the conjunction of *prakṛti* with the self like the colour produced by heat (*pākajarūpa*). Should it be understood to be *pākaja*, it would continue to exist even after the disjunction of *prakṛti* has taken place.[5]

The view that the modifications of the intellect such as non-discrimination, pleasure, pain, etc. are reflected in the individual self which is of the nature of consciousness is considered to be a unique feature of Vijñānabhikṣu's philosophy of liberation. But in this regard Vijñānabhikṣu substantiates his view by invoking the theory of superimposition held by the Advaitins. The view the latter hold is that the objects of cognition are as they are superimposed on the (individual) consciousness. The act of superimposition itself presupposes the reflection of objects in the individual self. Should

---

1. घटाद्यसंयोगाद्यैराकाशस्य द्वित्वादिभिश्च पुरुषस्य परिणामित्वव्यवहाराभावात्, पद्मपत्रस्थतोयेन पद्मपत्रस्यापरिणामासंयोगश्रवणाच्च । *YV* in *SYD*, p. 191.
2. जन्मापरनाम्नः स्वस्वबुद्धिभावापन्नप्रकृतिसंयोगविशेषस्यैव अत्र संयोगशब्दार्थत्वात् । *SPB* (under *sūtra* I-19), p. 18.
3. बुद्ध्युपाधिनैव पुरुषे दुःखयोगाच्च । *Ibid.*, p. 18. And see—तस्मात्पुरुषार्थनिमित्तको बुद्धिपुरुषयोः संयोगो भवति, स च जन्मरूपतया दुःखहेतुरिति सिद्धम् । *YV* in *SYD*, p. 192.
4. तस्माच्च संयोगादुत्पद्यमानस्य प्राकृतदुःखस्य पुरुषे यः प्रतिबिम्बः स एव दुःखभोगो दुःखसम्बन्धः । *SPB* (under *sūtra* III-74), p. 151.
5. यदि हि बन्धः प्रकृतिसंयोगजन्यः स्यात् पाकजरूपवत् तदा तद्वदेव तद्वियोगेऽप्यनुवर्तेत । *Ibid.* (under *sūtra* III-19), p. 16.

the cognition itself be taken as superimposition, the fault known as circular argument (*ātmāśraya*) would be incurred inasmuch as the cognition or knowledge which owes its emergence to the superimposition is itself understood as the latter.[1] He cites a verse from *Yogavāsiṣṭha* in support of his point of view. The verse when translated reads thus:

"In the mirror of consciousness all these mental modes (*dṛṣṭis*) of objects are reflected as trees standing on the bank are reflected in the lake."[2]

The word '*dṛṣṭi*' occurring in the verse, connotes according to Vijñānabhikṣu, 'a mental mode in general' on the basis of similarity. And the reflection is of the nature of the original intellectual modes in different adjuncts. As a consequence, the individual self's association with pain does exist in itself in the shape of reflection.[3] He buttresses his viewpoint by further pointing out that everybody is familiar with the fact that pain is a property of the mind and that in conformity with the rule that action takes place in the same locus where its cause resides, bondage in the form of the conjunction of pain is a property of the intellect. The reason is that the non-discrimination which causes the conjunction resides in the mind. As a result, it comes to mean that bondage, in reality, belongs to the mind only.[4] But if the view that bondage relates to the mind only were admitted, two unreasonable consequences would follow: One, the scriptural enunciations enjoining upon men to strive for liberation are relegated to insignificance. Obviously so, because bondage does not concern the individual self at all, so far as this view on bondage is concerned. Two, the variety of worldly experiences fails to be accounted for adequately. For, in case the experience of pain

---

1. वेदान्तिभिरपि चेतनेऽध्यस्ततयैव दृश्यभानमुच्यते, स चाध्यासः प्रतिबिम्बं विना न घटेत। ज्ञानमात्रस्याध्यासत्वे आत्माश्रयात्, अध्यासाज् ज्ञानं ज्ञानमेव चाध्यास इति । *SPB* (under *sūtra* I-1), p. 9.
2. तस्मिंश्चिद्दर्पणे स्फारे समस्ता वस्तुदृष्टयः ।
इमास्ता प्रतिबिम्बन्ति सरसीव तटद्रुमाः ।। *Yogavāsiṣṭha*, Upaśama, XCI, 123.
3. अत्र हि दृष्टिशब्दो बुद्धिवृत्तिसामान्यपरो युक्तिसाम्यात् । प्रतिबिम्बश्च तत्तदुपाधिषु बिम्बाकारश्चित्तपरिणाम इति । तस्मात्प्रतिबिम्बरूपेण पुरुषे दुःखसम्बन्धो भोगाख्योऽस्ति । *SPB* (under *sūtra* I-1), p. 9.
4. नन्वेवं दुःखयोगरूपोऽपि बन्धः कर्मसामानाधिकरण्यानुरोधेन चित्तस्यैवास्तु, दुःखस्य चित्तधर्मतायाः सिद्धत्वात् । *Ibid.* (under *sūtra* I-16), p. 15.

by the individual self be admitted in the absence of the conjunction of pain, the pain experienced by all the individual selves would become the object of experience of all the selves, as there remains nothing that can determine that the experience of pain should belong to a particular self only.[1] Hence, to explain the diversity of worldly experiences, bondage in the shape of the conjunction of pain should be admitted to exist in the individual self. It will serve two purposes: (1) That the experience of pain belongs to a particular self could be determined by it[2] and thus the contingency of the experience of all pain falling to the lot of all men is avoided.[3] (2) At the same time it would give meaning to the scriptural statements exhorting man to strive for the absolute freedom from pain as the experience of pain belongs to the individual self, at least in the form of reflection. Vijñānabhikṣu adduces one more argument to show why it is necessary that the intellectual modes be accepted as reflected in the individual self. He observes that experience consists in the reception of pleasure, pain, etc. and this reception means transformation of the intellect into their form. But such modification of the intellect into the form of objects apprehended by it is not possible in the case of immutable consciousness for fear that it would be rendered mutable and hence non-eternal. And thus there being no other alternative, 'mutation into their shape' is necessarily construed in the case of the eternal individual self as nothing but the nature of an image.[4]

In consonance with his view that non-discrimination (*aviveka* or *avidyā*) is empirically real,[5] Vijñānabhikṣu asserts that bondage is also real on the empirical plane,[6] and that non-discrimination becomes a characteristic of the individual self by the relation of objectivity,[7] likewise bondage (pain) and freedom from it also

---

1. दुःखयोगरूपबन्धस्य चित्तमात्रधर्मत्वे विचित्रभोगानुपपत्तिः । पुरुषस्य हि दुःखयोगं विना दुःखसाक्षात्काराख्यभोगस्वीकारे सर्वपुरुषदुःखादीनां सर्वपुरुषभोग्यता स्यान्नियामकाभावात् । *SPB* (under *sūtra* I-17), p. 16.
2. अतो भोगवैचित्र्योपपत्तये भोगनियामकतया दुःखादियोगरूपो बन्धः पुरुषेऽपि स्वीकार्यः । *Ibid.*, p. 16.
3. प्रतिबिम्बश्चोपाधिवृत्तेरेव भवतीति न सर्वपुंसां सर्वदुःखभोग इति भावः । *Ibid.*, p. 16.
4. सुखादिग्रहणं हि भोगः । ग्रहणं च तदाकारता । सा च कूटस्थचितौ बुद्धेरर्थाकारवत् परिणामो न संभवतीति अगत्या प्रतिबिम्बस्वरूपतायामेव पर्यवस्यति । *Ibid.* (under *sūtra* I-1), p. 9.
5. *Ibid.* (under *sūtra* VI-20), p. 21.
6. बन्धमोक्षौ तु व्यावहारिकावित्यविरोधः । *Ibid.* (under *sūtra* VI-20), p. 226.
7. विषयतासम्बन्धेनाविवेकस्य पुरुषधर्मत्वात् । *Ibid.* (under *sūtra* I-55), p. 31.

become the objects to be achieved by the same relation of objectivity.[1]

In short, non-discrimination being a characteristic of the individual self by the relation of objectivity gives rise to conjunction in the form of birth. It is this birth-conjunction that causes the individual self to be in contact with the reflection of intellectual modes cast in it. The mental modes as reflected in the individual consciousness hide[2] its true nature and make the individual self feel as if it were experiencing what actually occurs in the intellect. As such bondage consists in individual self's erroneously identifying itself with the reflection of the mental modes.[3]

III

The cause and the nature of bondage have been dwelt upon in the previous sections. Now, in this section, the nature and the cause of liberation are being taken up for discussion.

The nature of liberation is closely related to that of bondage inasmuch as while bondage consists in the individual self's experiencing the contact with pain in the form of reflection of the intellectual modes, liberation is constituted by the cessation of experiencing such a contact.[4] And this contact endures so long as mutations take place in the intellect under the impact of non-discrimination. No sooner do the modes get subdued completely than their reflection ceases to be cast on the individual self.[5] It is at this total cessation of modifications of the mind that the individual self is said to have

---

1. दुःखनिवृत्तेः पुरुषार्थत्वं विषयतासम्बन्धेनैव बोध्यम् । *SPB* (under *sūtra* I-1), p. 10.
2. *Ibid.* (under *sūtra* VI-20), p. 226.
3. बुद्धिपुरुषयोर्नोपरागः, किन्तु बुद्धिप्रतिबिम्बवशादुपरागाभिमानोऽविवेकवशादित्यर्थः । *Ibid.* (under *sūtra* VI-28), p. 228.
4. भोगश्च प्रतिबिम्बरूपेण दुःखसम्बन्धः इत्यतः प्रतिबिम्बरूपेण दुःखनिवृत्तिः यथार्थैव पुरुषार्थः । *Ibid.* (under *sūtra* VI-21), p. 227.

   And also–प्राकृतदुःखस्य यः प्रतिबिम्बः स एव दुःखभोगो दुःखसम्बन्धः तन्निवृत्तिरेव च मोक्षाख्यः पुरुषार्थः ।

   Ibid. (under *sūtra* III-74), p. 151 and compare *ibid.* (under *sūtra* III-72), p. 150.
5. बिम्बनिरोधे प्रतिबिम्बस्यापि निरोधः । *Ibid.*, p. 221.

attained its true nature.[1] But at the same time it should not be left out of the purview of the discussion about the nature of liberation that the cessation of mutations of the intellect entirely depends on the role of *prakṛti*. Vijñānabhikṣu says that it is its nature that it swings into action and stops doing so. Despite this being the fact, its continued activity depends on its having not shown itself as discriminated from the individual self and the knowledge of discrimination, (that is, when it has shown itself as discriminated from the individual self) makes it cease doing so. He elucidates *prakṛti* discharging these two functions by a dancer's illustration. It is natural for a dancer that she takes upon herself the role of showing dance-performance to the audience and stops doing so after she has performed it. In the same manner, though activity and cessation therefrom constitute *prakṛti's* nautre, it is teleologically determined to perform these functions for the sake of the individual self.[2]

Vijñānabhikṣu throws further light on the nature of liberation saying that it is neither the present nor the past pain from which freedom is to be attained but it is the future pain, absolute release from which constitutes the nature of liberation. So far as the present and the past pains are concerned, he says that both the pains do not call for the effort for their termination as the latter already stands annihilated while the former will terminate by itself in the following moment. In this regard he makes it absolutely clear that the future pain should not be considered non-existent like the sky-flower as it exists in the mind in a potential form and that the entity of the potential pain co-exists with its locus. It comes to this that the entity of future pain continues to be inferred till the mind endures and it is in this sense that the striving to attain freedom from the future pain existing in a subtle form assumes significance. Vijñānabhikṣu further observes that freedom from the coming pain does not mean its being blotted out of existence but its receding into the past state. It is so, because the consequent non-existence (*dhvaṃsābhāva*) and

1. वृत्त्यपाये वृत्तिप्रतिबिम्बशून्ये स्वरूपेऽवस्थानमिति भावः । *YV* in *SYD*, p. 18.
And also 'मुक्तिर्हित्वाऽन्यथाभावं स्वरूपेण व्यवस्थितिः' इत्यादिवाक्यैरात्यन्तिकस्य स्वरूपावस्थानस्यैव मोक्षत्वादिति दिक् । *Ibid.*, p. 11.
2. पुरुषार्थमेव प्रधानस्य प्रवृत्तिस्वभावो न सामान्येन । अतः प्रवृत्तस्यापि प्रधानस्य पुरुषार्थसमाप्तिरूपे चरितार्थत्वे सति निवृत्तिर्युक्ता यथा परिषद्भ्यो नृत्यदर्शनार्थं प्रवृत्ताया नर्तक्यास्तत्सिद्धौ निवृत्तिरित्यर्थः । *SPB* (under *sūtra* III-69), p. 149.

prior non-existence (*prāgabhāva*) are in essence not different from the past and future states respectively and because non-existence is not accepted as a category by those who hold the view that effects pre-exist in their causes before manifestation.[1]

Referring to the illustration cited by the Advaitins to explain the phenomenon of liberation of the individual self, which is ever free on their view, Vijñānabhikṣu proceeds to refute their view in the following manner. In cases of sudden forgetfulness, such as of an article of ornament hanging round the neck, one commences searching for it as it is mistakenly believed to have been lost and so may be the case in the context of individual self's liberation. He says that this view does not hold ground when closely examined. To impart importance to the pursuit for liberation, if it is said that it may be believed by error that the individual self is not of the nature of painlessness, though it has already been demonstrated that no pain is produced in the individual self as it is assumed to be free from being modified and influenced by the external stimuli, we may rejoin like this. Had this actually been the case, the error would have ended the moment one learns that the individual self is ever free from pain and consequently reflection and subsequent effort for steady meditation would have been rendered meaningless. For, one proceeds to exert so much to attain a goal only when one is sure about the result to be achieved. But in the present case the knowledge of the absence of pain in the immutable self has already been obtained from the authoritative sources (*śravaṇa*) and reflection (*manana*). This is why it has been stated here that such certainty about the absence of non-generation of pain in the individual self is not unaffected by false knowledge.[2]

The Advaitins maintain that it is erroneously believed that the self

---

1. तत्र स्थूलं दुःखं वर्तमानावस्थं तच्च द्वितीयक्षणादुपरि स्वयमेव नङ् क्ष्यति, अतो न तत्र ज्ञानापेक्षा । अतीतं तु प्रागेव नष्टमिति न तत्र साधनापेक्षेति परिशेषादनागतावस्थसूक्ष्मदुःखनिवृत्तिरेव पुरुषार्थतया प्रकृते पर्यवस्यति । . . . .निवृत्तिश्च न नाशोऽपित्वतीतावस्था, ध्वंसप्रागभावयोरतीतानागतावस्थास्वरूपत्वात् सत्कार्यवादिभिरभावानङ्गीकारात्. . . अतो यावच्चित्तसत्ता तावदेवानागतदुःखसत्तानुमीयते तन्निवृत्तिश्च पुरुषार्थ इति । *SPB* (under *sūtra* I-1), p. 8.
2. यत्तु कण्ठचामीकरवत् सिद्धेऽप्यसिद्धत्वभ्रमात् पुरुषार्थता स्यादिति, तन्न, एवमपि पुमान् निर्दुःख इति श्रवणमननोत्तरं दुःखहानार्थं निदिध्यासनादौ प्रवृत्त्यनुपपत्तेः । बह्वायाससाध्ये ह्युपाये फलनिश्चयादेव प्रवृत्तिर्भवति, प्रकृते तु श्रवणमननाभ्यां सिद्धत्वज्ञानान्नाप्रामाण्यज्ञानानास्कन्दितफलस्यासिद्धत्वनिश्चयोऽस्तीति । *Ibid.* (under *sūtra* I-1), p. 8.

is not of the nature of painlessness and that it is, therefore, meaningful to strive to attain the state of painlessness. Vijñānabhikṣu invokes the theory of double reflection, rejects the view of Advaitins and avers that pain does exist in the individual self in the form of reflection. Had this reverse reflection of the intellectual modes in the self not been postulated, the experienciability of pleasure and pain would not have been explained satisfactorily.[1]

Vijñānabhikṣu throws some more light on the nature of liberation when he says that it is nothing but the destruction of an obstacle. He explains its nature by offering the illustration of a crystal. Just as the crystal which possesses natural whiteness appears to be red because of the proximity of a China-rose, the appearance of redness is a mere obstacle in the sense that it hides the natural whiteness of the crystal. But it should not be understood that the whiteness of the crystal is destroyed by the nearness of the China-rose and that it is produced again when the China-rose is removed from its vicinity. In a similar way in the case of individual self which is by nature absolutely free from pain, the adjunctival reflection of the intellect constitutes an obstacle in the sense that it hides the painless nature of the individual self. The state of painlessness being veiled by the reflection in the self on account of the proximity of the adjunct in the form of intellect, it should not be presumed that pain is produced in the self by the proximity of the mind and that it is annihilated when the intellect stands distinguished from the self.[2] When the obstacle is removed, that is, when the contact of the individual self with the reflection of mental modes has ceased, the realization of the really meaningful objective, that is, absolute cessation of pain ensues.[3]

The cessation of pain, according to Vijñānabhikṣu, connotes the cessation of the experience of pain, as man is generally seen to pray, "Let me not suffer pain". He observes that the termination of the

1. तथा हि प्रतिबिम्बरूपेण पुरुषे सुखदुःखे स्तः । अन्यथा तयोः भोग्यत्वानुपपत्तेः । *SPB* (under *sūtra* I-1), p. 9.
2. वक्ष्यमाणान्तरायस्य ध्वंसादतिरिक्तः पदार्थो न मुक्तिरित्यर्थः । यथा हि स्वभावशुक्लस्य स्फटिकस्य जपोपाधिनिमित्तं रक्तत्वं शौक्ल्यावरकरूपं विघ्नमात्रं, न तु जपोपधानेन शौक्ल्यं नश्यति जपापाये चोत्पद्यते तथैव स्वभावनिर्दुःखस्यात्मनो बुद्ध्युपाधिकं दुःखप्रतिबिम्बं तदावरकरूपं विघ्नमात्रं न तु बुद्ध्युपधानेन दुःखं जायते तदपाये च नश्यतीति । *Ibid.* (under *sūtra* VI-20), p. 226.
3. भोगश्च प्रतिबिम्बरूपेण दुःखसम्बन्ध इत्यतः प्रतिबिम्बरूपेण दुःखनिवृत्तिर्यथार्थैव पुरुषार्थः । स एवान्तरायध्वंसः तादृशश्च मोक्षो यथार्थ एवेति भावः । *Ibid.* (under *sūtra* VI-21), p. 227.

experience of pain could not become an object of voluntary pursuit, were it only a means to an ulterior end. It follows, therefore, that it is by itself the object of pursuit. The cessation of pain, on the other hand, like the removal of thorns, etc. amounts to an end but is not in itself an object desired by the individual self. Similar is the case with pleasure also. It is the experience of pleasure and of cessation of pain as such that happens to possess the characteristic of being an object desired in itself by man. Hence the scriptural enjoining upon attaining the absence of pain should be understood in relation of pain being an object of experience.[1]

Vijñānabhikṣu alludes to the Buddhist's view that pain is natural, that the self is nothing but mind and that liberation ensues when the mind has been annihilated, and criticizes it pointing out that liberation which consists in the annihilation of the mind, that is, self, cannot claim to constitute a human value. He further maintains that the absolute freedom from pain deserves to become an object fit to be pursued vigorously for attainment only when bondage and liberation occur in one and the same locus as is evidenced in the usage 'I am bound; I shall be released'.[2] Vijñānabhikṣu hastens to clarify that he does not deny pain being natural to the mind and adds that for something to be natural it does not mean that it is to be experienced at all times. It would, therefore, not sound reasonable to hold that, on the view of pain being natural to the mind, the incidence of pain being experienced always rendering liberation meaningless would be entailed, since, though the pain is natural to the mind, it happens sometimes that it (pain) is not experienced on account of the preponderance of *sattva*. Similarly, it is possible that the individual self also does not experience pain some time or the other.[3] What Vijñānabhikṣu wants to drive home here is that it is not

1. अत एव दुःखं मा भुञ्जीयेति प्रार्थनाप्यापामरं दृश्यते । तच्च दुःखभोगनिवृत्तेः पुरुषार्थत्वमन्यशेषतया न सम्भवतीति सैव स्वतः पुरुषार्थः दुःखनिवृत्तिस्तु कण्टकादिनिवृत्तिवत् तादर्थ्येन न स्वतः पुरुषार्थः । एवं सुखमपि न स्वतः पुरुषार्थः किन्तु तद्भोग एव स्वतः पुरुषार्थत्वं यातीति. . . . अतः श्रुतावपि दुःखनिवृत्तेः पुरुषार्थत्वं विषयतासम्बन्धेनैव बोध्यम् । *SPB* (under *sūtra* I-1), pp. 9-10.
2. दुःखस्वाभाविकत्ववादिभिः बौद्धैश्चित्तस्यैवात्मताभ्युपगमाच्च । अथैवमात्मनाशादेव मोक्षोऽस्त्विति चेन्न, अहं बद्धो विमुक्तः स्यामिति बन्धसामानाधिकरण्येनैव मोक्षस्य पुरुषार्थत्वादिति । *Ibid.* (under *sūtra* I-7), p. 13.
3. ननु सर्वदोपलम्भापत्तेः दुःखस्य स्वाभाविकत्वशङ्कैव नास्ति इति चेत्, न, त्रिगुणात्मकत्वेन चित्तस्य दुःखस्वभावत्वेऽपि सत्त्वाधिक्येनाभिभवात् सदा दुःखानुपलब्धिवदात्मनोऽपि तदनुपलब्धिसम्भवात् । *Ibid.* (under *sūtra* I-7), p. 13.

possible to justify the significance of the pursuit for liberation in case the Buddhists' view that the mind is self and pain is its natural characteristic is taken into consideration. But on the other hand, it can be explained logically that striving to attain the absolute freedom from pain is a human value should Vijñānabhikṣu's view that the individual self is other than the mind which, of course, possesses pain as a natural characteristic be taken cognizance of. The argument in favour of his point of view runs like this: The mind which is *prakṛti* in its causal state ceases to be modalized into the forms of different objects the moment non-discrimination is destroyed at the dawn of discrimination-knowledge. It is at this stage that the self is restored to its pristine purity and painlessness as the intellectual mutations are no longer reflected in it. And this is nothing but the *summum bonum*, effort to attain which should be of the highest value.

Vijñānabhikṣu argues further that though he admits pain and bondage being natural to the mind, he does not subscribe to the view that they are natural to the self too. If bondage were natural to the self, as the Buddhists hold, it would continue to exist till the individual self endures. For, the release, like the separation of fire from its natural hotness, is not possible because that which is natural to a thing is coexistent with it.[1] To corroborate his own point of view, he cites a verse[2] from *Īśvaragītā* in the *Kūrma Purāṇa* and incidentally defines the natural characteristic of a thing. One thing is said to be natural to another, when, the former existing, no delay occurs in the production (manifestation) of the latter, from the delay (in the appearance) of the cause.[3]

Keeping in view the whole gamut of arguments detailed by Vijñānabhikṣu, it may safely be concluded that though pain and bondage are real and natural to the mind, they are not the natural characteristics of the individual self, since non-acceptance of the latter viewpoint would jeopardize the authenticity of scriptural

---

1. न ह्यग्नेः स्वाभाविकाद् औष्ण्यान्मोक्षः सम्भवति स्वाभाविकस्य यावद्द्रव्यभावित्वात् । *SPB* (under *sūtra* I-7), p. 13.
2. यद्यात्मा मलिनोऽस्वच्छो विकारी स्यात् स्वभावतः ।
   न हि तस्य भवेन्मुक्तिर्जन्मान्तरशतैरपि ।। Quoted *ibid.*, p. 13.
3. यस्मिन् सति कारणविलम्बाद् विलम्बो यस्योत्पत्तौ न भवति तस्य तत् स्वाभाविकमिति स्वाभाविकत्वलक्षणम् ।
   Ibid., p. 13.
   Also see Nandalal Sinha, *The Sāṃkhya Philosophy*, Munshiram Manoharlal, 1979, p. 27.

enunciations which describe the steps towards the attainment of liberation.[1] Vijñānabhikṣu's view about the point at issue may be summed up as follows: Pain and other modifications of the intellect are not absolutely annihilated but they merge into, and indistinguishably become one with, the cause. The individual self terminates its relationship with the felt pain.[2] Individual self's freedom from the felt pain leads to its freedom from the mind (*buddhi*). And thus it (individual self) attains liberation.

Before we take up the cause of liberation for explication two other important aspects of liberation need elaboration. One of them relates to the Vaiśeṣika view about the nature of liberation, viz. that the total extinction of the special attributes of individual self is what merits the designation of liberation. Vijñānabhikṣu does not accept this view and asserts that there is no question of the annihilation of the special attributes of self as it has been postulated and proved that the self is without any attribute. It is in this light that he cannot afford to accept the view of Vaiśeṣikas that the special attributes are produced in the self[3] during the epistemological process. The opponent has a poser for Vijñānabhikṣu stating that the absence of pain may be said to constitute a characteristic of being an attribute of the self. The latter answers the rejoinder clarifying that the absence of pain does not possess a characteristic of being an attribute as the non-existence of pain is mentioned as an object of experience by the individual self and not as its special attribute which is accepted as produced in the self during the cognitive process.

The second point relates to the bliss-aspect of liberation as held by the Advaitins. Vijñānabhikṣu does not accept the view that the individual self discovers itself as bliss after the cause of bondage has been destroyed. The Advaitins, on the other hand, hold the view that bliss also constitutes the nature of liberation as bliss is the nature of self. Vijñānabhikṣu rejects this view and explains that bliss being a transformation of the intellect because of the preponderance of

---

1. तस्य बन्धस्य पुरुषे न स्वाभाविकत्वं वक्ष्यमाणलक्षणमस्ति, यतो न स्वभावतो बद्धस्य मोक्षाय साधनोपदेशस्य श्रौतस्य विधिरनुष्ठानं नियोज्यानां घटते । *SPB* (under *sūtra* I-7), p. 12.
2. *SP*, p. 140.
3. अशेषविशेषगुणोच्छेदोऽपि न मुक्तिस्तद्वद् निर्धर्मत्वादेवेत्यर्थः । ननु तर्हि दुःखनिवृत्तिरेवं कथं मोक्ष उक्तः, दुःखाभावस्य अपि धर्मत्वादिति चेन्न, अस्माभिर्भोग्यतासम्बन्धेनैव दुःखाभावस्य पुरुषार्थतावचनादिति । *SPB* (under *sūtra* V-75), p. 196.

sattva, cannot, as such, belong to the self as its modifiable property. Should it be so, the individual self would be rendered liable to mutation. It is to avoid the entailment of mutation in the self that he does not subscribe to the view that bliss also constitutes the nature of self.[1] So far as the scriptural statements describing the nature of individual self and that of liberation as bliss are concerned, it may be said that bliss, a property of the intellect, is attributed to the self in a secondary sense.[2]

Then why is the individual self without bliss dear to all? He answers it syllogistically. The subject of the syllogism is the individual self for which the existence of natural love is to be proved. The probans (*hetu*) here is soulhood which makes one love the self as the quality of pleasure (*sukhatva*) causes one to love pleasure, or it may be said that soulhood being of the nature of painlessness spurs one to love it.[3] As a consequence of the syllogistic demonstration, the individual self being without bliss, cannot discover itself as bliss and liberation on that account cannot be of the nature of bliss. All the more so, since the individual self, though receiving the reflection of pleasure, cannot enter into relationship with pleasure itself and also because all the mutations of the adjunct in the form of intellect are totally subdued during the state of liberation. Moreover, were it conceded that the individual self possesses pleasure as its natural attribute, its experienciability being incongruous in the state of emancipation would make it unfit for being an object of voluntary pursuit. The reason for this anomaly is that if it were to become the object of its own direct perception, the fault of subject-object-contradiction would be incurred as the adjunct responsible for the epistemological processes has already submerged in its cause.[4]

---

1. Cf. आत्मन्यानन्दरूपोऽभिव्यक्तिरूपश्च धर्मो नास्ति; स्वरूपं च नित्यमेवेति न साधनसाध्यम् । अतो नानन्दाभिव्यक्तिर्मोक्ष इत्यर्थः । *SPB* (under *sūtra* V-74), p. 196.
   Also cf. तृष्णाक्षयस्यैते नार्हतः षोडशीं कलाम् । *VAB*, p. 34.
2. *VAB*, p. 34.
3. आत्मनो निरुपाधिप्रियत्वं वा सुखत्ववद् आत्मत्वस्य प्रेमप्रयोजकत्वात् दुःखनिवृत्तिरूपत्वाद् वा बोध्यम् । *Ibid.*, p. 34.
4. एतेन मोक्षस्य सुखरूपत्वमप्यपास्तम्, आत्मनश्च सुखासम्बन्धात् उपाधिधर्माणामत्यन्तोच्छेदाच्च । किं चात्मनः सुखरूपत्वेऽपि मोक्षावस्थायां तस्य भोग्यत्वानुपपत्त्या पुरुषार्थत्वं न सम्भवति, स्वस्य साक्षात् स्वविषयत्वे कर्मकर्तृविरोधात्, उपाधेश्चात्यन्तविलयादिति । *Ibid.*, p. 34.
   It may be noted here that Vijñānabhikṣu holds the view that even the individual self can perceive itself but only through the medium of intellect, which is contrary

Vijñānabhikṣu differs with the Advaitins in one more respect, viz., the cause of liberation. This difference of opinion about what destroys bondage and brings about emancipation is traceable to the difference in their metaphysical views on the nature of the Absolute. For Śaṅkara It is one undivided whole and the individual self, therefore, is identical with it.[1] Vijñānabhikṣu, on the other hand, holds that the Absolute is integrally non-dual in which *prakṛti* and the individual selves inhere as Its real powers which, though ontologically different, are not separate from It. It is because of this difference in their metaphysical views, specially on the nature of the Absolute, that the cause of liberation differs in both the cases. It is the knowledge of identity between the individual self and the Absolute which is said to liberate the former from bondage. This is the view of Śaṅkara. But on the other hand, Vijñānabhikṣu believes that it is the discrimination-knowledge in the form 'I am not the intellect, etc.' which frees the individual self from bondage.

Incidentally Vijñānabhikṣu delineates two kinds of liberation in conformity with his conception of the individual self. He elaborates that the individual self (*jīva*) is the soul of the body, senses, intellect, etc., since it constitutes the locus of their emergence and dissolution and also since it witnesses and supervises them. When the individual self equipped with the knowledge of discrimination perceives itself as discriminated from the body, senses, intellect, etc., its erroneous identification with them ends. It is the Sāṅkhya view according to Vijñānabhikṣu. To describe the second type of liberation, he says that the Absolute is the Ultimate Soul[2] because It is the locus of emergence and submergence of all the individual selves and because It witnesses and controls them. As such, the individual self attains absolute freedom from bondage when it knows that it is distinct from

---

to the Advaitic view of individual self's self-luminosity. He explains his view: the self as the original perceives the reflection of the intellect modalized into its own form. In this way the original becomes the subject while its reflection assumes objectivity and thus the contradiction of the subject also being an object is not involved.

1. जीवात्मनोरनन्यत्वभेदेन प्रशस्यते । *Māṇḍūkyopaniṣad*, III-13.
Here *ātman* means the Supreme Self. And also see Śaṅkara's commentary thereon. Cf. also on this point, Veermani Prasad Upādhyāya, *Lights on Vedānta*, Varanasi, 1959, p. 195.
2. Cf. यो यत आगत्य यदधिष्ठितं यत्र जीवित्वा यत्र लीयते समुद्रतरंगादिवत् जीवात् तद्बुद्ध्यादिवच्च स तस्यात्मा भवति । *VAB*, p. 28.

the Absolute and that It is the only soul in reality. Then its false identification[1] with the Ultimate Soul, that is, the error that it possesses soulhood, having ended, the individual self is merged into It indistinguishably as pure water poured into pure water.[2]

It would be appropriate at this juncture to interpret the termination of both kinds of false identification mentioned in the preceding para in a way that it may fit in well with liberation interpreted as destruction of non-discrimination. Should both false identification and non-discrimination be studied minutely, it would become clear that both mean one and the same thing. Non-discrimination consists in individual selves not knowing themselves as distinct from the body, senses, intellect, etc. on the one hand and from the Absolute on the other. False identification connotes that the individual selves know themselves as one with the intellect and the Ultimate Soul. Essentially both the meanings are identical. The lower kind of liberation consists in individual self's knowing itself as discriminated from the body, senses, intellect, etc. And the higher kind of emancipation ensues when the individual self comes to know that it is different from the Absolute and that its soulhood is derived from that of the Absolute. Consequently the individual self ceases to be falsely identified with the Ultimate Soul and submerges in It like salt dissolved in the sea[3] and like rivers which lose their identity into the ocean.[4]

Though not vitally relevant to the present topic, it may be mentioned that Vijñānabhikṣu ascribes to the Absolute the power of binding and releasing the individual selves, thereby bringing into

---

1. यथा हि देहेन्द्रयादीनां बुद्धिपर्यन्तानामुत्पत्तिलयाधारतया तत्साक्षित्वेनाधिष्ठातृत्वादिना च जीवस्तेषामात्मा तत्स्वरूपज्ञानाच्च तेषु अहमित्यभिमानो निवर्तते 'नाहं बुद्ध्यादिरिति' विद्ययेति सांख्यसिद्धान्तः । तथैव जीवानां चिन्मात्रस्वरूपाणामुत्पत्तिलयाधारतया तत्साक्षित्वेन तदधिष्ठातृत्वादिना चेश्वरः तेषामात्मा तत्स्वरूपज्ञानादेव च जीवेषु अहमित्यभिमानो निवर्तते ब्रह्मात्मविद्ययेति ब्रह्ममीमांसासिद्धान्तः ।
VAB, p. 29.
And also cf. ब्रह्मात्मज्ञानादेवौपाधिकसंसारवज्जीवमारभ्य स्थूलदेहपर्यन्तेषु अभिमाननिवृत्तेः । अत इदं ब्रह्मज्ञानं विविक्तजीवज्ञानात् सांख्योक्तादपि श्रेष्ठं, नातोऽधिकं ज्ञानमस्ति । *Ibid.*, p. 28.
2. यथोदकं शुद्धे शुद्धमाक्षिप्तं तादृगेव भवति एवं मुनेर्विजानत आत्मा भवति गौतम । *Ibid.*, p. 21.
3. लवणस्य समुद्रे अविभागव्यवहारस्यापलपितुमशक्यत्वात् । *Ibid.*, p. 26.
4. समुद्रेण नदनदीनामिवाविभागेन लक्षणानन्यत्वरूपेणात्यन्तिकलयरूपैव मुक्तिः । *Ibid.*, p. 332.

open his strong theistic inclination.[1] Nonetheless it does not affect our treatment of the problem of bondage and liberation, as the Absolute directs *prakṛti* to swing into action and the latter becoming active enables itself to bind the individual self in respect of which it has not yet shown itself as discriminated from it. Resultantly, it is non-discrimination which brings about the bondage of individual self as has been shown earlier.

IV

Liberation ensues the moment ignorance or non-discrimination that brings about bodily existence is annihilated.[2] But the phenomenon of liberation during life appears to be problematic since even after the cause of bodily existence is destroyed, the individual self continues to remain in conjunction with the body, senses, intellect, etc. The individual self's remaining in conjunction with the psycho-physical organism is due to non-discrimination, which when destroyed ceases to be the cause of the conjunction. It is in this context that the incidence of liberation during life assumes an enigmatic aspect as it brings upon itself the inevitable consequence of inconstancy of co-absence (*vyatireka-vyabhicāra*). It means that the phenomenon of liberation during life entails deviation of the accepted principle that the absence of cause necessarily leads to the absence of its effect. An extension of the application of this principle to the liberated state of life renders untenable the embodied existence of the liberated self even when its cause, non-discrimination, has already been done away with. But instances of the embodied existence of the liberated selves are cited in the philosophical literature. To explain this phenomenon, philosophers quote several instances from worldly experiences. One of them is that of rotation of the wheel that continues to whirl from the effect of the impulse previously given to it.[3]

---

1. यस्मात् ततः परमेश्वराभिध्यानादेव जीवस्य मनोविकारैः बन्धः तद्विपर्ययो विकारविलयेन चिन्मात्ररूपतया अवस्थानं मोक्षश्च भवति । *VAB*, p. 237.
2. Cf. *SP*, p. 157, section 47.
3. तिष्ठति संस्कारवशाच्चक्रभ्रमिवद् धृतशरीरः । *Sāṅkhyakārikā*, 67.
   Also compare *Śāṅkarabhāṣya* on *Brahmasūtra*, IV-1-15.

Even then, to avoid the principle of cause and effect being violated, should the phenomenon of *jīvanmukti* (liberation during life) be considered worth dispensing with,[1] it would render untenable the act of teaching seekers the steps to attain the *summum bonum.* There would be no living liberated being to do so, as on this view the individual self has to relinquish the psycho-physical organism simultaneously with the dawn of knowledge. Pratyagrūpa's observation in this context deserves attention. He says that it is only for the sake of proving (or substantiating) the incidence of *jīvanmukti* that such an analytical discourse as 'If there is no *jīvanmukti* there is no *mukti* and vice versa' continues to prevail in the philosophical tradition. Further, it also proves that the transmission of knowledge does take place. The point which Pratyagrūpa wants to drive home is that both the acquisition and the dissemination of knowledge acquire significance, in case liberation is accepted as an event in this very life even before the bodily existence comes to an end.[2] Otherwise the view that liberation brings about the total annihilation of all *karmas,* even including the *prārabdha* and that it is immediately followed by the termination of the embodied existence,[3] renders inauthentic, and hence redundant, all injunctions and enunciations which lay down the steps to liberation.

Citsukhācārya attempts to shed light on the enigmatic feature of *jīvanmukti* by saying that a little fraction of ignorance does continue to exist even during the liberated state of life. The residual little fraction of ignorance, according to him, accounts for the carrying out of day-to-day activities even after attaining the absolute freedom from bondage. He further remarks that the embodied existence is also accounted for by the remaining powerful *prārabdha karma* which obstructs true knowledge.[4] He avers that this little fraction of *avidyā*

---

1. V.P. Upādhyāya, *Lights on Vedānta,* Varanasi, 1959, p. 248.
2. Cf. जीवत एव ज्ञानोत्पत्तिः, इतरथा तदुत्पादककरणाभावेन अनुत्पत्तिप्रसङ्गात्, तद् यदि मुक्तिरस्ति अस्त्येव जीवन्मुक्तिः । अथ यदि न जीवन्मुक्तिः, नास्त्येव मुक्तिरिति मुक्तिसिद्ध्यर्थमेवायं विचारः विद्यासम्प्रदायसिद्ध्यर्थम्, इतरथा हि तत्त्वविदः सद्यः शरीरपाते शिष्याद्यप्रतिभासादसाक्षात्कृततत्त्वस्य चानुपदेष्टृत्वाद् विहीनसम्प्रदायतया निर्मोक्ष एव पर्यवस्येत् ।

   Pratyagrūpa's *Nayanaprasādinī* on *Tattvapradīpikā,* Svāmī Yogīndrānanda's edition, 1974, p. 604.
3. V.P. Upādhyāya, *Lights on Vedānta,* p. 248.
4. This observation of Citsukha needs scrutiny, see fns. 1 and 2 on p. 150.

left unaffected by the attainment of knowledge is one of the many forms of *avidyā*.[1]

Vijñānabhikṣu joins the issue with Citsukhācārya and Advaitins of his sort and discusses at length why he does not find acceptable their view about the point at issue. He says that if, in order to explain the plausibility of continued bodily existence, a little fraction of ignorance (*avidyā*) is assumed to continue to be operative with regard to the individual self so long as the body endures, even after the attainment of liberating knowledge, there is nothing which vouchsafes its termination even when the body falls off. All the more so, since there is no evidence to substantiate the view that it is the spent-up *prārabdha* that terminates the remaining trace of ignorance at the end of the embodied existence. In the absence of any determining factor in this regard, even the ignorant may cease to be born again as in his case the exhaustion of the *prārabdha karma* could also put an end to his potential ignorance though he is yet to attain the discrimination-knowledge logically responsible for the attainment of liberation.

Vijñānabhikṣu continues his criticism of Citsukha's view of the liberated state of life by further pointing out that if he feels compelled to postulate that the residual little fraction of ignorance is annihilated by itself, the incidence of liberation might occur even without attaining discrimination-knowledge. Besides, the principle of cause and effect would be violated. To put it differently, discrimination-knowledge could cease being the terminating cause of ignorance.[2]

Vijñānabhikṣu traces the inadequacy of Citsukha's explanation of *jīvanmukti* to his conception of bondage and liberation. The Advaitin holds that ignorance is the direct cause of bondage without any intermediary factor, and that as a consequence of this, liberation

---

1. V.A. Sharma, *Citsukha's Contribution to Advaita*, p. 218. Also compare—
अत्र विदाम:-
अविद्यालेशशब्देन मोहाकारान्तरोक्तित: ।
ज्ञानस्य प्रतिबन्धाच्च प्रबलारब्धकर्मभि: ।।
लेशानुवृत्तौ तज्जन्यकर्मादेरनुवृत्तित: ।
उत्पन्नावबोधस्य जीवन्मुक्ति: प्रसिद्ध्यति ।। *TP*, p. 604.

2. ज्ञानपरिपाकोत्तरमपि यावद्देहपातमविद्यालेशस्वीकारे च स च लेशो न नश्येतैव, देहारम्भककर्मनाशस्य वासनानाशकत्वे प्रमाणाभावात्, अविदुषोऽपि पुनर्जन्मासंभवाच्च ।स्वयं विनाशे कदाचित् ज्ञानं विनाऽपि मुक्ति: स्यात् । अज्ञानज्ञाननाश्यनाशकभावे व्यभिचारप्रसङ्गाच्च । *VAB*, p. 11.

has been described as the removal of ignorance (*avidyānivṛtti*).[1] He emphatically says that if the view that non-discrimination by means of birth conjunction causes bondage were accepted, the inadequacy of explanation of the state of liberation during life would not arise at all. To put it differently, *avidyā*, according to Vijñānabhikṣu is held to be the cause of bondage through a particular conjunction,[2] and thus he claims to adequately account for the incidence of liberated state of life, since the conjunction in the form of birth does not necessarily end at the dawn of discrimination-knowledge. The reason is that the *prārabdha karma* still remains to be exhausted.[3] But Vijñānabhikṣu postulates that this conjunction which explains adequately the phenomenon of *jīvanmukti* is other than the relation of egoity (I-sense, *abhimāna*), which if admitted to be a relation between the individual self and the body, senses, intellect, etc. fails to substantiate the authenticity of liberation during bodily existence.[4] He holds the view that a specific conjunction, which is certainly not the one that causes mutation for the obvious reason of the incurrence of mutation in the individual self, takes effect between the individual self and the psycho-physical organism because of non-discrimination. Vijñānabhikṣu remarks that it is this specific conjunction which terminates only when the *prārabdha karma* has spent its force. Otherwise, the incidence of knowledge, its acquisition and dissemination, and continued bodily existence after the attainment of liberation would continue to resist being adequately accounted for.[5] It may be mentioned here that the burning

---

1. *CCA*, p. 215.
2. संयोगद्वारैवाविद्याकर्मादीनां बन्धहेतुत्वात् । *SPB* (under *sūtra* I-24), p. 22.
3. अपि चाविद्याया: साक्षादेव दु:खयोगाख्यबन्धहेतुत्वे ज्ञानेनाविद्याक्षयानन्तरं प्रारब्धभोगानुपपत्ति:, बन्धपर्यायदु:खभोगस्य कारणनाशादिति । अस्मदादिमते तु नायं दोष: । संयोगद्वारैवाविद्याकर्मादीनां बन्धहेतुत्वात् । जन्माख्यसंयोग: प्रारब्धसमाप्तिं विना न नश्यतीति । *Ibid.*, p. 22.
   See also *ibid.* (under *sūtra* I-55), p. 31.
   It may be mentioned here that Vijñānabhikṣu holds the view that the annihilation even of the remaining *prārabdha* may be brought about instantaneously by the *asamprajñāta-yoga*. *Yogasārasaṅgraha*, tr. Ganganath Jha, 1986, p. 7.
4. ये त्वभिमानमेव बुद्ध्यात्मनो: सम्बन्धं मन्यते तेषामेव ज्ञानेन सवासनाज्ञाननिवृत्त्या विदुषां भोगानुपपत्ति: । *VAB*, p. 11.
5. Cf. ननु तथापि देहेन्द्रियादिभि: सम्बन्धाभावाद् विदुषां कथं प्रवृत्ति: ? न हि असङ्गस्यात्मनो देहादिभि: सहाभिमानातिरिक्त: सम्बन्ध: सम्भवतीति चेन् न–विदुषां ज्ञानोत्पत्त्यर्थम् असङ्गवाक्यैर्लेपाख्यस्य विकारहेतुसंयोगस्यैव निषेधात्, न तु पुष्करपत्रे जलस्येवासङ्गेऽपि चेतने स्वोपाधे: संयोगविशेष: प्रतिषिध्यते 'आत्मेन्द्रियमनोयुक्तं भोक्तेत्याहुर्मनीषिण:' इति श्रुते: । स च संयोगविशेष: प्रारब्धकर्मक्षयादेव नश्यतीति सर्वैरेवाभ्युपेयम् अन्यथा ज्ञानाद्यनुपपत्तेरिति । *Ibid.*, p. 11.

of seeds, as the state of liberation is generally described, means, in this context, that the accompanying cause of pain, that is, ignorance, has been destroyed as it has already been demonstrated conclusively on the empirical plane that it is the knowledge that annihilates ignorance immediately but which has no direct bearing on the pain which terminates only when its locus has merged in its cause at the end of the embodied existence.[1]

Here Vijñānabhikṣu recounts the view that freedom from pain means freedom from the experience of pain. And the experience of pain consists in comprehending the reflection of the adjunctival modes of pain, pleasure, etc. Thus the application of the bondage consisting in receiving the reflections of objects may smoothly be extended to the liberated individual self[2] since the experience connoting the reception of reflections of the mental modes of the form of objects continues to operate so long as the intellect endures on account of the force of the *prārabdha karma* yet to be exhausted.

V

Let us now take up another significant problem related to the doctrine discussed in the preceding sections. It concerns the status of *karma* and *jñāna* (knowledge) vis-a-vis the state of liberation and its attainment. In this regard each of the *āstika* philosophical school has its own views. They conform to the respective metaphysical principles. If the Absolute is conceived as an integral whole of different real entities as held by Vijñānabhikṣu then the validity of *karma* may remain on a par with that of *jñāna* (knowledge). On the other hand, if It is conceived as one undivided whole and the individual self and the world as unreal entities, then the validity of *karma* will not remain on a par with that of knowledge. The second is the view held by Śaṅkara, who criticizes the theory of combination of knowledge and action as held by the Bhedābhedavādins, like, for example, Bhartṛprapañca.[3]

---

1. बीजदाहश्चाविद्यासहकार्युच्छेदमात्रम् । ज्ञानस्याविद्यामात्रोच्छेदकत्वस्य लोके सिद्धत्वात् । अत एव चित्तेन सहैव दुःखनाशः । ज्ञानस्य साक्षाद्दुःखनाशकत्वे प्रमाणाभावादिति । *SPB* (under *sūtra* I-1), p. 8.
2. विषयैः प्रतिबिम्बरूपस्य बन्धस्य ज्ञानिसाधारण्याद् विषयभोगोऽपि ज्ञानिनामुपपन्नः स्वप्रतिबिम्बितोपाधिसुखस्य भानमेव भोगः । *VAB*, p. 11.
3. *Naiṣkarmyasiddhi of Sureśvarācārya*, ed. M. Hiriyanna, BORI, Poona, 1980, Introduction, p. xxix.

In the prelude to his commentary (*bhāṣya*) on the *Bhagavadgītā* II-11, Śaṅkara dwells on the problem and presents his view on this contentious issue. He says that the discipline of knowledge (*jñānaniṣṭhā*) and that of action (*karmaniṣṭhā*) are derived from two kinds of understanding. They are, therefore, clearly distinguished from each other.[1] He further states that the Lord elucidates the Sāṅkhya knowledge about the Eternal Truth in the ślokas of *Bhagavadgītā* from II-11 to II-31 and teaches therein that the self is free from the six-fold transformation and is, therefore, beyond the phenomenon of change. It is devoid of any agency whatsoever (*kartṛtvabuddhi*). The knowledge that dawns on studying this text is designated as the Sāṅkhya knowledge.[2] It is only prior to the birth of this knowledge that the self may have to pass through the stage of Yoga characterized by the performance of Veda-enjoined acts. But such performance is based on two factors:

1. Discrimination between righteousness and unrighteousness.
2. The self is other than the body, intellect, etc. It is the agent of actions and reaps the fruits thereof.[3]

Śaṅkara clarifies here that the discipline of knowledge depends on the notion of the non-agency of self and on the perception of unity whereas the discipline of action (*karma-niṣṭhā*) is based on the notion that self is an agent, and on the perception of plurality in the world. That is why that both cannot remain present simultaneously in one and the same person.[4] He concludes by pointing out that if the combination of knowledge and acts (*śrautakarmas*) were intended by the Lord, the distinction drawn by him between the two would become illogical[5] and unnecessary.

---

1. ज्ञानकर्मनिष्ठयोः विभागवचनात् बुद्धिद्वयाश्रययोः । *Śāṅkarabhāṣya* on *Bhagavadgītā*, II.11
2. तद्विषया बुद्धिः आत्मनः जन्मादिषड्विक्रियाभावात् अकर्ता आत्मा इति प्रकरणार्थनिरूपणात् या जायते सा सांख्यबुद्धिः । *Loc. cit.*
3. एतस्याः बुद्धेः प्राक् आत्मनः देहादिव्यतिरिक्तत्वकर्तृत्वभोक्तृत्वाद्यपेक्षः मोक्षसाधनानुष्ठानलक्षणः योगः । तद्विषया बुद्धिः योगबुद्धिः । *Loc. cit.*
4. एवं सांख्यबुद्धिं योगबुद्धिं चाश्रित्य द्वे निष्ठे विभक्ते भगवता एव उक्ते ज्ञानकर्मणोः कर्तृत्वाकर्तृत्वैकत्वानेकत्व-बुद्धिद्वयाश्रययोः युगपत् एकपुरूषाश्रयत्वासंभवं पश्यता । *Loc. cit.*
5. तदेतत् विभागवचनम् अनुपपन्नं स्यात्, यदि श्रौतकर्मज्ञानयोः समुच्चयः अभिप्रेतः स्यात् । *Loc. cit.*

It may also be mentioned here that the need for meditation is admitted practically by all Vedāntins. It is only Śaṅkara and his followers who maintain that the knowledge of the Upaniṣadic propositions like *tat tvam asi* does not stand in need of any assistance from meditative practices for imparting an immediate knowledge of Brahman. But since all are not qualified to grasp this teaching directly, in such cases meditational practices serve as the means of securing the necessary qualification. These are only a contributory aid to the right and immediate apprehension of the meaning of the Upaniṣadic propositions.[1] The point that the Advaitins here intend to make is that the Veda-enjoined acts (*śrautakarmas*) are obligatory only for those who have not yet transcended the sense of agency and are, therefore, yet to acquire the capacity to grasp the Truth immediately. The Advaitins' position on this issue can be summed up like this:

1. The combination of knowledge and action is not necessary. It is only knowledge that liberates.
2. Veda-enjoined acts (*śrauta-karmas*) no longer hold validity in the case of the liberated selves.

It is not only in conformity with his conception of the Absolute but also on the basis of scriptural evidence that Vijñānabhikṣu does not agree with the Advaitins on these views. Among his published works, it is *Vijñānāmṛtabhāṣya,* specially his commentary on the first *sūtra* and the fourth section of the third chapter of *Brahmasūtra* wherein he takes up this issue for discussion and presents his viewpoint.

The scriptures do not enjoin total renunciation of acts.[2] Rather the *Bhagavadgītā* clearly states that the embodied man cannot indeed totally renounce acts.[3] Moreover, total renunciation of external acts cannot be the purport of scriptural injunctions. This is so because the absence of performance of enjoined acts is already given in the case of the seeker who is either engrossed in deep meditation or suffers from some incapacitating disease.[4] For, the essence of Vedic injunctions lies in making known a matter that was not known

---

1. *Naiṣkarmyasiddhi,* p. xxvi.
2. संन्यासिनां सर्वकर्मत्यागोऽशास्त्रार्थः । *VAB,* p. 4.
3. न हि देहभृता शक्यं त्यक्तुं कर्माण्यशेषतः । *Bhagavadgītā,* XVIII-11.
4. समाधिप्रयुक्ताशक्त्या रोगादिदारिद्र्याद्यशक्त्या चैव हि बाह्यकर्मत्यागसिद्धिः । *VAB,* p. 7.

(or given) before.[1] As such scriptures do not enjoin renunciation of enjoined external acts.

But the opponent takes recourse to the implied meaning and seeks to prove that the scriptures do enjoin renunciation of acts in the case of sannyāsins and the liberated ones. The basis for the implication is the assumption that knowledge and action cannot remain together simultaneously in one and the same person. Vijñānabhikṣu rejects the contention of the Advaitin and replies: Even if knowledge were taken to mean experience (of the Truth), then also it is the sense of ego that would be incompatible with it and not the acts themselves since even the liberated souls like Jaḍa Bharata used to beg alms and perform internal rites. They also did not do without performing acts.[2] Then how does action contradict knowledge and vice versa? It is right that they did not perform any such acts during the state of samādhi. But it is not within the purview of the scriptural injunctions as has been made clear in the preceding para.

Vijñānabhikṣu also takes this opportunity to stress the point that moral principles ought to pervade the whole life whether one is liberated or not. Even Jaḍa Bharata, Dattātreya, Ṛṣabhadeva, etc. who were liberated souls accorded equal value to the moral code.[3] His concern for scriptural injunctions (ethical code) becomes more pronounced when he does not discount the possibility that even the realized selves may bring upon themselves the demerit caused by the non-performance of obligatory duties due to dereliction. It is this obstacle in the form of demerit that is removed by performing the Veda-enjoined obligatory acts (*nityakarmas*). This removal of the

---

1. *The Arthasaṃgraha of Laugākṣi Bhāskara*, ed. and tr. A.B. Gajendragadkar and R.D. Karmarkar, 1984, p. 97.
2. ननु श्रुतिस्मृतीनां कर्मत्यागाविधायकत्वेऽपि ज्ञानिनामर्थादेव कर्मत्यागो लभ्यते ज्ञानकर्मणोरेकदा विरोधादिति, मैवम्, यदि पुनर्ज्ञानशब्देनानुभवमात्रमुच्यते तदा तेन सह कर्माभिमानस्यैव विरोधान्न तु कर्मणः । जडभरतादीनां भिक्षाटनादेर्भवतामप्यभ्युपगमात् । *VAB*, p. 9.
   And also cf. समाधिनैव सह कर्मणां विरोधो न तु ज्ञानेन। ज्ञानेन च सह कर्माभिमानस्यैव विरोधः । *Ibid.*, p. 285.
3. विद्यायाः प्राधान्येऽप्याचारदर्शनं तुल्यमेव जडभरतदत्तात्रेयऋषभदेवादीनां विद्याप्राधान्यदर्शनात् । *Ibid.*, p. 285.
   Also cf. किं च एवं ज्ञात्वा कृतं कर्म पूर्वैरपि मुमुक्षुभिरित्यादिवाक्येभ्यो निर्गुणात्मज्ञानस्य कर्मशेषत्वमवगम्यते, तथा जनकादीनां ज्ञानिनामपि कर्म श्रूयते, अन्यथा भिक्षादिकमपि जडभरतादीनां नोपपद्येत । *Ibid.*, p. 285.

obstacle gives the scriptural injunctions their meaning.[1] According to Vijñānabhikṣu the validity of scriptural injunctions with reference to the liberated selves is inferred from the fact that the demerit brought about by the neglect of obligatory acts is to be destroyed by the performance of the acts enjoined by the scriptures.[2] This is as far as the compatibility of knowledge with acts during the liberated state of life is concerned.

So far as his view about the compatibility of action with knowledge as means to liberation is concerned, it becomes clear when he seeks to reconcile Pūrvamīmāṃsā with Uttaramīmāṃsā[3] saying that difference in their approach is based on the difference in their ideals, *Karmakāṇḍa* and *Jñānakāṇḍa*, and that as such they should not be understood as mutually contradictory. It means that he lays equal emphasis on both *karma* and *jñāna*. His preference for yogic discipline in order to attain the state of *asamprajñāta samādhi* buttresses this since it is his considered opinion that *asamprajñāta samādhi* exhausts the residual *prārabdha* instantaneously and liberates the self immediately.[4] Thus it can be said that he upholds the theory of the combination of knowledge and action with respect to both the state of liberation and its attainment.

---

1. अविद्यया कर्मणा मृत्युं पुरुषार्थघातकं विघ्नं तीर्त्त्वा विद्यया मोक्षं प्राप्नोतीति श्रुत्यर्थः । ननूत्पन्नज्ञाननिष्ठस्य कीदृशः प्रतिबन्धः कर्मणा परिह्रियत इति चेत्, नित्यकर्माकरणजप्रत्यवायेन मिथ्याज्ञानवासनाक्षये प्रारब्धभोगसमाप्त्यादौ च प्रतिबन्धो नित्यकर्मणा परिह्रियते तत्प्रतिबन्धकप्रत्यवायानुत्पादात् । न च ज्ञानिनां कथं स्यादिति वाच्यम्, ज्ञानिनामपि वृथा स्वाच्छन्द्यात् प्रत्यवायोत्पत्तेः कर्मविध्यनुमेयत्वात् । *VAB*, p. 298.
2. See the preceding footnote.
3. *VAB*, p. 284.
4. आशुमोक्षहेतुरसम्प्रज्ञातयोगश्च प्रदर्शितः । *YV* in *SYD*, p. 136.

7

CRITICAL REMARKS

It was probably between 1550 and 1623 A.D. when Vijñānabhikṣu wrote his commentarial works. It is evident from them that he was influenced in his thinking by the cult of devotion[1] which, of course, requires an intense I-and-Thou relationship between the Lord and His devotee. It is in this background that he conceived the system of *avibhāgādvaita* (Integral Non-dualism). According to it there are three ontologically real entities: the Absolute, individual selves and *prakṛti*. According to Vijñānabhikṣu the all-encompassing Absolute is an integral whole in which *prakṛti* and the selves inhere as Its powers distinguishably during creation and indistinguishably after dissolution and before creation. In order to make his system of Integral Non-dualism coherent, he also has defined the concepts of the Absolute, *ātmatva*, Locative Causality, reality, existence, etc. and tried to justify that his interpretation of the *Brahmasūtras* is the genuine one, especially when compared with that of Śaṅkara.

As we study his works, we come to know that on the one hand Vijñānabhikṣu does not admit the concepts of *māyā* and undivided oneness of the Ultimate Reality as advocated by the Advaitins and on the other he rejects Rāmānuja's concept of the atomic nature of the individual self. A perusal of his published works[2] shows that he has actually synthesized the tenets of Sāṅkhya, Yoga and Vedānta into

---

1. प्रीयतां मोक्षदो हरिः । *SPB*, p. 2.
सोऽस्मान् बुद्धिगुणैः स्वयं निगडितान् स्वांशान् कृपासागरो
दीनान् मोचयतु प्रभुर्गुणमयं पाशं दहल्ँलीलया । *YV* in *SYD*, p. 2.
And the fact that he has also drawn heavily on the Purāṇas to present and defend his standpoint.
2. (1) *Vijñānāmṛtabhāṣya*, (2) *Yogavārttika*, (3) *Sāṅkhyapravacanabhāṣya*, (4) *Sāṅkhyasāra* and (5) *Yogasārasaṃgraha*.

avibhāgādvaita. The grafting of the Sāṅkhya principles on the Vedānta and of those of the Vaiśeṣika on the Sāṅkhya concept of *prakṛti* will become manifest in the process of discussing the viability of his thought as a system. For a proper assessment let us examine the key concepts of his philosophical system.

To begin with, let's take the concept of Locative Causality since it is very significant so far as determining the relation of the Absolute with selves and *prakṛti* is concerned. It also explains how all the three form one integral whole even as they remain ontologically different. He uses this concept to tide over the dichotomy in assuming the changeless Absolute while *prakṛti* inhering in It is constantly in a state of flux. Rāmānuja encountered almost the same problem and resolved it by assuming both *cit* (selves) and *acit* (*prakṛti*) as modes of the Lord[1] since on this view a change in the modes does not necessarily warrant a change in the Lord even though the modes remain with Him in a state of non-differentiation. Probably in the same way Vijñānabhikṣu tries to drive home the point that a change or transformation of the subsisting entities does not at all involve a modification of the locus. But it is not a tenable proposition for the following reason:

The Absolute is described by Vijñānabhikṣu as an integral whole in which different entities, *prakṛti* and individual selves, inhere as Its powers. It can, somehow, be understood that selves do not undergo any modification even when the *sattva, rajas* and *tamas* constituents of *prakṛti* constantly remain in a state of flux. The reason is that the modification of intellect (a product of *prakṛti*) are cast on to the self in the form of reflections only and consequently do not bring about any real change in it. But it is not the case with the Absolute vis-a-vis *prakṛti.* Vijñānabhikṣu holds that *prakṛti* is a real entity inhering in the Absolute whereas the intellect undergoing transformation is not postulated to be inhering in the self in the primary sense. It is in this light that the view that the Absolute remains unchanged while *prakṛti* undergoes modification is not logically sound since the assumption of absence of change in Brahman notwithstanding the transformation in the entities which inhere in It would render Vijñānabhikṣu liable to the charge of *ardhajaratīnyāya* which the Advaitins often level against the Sāṅkhya concept of eternal and transforming (*pariṇāminitya*) *prakṛti.*

---

1. P.N. Srinivasachari: *The Philosophy of Viśiṣṭādvaita*, Madras, 1978, p. 105.

Or, it may be said that Vijñānabhikṣu in this context, has been influenced by the *brahmapariṇāmavāda* of the *Bhedābhedavādin*[1] and in his attempt to tide over the contingency of change in the Absolute, he has postulated the new category of Locative Cause[2] which is over and above that of threefold causality of the Nyāya system of philosophy.[3] He explains it by giving the illustrations of other locative causes. Water is the locative cause of the great earth at the beginning of creation since the subtle constituents of earth remaining non-separately with water were responsible for the production of gross earth.[4] But there is an anomaly in this illustration. He has conceived the category of Locative Cause (*adhiṣṭhānakāraṇa*) to describe the Absolute as the unchanging Locative Cause of all manifestations while at the same time *prakṛti* as Its inherent power continues to undergo transformation. But the definition of the Locative Cause as given by Vijñānabhikṣu, and as it is applied to Brahman suffers from over-pervasion, as in the illustration just given, it extends to water. Likewise, it would overpervade to the series of causes beginning with *prakṛti* in the process of evolution. In order to do away with the defect of overpervasion he has inserted three additions in the definition of the Locative Cause as applied to Brahman. In addition to the definition of the Locative Cause as given by him Brahman should be viewed as the original cause, as the all- comprehensive cause of creation and also as the cause which is endowed with the property of witnesshood.[5] Were these amendments added to the definition of the Locative Cause, it would add to the cumbersomeness of the conception of Locative Causality which is already cumbersome and vague. To further distinguish the unchanging Locative Cause from that which undergoes modifications with the process of creation, Vijñānabhikṣu further resorts to

1. *The Philosophy of Viśiṣṭādvaita*, p. 104.
2. *VAB*, p. 17.
3. अस्माभिस्तु समवाय्यसमवायिभ्यामुदासीनं निमित्तकारणेभ्यश्च विलक्षणतया चतुर्थमाधारकारणत्वमिति । *Ibid.*, p. 18.
4. यथा सर्गादौ जलाविभक्ताः पार्थिवसूक्ष्मांशास्तन्मात्राख्याः जलेनैवोपष्टम्भात् पृथिव्याकारेण परिणमन्ते इत्यतो जलं महापृथिव्या अधिष्ठानकारणमिति । *Ibid.*, p. 17.
5. अधिष्ठानकारणत्वमिति मूलकारणत्वमिति चोच्यते । *Ibid.*, p. 17.
   जगतः सर्वप्रकारकारणत्वमपि ब्रह्मलक्षणं कर्तुं शक्यते । *Ibid.*, p. 18.
   सर्गात्पूर्वमन्येषां साक्षित्वासंभवात् । *Ibid.*, p. 17.

postulating the relationship of sameness (*svarūpa-sambandha*).[1] He explains that the unchanging cause is non-separately related to its effects. He considers this relationship to be a kind of *svarūpa-sambandha* (Ingalls describes it as a peculiar relation)[2] like *ādhāratā*. In other words, the cause which is inherently related to its effects could be understood to undergo modification whereas the cause which is related to its products with the relation of sameness (*svarūpa-sambandha*) may be considered not to undergo any change.[3] He adduces an argument to support his contention: The changing material cause produces effects having the same genus as that of the material cause, while the Locative Cause is assumed to give rise to the products of even a different class. He does not support the view that both should be classified under the category of material cause.[4]

Vijñānabhikṣu evidently tries to resolve the dilemma by assuming a changeless cause while its constituent undergoes modification by postulating two different additional categories, viz., Locative Cause and *avibhāga* as a *svarūpa-sambandha* (peculiar relation or the relation of sameness). But he does not appear to have succeeded in this since he fails to provide an adequate lucid explanation for his assumption. While explaining the nature of *avibhāga* as the self-same relation (*svarūpasambandha*), he likens it to *ādhāratā*. To clarify he further likens it to the state of sameness (harmony or rather the state where distinction cannot easily be made) caused by intense mixing of milk with water. But it is hard to think that the relationship such as *ādhāratā* has been conceived in the sense in which Vijñānabhikṣu has assumed *avibhāga* as a relation.

Moreover, the relation of inherence conceived by the Naiyāyikas for various reasons subsists between two terms which remain inseparable prior to their destruction. Likewise the relation of sameness conceived mainly to account for the relation of the absence of an object with its locus also subsists between two real terms. In case the conception of *prakṛti, puruṣa* and creation is to be understood to be

---

1. अविभागश्चाधारतावत् स्वरूपसम्बन्धविशेषोऽत्यन्तसंमिश्रणरूपो दुग्धजलाद्येकताप्रत्ययनियामकः । *VAB*, p. 17.
2. *Materials for the Study of Navya-Nyāya Logic*, p. 58.
3. तत्र समवायसम्बन्धेन यत्राविभागस्तद्विकारिकारणम् । यत्र च कार्यस्य कारणाविभागेनाविभागस्तदधिष्ठानकारणम्, यथा जलं पृथिव्याः । *VAB*, p. 17.
4. न च द्वयोरेवोपादानत्वम्, विजातीयानामनारम्भकत्वात् । एवमाकाशादीनां वाय्वाद्युपादानत्वमधिष्ठानतयैव द्रष्टव्यम् । *Ibid.*, p. 17.

similar to the Nyāya-Vaiśeṣika conception of absence, Vijñānabhikṣu had better not disagree with the Advaitins on the conception of *māyā,* or, if he firmly believes that the Absolute is related to the individual selves, *prakṛti* and creation with a relation of inseparability, he should have conceded to the view of *brahmapariṇāmavāda* of the Bhedābhedavādins. But actually he appears to have been caught between *brahmapariṇāmavāda* and *brahmavivartavāda* and consequently felt the compulsion for such assumptions as do not at all lend logical coherence to his philosophy of Integral Non-dualism.

An examination of Vijñānabhikṣu's views on the concepts of reality, existence and *ātmatva* is also helpful in assessing the value of his philosophy. He conceives both reality and existence in terms of a meaningful activity (*artha-kriyā-kāritva*) which consists, at least, in having a mental mode. This is precisely the reason why he assumes that the Absolute is eternally invested with the Pure-*Sattva*-Adjunct, but for which the Absolute would stand divested of the status of reality, even that of existence. To explain, the individual self enjoys the status of being real, having its *upādhi* in the form of intellect. But this adjunct (intellect) submerges in its cause, *prakṛti,* at the time of dissolution.[1] With the submergence of its *upādhi* (intellect) in *prakṛti,* the self stops performing any meaningful activity and as a consequence ceases to be real. Since it requires both the individual self and its *upādhi* for the meaningful activity to take place, both cease to be real, nay, even to exist, since existence is also construed in the same sense. With the individual selves and *prakṛti,* which lie dormant in the Absolute at the time of dissolution, being thus rendered unreal at the ultimate level, the very basis of his conceiving the Absolute as integrally non-dual is jeopardized.

Likewise the individual self is considered to possess *ātmatva* in that the intellect and other organs emerge from it and are sustained by and submerged in it.[2] But the individual selves themselves are said to have been invested by the Absolute with the property of consciousness and this is the reason why Vijñānabhikṣu calls them *ātman* in the secondary sense like *prāṇa* which has been so called with respect to

---

1. ब्रह्मचैतन्यं हि विश्वावभासनरूपं कार्यं प्रलयेऽपीदानीमिवैव कुर्वदास्ते प्रकृतिपुरुषादयस्तु सृष्ट्यादिलक्षणस्वकार्येभ्य उपरता एव सुषुप्तास्तिष्ठन्तीति । *VAB*, pp. 57-58.
2. यो यत आगत्य यदधिष्ठितं यत्र जीवित्वा यत्र लीयते समुद्रतरङ्गादिवत् जीवात् बुद्ध्यादिवच्च स तस्यात्मा भवति । *Ibid.*, p. 28.

the sense-organs since it possesses the characteristic of superintending over the latter.[1] The property of superintendence becomes the criterion of *ātmatva* in the latter case whereas in the former case it is the property of consciousness. Since the Absolute creates, sustains and engulfs all, It is the Ultimate *Ātman* in the primary sense.[2] It becomes clear from the foregoing discussion that Vijñānabhikṣu holds the view that it is only Brahman Which perfectly fits in with the criteria of reality, existence and *ātmatva* as conceived by him.

In spite of his views on the Absolute referred to just now, Vijñānabhikṣu tries to maintain that the world and its objects are real since these are not sublated though their reflections in the individual consciousness cease to be cast either at the time of dissolution or when individual self's *aviveka* terminates. He thus criticizes the Advaitins' view that the visible phenomenon is illusory like a mirage.[3] His way of thinking clearly bears out the influence of Sāṅkhya and it conflicts with his views on the Absolute Which is the only reality, soul and existent entity as has been explained above.

Confronted with this dichotomy, Vijñānabhikṣu attempts at reconciliation and in the process attributes a dual status of reality and unreality, existent and non-existent to the objects of the world.[4] He suggests further improvement saying that they should be understood to be less real and less existent than the Absolute since they are destined to submerge in It in the end.[5] Similarly he considers the individual selves to be less real than the Absolute in respect of existence, reality and *ātmatva*. If we analyze his views, we come to the conclusion that he accepts the grades of reality, to all intents and purposes and inadvertently lands himself in a position he is seen contesting throughout his commentarial works.

That Vijñānabhikṣu does not accept bliss as a characteristic of the

---

1. जीवाश्च चित्शक्तिगुणयोगाद् गौणात्मान एव यथाध्यक्षत्वगुणयोगेन प्राणः करणानामात्मा तद्वद् । *VAB*, p. 29.
   Also see यथा हि देहेन्द्रियादीनां बुद्धिपर्यन्तानामुत्पत्तिलयाधारतया तत्साक्षित्वेन अधिष्ठातृत्वादिना च जीवस्तेषामात्मा । *Ibid.*, p. 29.
2. मुख्यस्त्वात्मेश्वर एव । *Ibid.*, p. 29.
3. अन्यत् सर्वं दृश्यजातं मरीच्युदकादिवत्तुच्छमित्याधुनिका विवर्तवादिनोऽभ्युपगच्छन्ति, तन्न, तथापि बिम्बरूपाणां विषयाणामेव प्रतिबिम्बरूपेण भानात् प्रतिबिम्बरूपतया चैतन्ये बाधेऽपि स्वतो बाधाभावात्। *Ibid.*, p. 41.
4. सदसद्रूपत्वमेव च व्यावहारिकसत्त्वम् । *Ibid.*, p. 55.
5. अथवा लयवत्त्वेन परमात्मापेक्षया तेऽप्यसन्त एव । *Ibid.*, p. 56.

Absolute in addition to those of existence and consciousness also shows his predilection for Sāṅkhya and Yoga metaphysics. And it is in consonance with this influence that he denies that bliss is on a par with existence and consciousness and explains it in terms of absence of pain. Were Vijñānabhikṣu's view on the bliss aspect of the Absolute accepted, it would be difficult to interpret in the negative terms all the scriptural enunciations[1] proclaiming bliss as the nature of Absolute when the intended meaning is so obviously affirmative. As such in the absence of some rational explanation of the Upaniṣadic statements, his view that the *Brahmasūtras* depict the Absolute as integrally non-dual also becomes suspect.

Another important problem we are now about to discuss concerns the aspect of self-luminosity of the Absolute, and also that of the individual self. According to Vijñānabhikṣu self-luminosity consists in knowing oneself through one's own mental mode, and not through another's. The Absolute becomes manifest to Itself through the mode of the Pure-*Sattva*-Adjunct and as such is assumed to be self-luminous.[2] He minces no words about his admitting that the attribute of knowability belongs to the Absolute. But such an assumption incurs the contingency of the subject-object-contradiction. To resolve this contradiction, he explains his standpoint by giving an example of the sun and its reflection in the water. He points out that the sun is the illuminator, i.e. the agency of the act of illuminating belongs to the sun, but in the form of its own reflection, it becomes the object of illumination.[3] In a similar way the Absolute reveals and also becomes an object of revelation in the form of Its reflection in the Pure-*Sattva-Upādhi.* It is in this context that he refers to the definition of self-luminosity given by Citsukhācārya in *Tattvapradīpikā.*[4] It denies that the Absolute becomes knowable. He criticizes and rejects it averring that he does accept that Brahman assumes the characteristic of being knowable[5] since It can become so in the fo m of Its own reflection in the Pure-*Sattva*-Adjunct.

---

1. विज्ञानमानन्दं ब्रह्म । *BṛhadUp,* 3.10.28.
   आनन्दो ब्रह्मेति व्यजानात् । आनन्दाद्ध्येव खल्विमानि भूतानि जायन्ते ।
   आनन्देन जातानि जीवन्ति । आनन्दं प्रयन्त्यभिसंविशन्तीति । *TaittUp, Bhṛguvallī, anuvāka* VI.
2. आत्मन: स्वप्रकाशत्वश्रुतिस्त्वनन्योपाधिप्रकाशादिपरा बोध्या । *SPB,* p. 236.
3. सूर्यो बिम्बरूपेण प्रकाशक: प्रतिबिम्बरूपेण च प्रकाश्य इति न कर्मकर्तृविरोध: । *VAB,* p. 42.
4. अवेद्यत्वे सति अपरोक्षव्यवहारयोग्यताया: तल्लक्षणत्वात् । *TP,* p. 16.
5. अज्ञेयत्वरूपं तावत्स्वप्रकाशत्वमस्मामिर्नाभ्युपगम्यते । *VAB,* p. 39.

Vijñānabhikṣu's standpoint on self-luminosity has far-reaching implications. The absoluteness of the Absolute stands compromised since the very term Absolute implies that It does not stand in need of anything extraneous for Its own revelation. It is not untrue that there are a great many scriptural enunciations that proclaim that the human psycho-physical organism functions because of the Absolute but to make the latter dependent on the Pure-*Sattva*-Adjunct for Its own revelation is to make all such statements lose significance.[1]

The Absolute as consciousness or knowledge should be self-revealing. Should this viewpoint be not admitted, then Vijñānabhikṣu's own point of view in this context becomes unjustifiable. For consciousness, different from the illuminating light of the sun, etc. illuminates all objects. It is an accepted fact that what illuminates others also illuminates itself without any external support. The self also knows/reveals its own mental states[2] which should be self-revealing; otherwise they cannot be always given to the self. If the mental mode (*vṛtti*) is not admitted to be self-revealing and immediately given to the self and if it is assumed to be given to the self through some other (medium) (in this context the mental mode as reflected in it), infinite regress would result. By implication, it is all the more understandable and plausible to accept that Absolute is self-luminous even without the aid of the Pure-*Sattva-Upādhi* since Vijñānabhikṣu's view on self-luminosity makes the subject knowable and jeopardizes the very concept of subject as such, not to speak of the concept of pure-subjectivity for which self-luminosity in the Advaitic sense is indispensable.

That Vijñānabhikṣu interprets the *Brahmasūtras* on the Sāṅkhya pattern is proved by his views on the concept of self. He holds that they are omnipresent and many. He also assumes that they are *aṃśas* (parts) of the Absolute. It may be pointed out here that he implicitly admits that the Absolute and the selves should be as whole and its parts equally omnipresent even if they are assumed to be related to each other. Even in the face of such an implication, he does not have any qualms about defining the concepts of part and whole. He defines the former (*aṃśa*) as an adjunct of the relation of insepara-

1. *Kena Upaniṣad*, I-4 to 7.
2. बुद्धिवृत्तयो ज्ञातारितष्ठन्ति । *SPB*, p. 220.

bility from a homogeneous whole.[1] The *aṃśī* has accordingly been defined as the subjunct of the relation of non-separateness (inseparability) from a homogeneous whole.[2] As a consequence *aṃśatva* has the implication for the self being homogeneous with the whole, i.e. the Absolute. It also implies that the former is an inseparable and hence integral part of the latter. To buttress his point of view on the relation of the self with the Absolute, he explains that this relationship is similar to that obtaining between body and its hair, between heap and its grain, and between father and ṣon.[3]

As the definitions of *aṃśa* and *aṃśī* show, Vijñānabhikṣu emphasizes self's likeness with the Absolute. But it does not make any sense for the following reasons:

1. The agency of epistemological processes belongs to the self only nominally since on Vijñānabhikṣu's view it belongs to the Absolute in the real sense. The reason is that these processes take place under Its control and supervision. Vijñānabhikṣu says that the self's psychological processes being controlled and supervised by the Absolute imply that their ownership and doership accrue to the Absolute. More so, since they are assumed to be Its instruments.[4]

2. As per Vijñānabhikṣu's view, the selves submerge in the Absolute and remain in It at the time of dissolution as the snakes which are dead lie in a ditch. They also become divested of their *upādhis,* which submerge into *prakṛti* at that time. Consequently, the selves cease to perform any meaningful activity[5] and hence cannot be called real.

3. The selves are understood to shed even the characteristic of consciousness at the time of dissolution. It means that they remain without consciousness at that time. It is implied that their having the characteristic of consciousness is contingent on the will of the

---

1. अंशत्वं च सजातीयत्वे सति अविभागप्रतियोगित्वम् । *VAB*, p. 26.
2. तदनुयोगित्वं चांशित्वम् । *Ibid.*, p. 26.
3. यथा शरीरस्य केशादिरंशो राशेश्चैकदेशोंऽशः. . . .पितुश्च पुत्र इति । *Ibid.*, p.27.
4. किंच जीवदर्शनश्रवणमननविज्ञानानामप्यन्तर्याम्यायत्ततया अन्तर्यामिण एव तानि भवन्ति तत्स्वामिकत्वात् तत्कर्तृकत्वाद् येन तु करणस्थानीयस्य जीवस्येति महिमोत्कीर्तनादिति । *Ibid.*, p. 273.
5. प्रकृतिपुरुषादयस्तु सृष्ट्यादिलक्षणस्वकार्येभ्य उपरता एव सुषुप्तास्तिष्ठन्ति इति । *Ibid.*, pp. 57-58.

Absolute. This view of the nature of self can hardly be distinguished from that of the Nyāya-Vaiśeṣika system, which holds that a substance which becomes the locus of knowledge (cognition) by the relationship of inherence is called *ātman.*[1] Except this, the self is an unconscious substance. Similarly Vijñānabhikṣu's view is that the selves are inert or unconscious entities to all intents and purposes except that they can assume the characteristic of consciousness when the Absolute wills so at the time of creation.

4. Vijñānabhikṣu opines that the genus soulhood (*ātmatva*) belongs to the self not in the primary sense. The dilemma that confronts Vijñānabhikṣu is that he postulates the Absolute as an integral whole consisting of selves and *prakṛti* and at the same time struggles hard to maintain that the latter are both existent and real. As it has been shown earlier that both existence and reality consist in a meaningful activity being performed and as both *prakṛti* and the individual selves cease to perform any meaningful activity at the time of dissolution, they, therefore, cease to be both existent and real, at least, at that time. How can, then, they be regarded as real and as existent as the Absolute. And when they do not enjoy the status of being existent and real, that is, when they are not on a par with the Absolute in terms of existence and reality, it hardly makes any sense in holding the Absolute as a unified whole of *prakṛti* and *puruṣas.*

Similar is the case with the conception of *ātmatva* as pointed out at the start of the preceding para. Vijñānabhikṣu defines *ātman* as an entity from which effects issue forth and wherein having been located and having lived they again submerge. As per this definition, the sea can be understood in the sense of *ātman* in respect of its waves since they rise in it and after having lived in it, they just disappear in it. In the same way the individual self (*jīva*) is taken to be endowed with *ātmatva* for it is responsible for the emergence, sustenance and submergence of intellect and other organs.[2] But the self equipped with the contingent property of consciousness is held to possess the genus, *ātmatva,* in a secondary sense just as the vital force (*prāṇa*) endowed with the property of superintendence is regarded as the

1. ज्ञानाधिकरणमात्मा । *TS*, p. 12.
2. यो यत आगत्य यदधिष्ठितं यत्र जीवित्वा यत्र लीयते समुद्रतरङ्गादिवत् जीवाद् बुद्ध्यादिवच्च स तस्यात्मा भवति । *VAB*, p. 28.

ātman of the sense-organs, etc.[1] It is implicit in the preceding statement of Vijñānabhikṣu that the self should be taken to possess *ātmatva* in terms of being the witness and superintendent of the intellect, sense-organs, etc. In other words, the emergence of the intellect, senses, etc., in a figurative sense, consists in their being controlled (superintended over) and witnessed by the self.

The crux of the matter is that Vijñānabhikṣu does not admit that the individual self is endowed with the soulhood (*ātmatva*) in the ultimate and primary senses since it is only the Absolute which is *ātman* in the primary and ultimate senses.[2] His views discussed above imply that he admits the grades of existence, reality, soulhood (*ātmatva*), etc. As such there is no point in holding that the Absolute, selves and *prakṛti* are three different real entities on the ontological level.

The attitude of accommodation that Vijñānabhikṣu has towards the philosophical systems other than the one propounded in the *Brahmasūtra* also needs to be discussed. Let us, to begin with, take the Nyāya-Vaiśeṣika schools of philosophy. Vijñānabhikṣu thinks that they pertain to the preliminary investigation into the nature of truth. They help man reflect that the self is distinguished merely from the physical organism and thereby prepare him to attain the capacity to practise reflection of higher stages. Their utility, in a sense, lies in the fact that it is not always possible for each and every seeker to be able to comprehend the ultimate nature of truth at the very outset.[3] In this context he points out that *Bhagavadgītā* III-20 has not been properly construed. It does not mean that the Naiyāyika and the Vaiśeṣika are rank ignorant. It should, instead, be considered to be of relative significance as compared to the philosophy of Sāṅkhya.[4]

---

1. जीवाश्च चित्शक्तिगुणयोगाद् गौणात्मान एव यथाध्यक्षत्वगुणयोगेन प्राण: करणानामात्मा तद्वद् । *VAB*, p. 29.
   Also cf. यथा हि देहेन्द्रियादीनां बुद्धिपर्यन्तानामुत्पत्तिलयाधारतया तत्साक्षित्वेन अधिष्ठातृत्वादिना च जीवस्तेषामात्मा । *Ibid.*, p. 29.
2. मुख्यस्त्वात्मेश्वर एव । *Ibid.*, p. 29.
3. न्यायवैशेषिकाभ्यां हि सुखिदु:ख्याद्यनुवादतो देहादिमात्राविवेकेन प्रथमभूमिकायामनुमापित: परसूक्ष्मे प्रवेशासम्भवात् । *SPB*, pp. 2-3.
4. प्रकृतेर्गुणसम्मूढा: सज्जन्ते गुणकर्मसु ।
   तानकृत्स्नविदो मन्दान् कृत्स्नविन्न विचालयेत् ।। इति गीतायां (III-20) कर्तृत्वाभिमानिनस्तार्किकस्याकृत्स्नवित्त्वमेव कृत्स्नवित्साङ्ख्यापेक्षयोक्तम्, न तु सर्वथाज्ञत्वमिति । *Ibid.*, p. 3.

The Nyāya system is meant for the lower kind of renunciation since it does not deny that agency belongs to the self.[1] But on the other hand the Sāṅkhya system is suited to the higher order of renunciation as it does not admit that the individual self is the real doer. The former is understood to be a step towards liberation whereas the latter is a direct means to it. And the *Bhagavadgītā* just quoted endorses the view that one who has understood that the self does nothing knows the whole of truth.[2] But it should not be understood to lead to the conclusion that both the Nyāya and Vaiśeṣika systems are worthless though it is true that the knowledge that the self is the doer as laid down in these systems is sublated at the higher level of meditation, yet on closer examination, it becomes quite clear that the knowledge that the self is distinct from the physical organism is not contradicted at any level and to that extent the purpose for which they have been written is thus fully served.[3]

The Sāṅkhya system, too, according to Vijñānabhikṣu, is not purported to say anything with regard to God since it does not form a part of the main subject-matter of this system. It is, therefore, reasonable that the Sāṅkhya philosophy should not be considered as inauthentic insofar as the denial of God is concerned. This view is based on the principle that the connotation of a word is that for which it has been primarily used. The Sāṅkhya system mainly undertakes to propound the nature of liberation and how it is to be attained[4] and for that reason it is unique in describing the nature of *puruṣa* and *prakṛti* for the sake of discrimination between them. Vijñānabhikṣu points out here that if an empirically given datum like the self possessing pleasure, etc. is mentioned in the śāstra, it should be assumed that it is merely a restatement, and does not constitute the main topic.[5]

---

1. तदीयमपि ज्ञानमपरवैराग्यद्वारा परम्परया मोक्षसाधनं भवत्येवेति । तज्ज्ञानापेक्षयापि च सांख्यज्ञानमेव पारमार्थिकं परवैराग्यद्वारा साक्षान्मोक्षसाधनं च भवति । *SPB*, p. 3.
2. उक्तगीतावाक्येनात्माकर्तृत्ववित्त्वस्यैव कृत्स्नवित्त्वसिद्धेः । *Ibid.*, p. 3.
3. न्यायवैशेषिकोक्तज्ञानस्य परमार्थभूमौ बाधितत्वाच्च । न चैतावता न्यायाद्यप्रामाण्यम्, विवक्षितार्थे देहाद्यतिरेकांशे बाधाभावद् । *Ibid.*, p. 3.
4. सांख्यशास्त्रस्य तु पुरुषार्थतत्साधनप्रकृतिपुरुषविवेकावेव मुख्यो विषय इतीश्वरप्रतिषेधांशेऽपि नाप्रामाण्यम्, 'यत्परः शब्दः स शब्दार्थः' इति न्यायात् । अतः सावकाशतया साङ्ख्यमेवेश्वरप्रतिषेधांशे दुर्बलमिति । *Ibid.*, p. 4.
5. आत्मनि सुखादिमत्त्वस्य लोकसिद्धतया तत्र प्रमाणान्तरानपेक्षणेन तदंशस्यानुवादत्वान्न शास्त्रतात्पर्यविषयत्वमिति । *Ibid.*, p. 3.

Since Vijñānabhikṣu is an upholder of the view that the śāstra is a unique means of knowledge, he holds that the *Brahmasūtra* and Sāṅkhya philosophy are not contradictory to each other. The reason is that the former mainly concerns itself with God Who is denied in the latter. Vijñānabhikṣu clarifies it saying that—whether Sāṅkhya denies the existence of God dogmatically or by way of giving concession to some prevalent view of the sort—the statement about God's denial is intended to serve the practical purpose that its own avowed purpose of describing the nature of liberation is not side-tracked and that liberation can be attained by the knowledge of discrimination between the individual self and *prakṛti*. And the practice of giving concession to the prevalent view or even to the ones propounded in other śāstras is not unseen in the śāstras.[1]

His attempt to syncretize these diverse systems does not stop here. In his commentary on the *Brahmasūtras* (*Vijñānāmṛtabhāṣya* or *Ṛjubhāṣya*) Vijñānabhikṣu makes the firm statement that no philosophical system contradicts another and that where there is some contradiction seen, it is not the main purport of that particular system. Since all philosophical systems have been written with the spirit of reconciliation, it does not seem proper to emphasize the contradiction aspect of these systems.[2] Syncretism reaches its zenith when Vijñānabhikṣu offers his considered view that every system of philosophy keeps within the limits of its own subject-matter and that it is not expected to contradict what it has undertaken to propound. He gives an example to clarify: If a system views that God exists and that the contrary is not true, it is perfectly right in that it is interpreting the subject-matter it has undertaken to elaborate and it should not, for that reason, be construed as contradictory to that system of philosophy which denies the existence of God.

The syncretic amalgamation of the tenets of different and divergent schools of thought appears to be a result of his professed predilection for the Purāṇic literature. But it lacks logical rigour.

---

1. तस्मादभ्युपगमवादप्रौढिवादादिनैव साङ्ख्यस्य व्यावहारिकेश्वरप्रतिषेधपरतया ब्रह्ममीमांसायोगाभ्यां सह विरोध: । अभ्युपगमवादश्च शास्त्रे दृष्ट: । *SPB*, p. 5.
2. सर्वाणि दर्शनानि तात्पर्यत: परस्परमविरोधीन्येव । यत्रांशे तु विरोधो दृश्यते, तत्र न तस्य दर्शनस्य तात्पर्यमिति दर्शनानामविरोधवाद एव परमार्थ: विरोधवादस्तु न तेषां मुख्य: कल्प इति वस्तुगत्याऽविरोध एवेति । *VAB*, Introduction, p. 14.
Also cf. स्वस्वविषयेषु सर्वेषामबाधात्, अविरोधाच्चेति । *SPB*, p. 5.

How can the seven categories propounded by the Vaiśeṣika philosophy, and not contradicted by Nyāya, be compatible with the two ultimate principles of the Sāṅkhya philosophy. His position looks all the more untenable when he himself mentions that genus, soulhood of the selves (*puruṣas*) is superseded by that of the *Brahmamīmāṃsā*[1] since such conflicting statements give rise to ambivalence. Even when the Purāṇic quotations used by him to justify his syncretism are taken into consideration, his position cannot be defended on that count, too. Take, for example, the widely recognized *Śrīmad-bhāgavata-purāṇa.* The philosophies named Sāṅkhya and Yoga do find place in it. But they have been ingeniously adapted to the principle of Non-dualism which has been described as Śrīkṛṣṇa Who has been further delineated as *āśraya* (the all-supporting Brahman). This has been done without making any mention of the supersession of one principle by another of a different system as Vijñānabhikṣu has done while comparing the philosophies of Sāṅkhya and Vedānta.

1. "सांख्यसिद्धपुरुषाणामात्मत्वं तु ब्रह्ममीमांसया बाध्यत एव ।" *SPB*, p. 6.

BIBLIOGRAPHY

Āraṇya, Svāmī Hariharānanda, *The Sāṁkhya-sūtras of Pañcaśikha and the Sāṁkhyatattvāloka*, Motilal Banarsidass, Delhi, 1977.

Athalye and Bodas, *Tarkasaṁgraha of Annambhaṭṭa*, BORI, Poona, 1974.

Bhattacharya, Ram Shankar, ed. *Sāṅkhyasūtras with the Vṛtti of Aniruddha*, Prācya Bhāratī Prakāshana, Varanasi, 1964.

——*Sāṅkhyasūtram with the Commentary of Vijñānabhikṣu*, Bharatiya Vidya Prakashan, 1976.

——with Vedāntakeshari Goswami Prahlad Giri, ed. *Yogasāra-saṁgraha*, Bharatiya Vidya Prakashan, 1989.

——Sāṅkhyasāra, Bharatiya Vidya Prakashan, 1978.

Bhattacharyya, K.D., *A Modern Understanding of Advaita Vedānta*, L.D. Series, 47, 1975.

Bhattacharyya, K.C., *Studies in Philosophy*, Motilal Banarsidass, Delhi, 1983.

Brahmasūtrasāṅkarabhāṣya with the Commentaries, *bhāṣyaratna-prabhā*, *bhāmatī* and *nyāyanirṇaya*, ed. J.L. Shastri, Motilal Banarsidass, Delhi, 1988.

Chakravarti, Pulinbihari, *Origin and Development of the Sāṁkhya System of Thought*, Oriental Books Reprint Corporation, Delhi, 1975.

Chattopadhyay, Narayan Kumar, *Indian Philosophy—Its Exposition in the Light of Vijñānabhikṣu's Bhāṣya and Yogavārttika*, Sanskrit Pustak Bhandar, Calcutta, 1979.

Chaudhuri, A.K.R., *Self and Falsity in Advaita Vedānta*, Progressive Publishers, Calcutta, 1955.

Chennakesavan, Sarasvati, *Concept of Mind in Indian Philosophy*, Motilal Banarsidass, Delhi, 1980.

Citsukhācārya, *Tattvapradīpikā*, Translated by Svāmī Yogīndrānanda, Ṣaḍdarśanaprakāśanapratiṣṭhāna, Varanasi, 1974.

Dvivedin, Pt. Vindhyeśvarī Prasād, *Nyāyavārttika*, Eastern Book Linkers, Delhi, 1986.

Gode, P.K., "The Chronology of Vijñānabhikṣu and His Disciple Bhāvāgaṇeśa, the Leader of the Citpāvan Brahmins of Benares", *Adyar Library Bulletin*, February, 1944, Vol. VIII.

Guha, D.C., *Navya Nyāya System of Logic*, Motilal Banarsidass, Delhi, 1979.

Gupta, Anima Sen, *Classical Sāṁkhya: A Critical Study*, Munshiram Manoharlal, Delhi, 1982.

———, *Sāṁkhya and Advaita Vedānta: A Comparative Study*, Published by Monoranjan Sen, 'Gour Ashram', Lucknow, 1973.

Gupta, S.N. Das, *History of Indian Philosophy*, Vol. I, Motilal Banarsidass, Delhi, 1988.

Hall, F.E., *An Introduction to Sāṅkhya Pravacana Bhāṣya of Vijñānabhikṣu*, Bharatiya Book Corporation, Delhi, 1979.

Ingalls, D.H.H., *Materials for the Study of Navya-Nyāya Logic*, Motilal Banarsidass, Delhi, 1988.

Īśvarakṛṣṇa, *Sāṅkhyakārikā* with Sāṅkhyatattvakaumudīprabhā by Adya Prasad Misra, Prem Prakashan, Allahabad, 1973.

James, William, *Principles of Psychology*, Dover Publication, USA, 1950.

Jha, Pt. Ganganath, tr., *Yogasārasaṅgraha*, Akay Book Corporation, Delhi, 1986.

Johnston, E.H., *Early Sāṁkhya*, Motilal Banarsidass, Delhi, 1974.

Karnataka, Vimla, *Vyākhyākāron kī Dṛṣṭi se Pātañjala Yogasūtra kā Samīkṣātmaka Adhyayana*, Kashi Hindu Vishvavidyalaya, Varanasi, 1974.

Keith, A.B., *A History of Sāṁkhya Philosophy*, Nag Publishers, Delhi, 1975.

Majumdar, A.K., *The Sāṅkhya Conception of Personality*, Bharatiya Book Corporation, Delhi, 1981.

Misra, Adya Prasad, *Sāṅkhya Darśana kī Aitihāsika Paramparā*, Akṣayavaṭa Prakashan, Allahabad, (year not mentioned).

Moore, Charles A., ed. *A Source Book in Indian Philosophy*, Princeton University Press, 1970.

The Naiṣkarmyasiddhi of Sureśvarācārya, ed. M. Hiriyanna, BORI, Poona, 1980.

Potter, Karl, H., *Encyclopedia of Indian Philosophies*, Motilal Banarsidass, Delhi.
Vol. I, 1983
Vol. II, 1977
Vol. III, 1981
Vol. IV, 1987

Radhakrishnan, Sarvepalli, ed. *A Source Book in Indian Philosophy*, Princeton University Press, 1970.

Rāmānujācārya, *Śrībhāṣya, Catuḥsūtrī*, Bharatiya Vidya Prakashan, 1983.

Rukmani, T.S., tr. *Yogavārttika of Vijñānabhikṣu*, Munshiram Manoharlal, Delhi, Vol. I, 1981.

Sadānanda Yati, *Advaita Brahma Siddhi*, ed. Vamana Shastri, Parimal Publications, Delhi, 1981.

Śāṅkarabhāṣya on Muṇḍaka Upaniṣad and Taittirīya Upaniṣad (Upaniṣadbhāṣyam), (Vol. I), Mahesh Research Institute, Varanasi, 1979.

Sarasvati Anandabodhendra, *Vāsiṣṭhamahārāmāyaṇatātparyaprakāśa on Yogavāsiṣṭha*, Motilal Banarsidass, Delhi, 1981.

Sarasvatī, Madhusūdana, *Advaitasiddhi*, ed. Ananta Krishna Sastri, Parimal Publications, Delhi, 1982.

Śāstrī, Śrī Gosvāmī Dāmodara, ed., *Sāṁgayogadarśana with Vyāsabhāṣya, Tattvavaiśāradī, Pātañjalarahasya, Yogavārttika and Bhāsvatī*, Jai Krishnadas Haridas Gupta, Chowkhamba Sanskrit Series Office, Benares, 1935.

Śāstrī, Udayavīra, *Sāṅkhya Darśana kā Itihāsa*, second edition, Virajānanda Vaidika Śodha Saṃsthāna, Ghaziabad, 1979.

Sharma, V.A., *Citsukha's Contribution to Advaita*, Kavyalaya Publishers, Mysore, 1974.

Shastri, Swami Dwarika Das, ed., *Sāṃkhya Sūtrāṇi with Sāṅkhyavṛttisāra*, Sudhi Prakashan, Varanasi, 1987.

Shiva Kumar, *Sāṁkhya Yoga Epistemology*, Eastern Book Linkers, Delhi, 1984.

——, *Sāṁkhya Thought in the Brahmanical Systems of Indian Philosophy*, Eastern Book Linkers, Delhi, 1983.

——, *Sāṁkhyasāra of Vijñānabhikṣu,* Eastern Book Linkers, Delhi, 1988.

Sinha, Jadunath, *The Philosophy of Vijñānabhikṣu,* Sinha Publishing House, Calcutta, 1976.

——, *Indian Psychology : Perception,* Kegan Paul, Trench, Trubner & Co., London, 1934.

Sinha, Nand Lal, *The Sāṃkhya Philosophy* (Translation of Aniruddha's *Vṛtti* and *Sāṅkhya Pravacana Bhāṣya* of Vijñānabhikṣu), Oriental Books Reprint Corporation, Delhi, 1979.

Solomon, Esther A., *The Commentaries of Sāṁkhya Kārikā—A Study,* Gujarat University, 1974.

Sovani, V.V., *A Critical Study of the Sāṃkhya System,* Oriental Book Agency, Poona, 1935.

Śrīmadbhāgavata Purāṇa, Gita Press, Gorakhpur, Saṃvat 2037.

Śrīmadbhagavadgītā with the *Bhāṣya* of Śrī Śaṅkarācārya, tr. Dr. A.G. Krishna Warrier, Sri Ramakrishna Math, Madras, 1983.

Srinivasachari, P.N., *The Philosophy of Viśiṣṭādvaita,* The Adyar Library and Research Centre, Madras, 1978.

Śrīvāstavya, Suresh Chandra, *A Study of Vijñānabhikṣu and His Place in Indian Philosophy,* Lok Bharati Prakashan, Allahabad, 1969.

Tripāṭhī, Pt. Kedāranātha, ed. *Vijñānabhikṣu's Vijñānāmṛtabhāṣyam,* Banaras Hindu University, Varanasi, 1979.

Udāsīna, Bālarāma, *Vidvattoṣiṇī,* Guru Mandalashrama, Hardwar, 1931.

Upādhyāya, V.P., *Lights on Vedānta,* Chowkhamba Sanskrit Series Office, Varanasi, 1959.

Vācaspati Miśra, *Sāṅkhyatattvakaumudī* on *Sāṅkhyakārikā,* Pandurang Jawaji, Nirnaya Sagar Press, Bombay, 1940.

Vidyāraṇya Muni, *Pañcadaśī with the Commentary of Rāmakṛṣṇa,* Chaukhamba Sanskrit Pratishthan, Delhi, 1987.

Winternitz, M., *History of Indian Literature,* Vol. III, Motilal Banarsidass, Delhi, 1985.

Yogavāsiṣṭha, Part I, ed. Vasudeva Laxmana Sharma Pansikar, Motilal Banarsidass, 1984.

Index